An iOS Developer's Guide to SwiftUI

Design and build beautiful apps quickly
and easily with minimum code

Michele Fadda

An iOS Developer's Guide to SwiftUI

Group Product Manager: Rohit Rajkumar

Publishing Product Manager: Vaideeshwari Muralikrishnan

Book Project Manager: Aishwarya Mohan

Senior Editor: Rakhi Patel

Technical Editor: Reenish Kulshrestha

Copy Editor: Safis Editing

Indexer: Pratik Shirodkar

Production Designer: Prafulla Nikalje

DevRel Marketing Coordinators: Anamika Singh and Nivedita Pandey

First published: May 2024

Production reference: 1050424

Published by Packt Publishing Ltd.

Grosvenor House

11 St Paul's Square

Birmingham

B3 1RB, UK

ISBN 978-1-80181-362-4

www.packtpub.com

Dedicated to my love, Stefania.

– Michele Giuseppe Fadda

Contributors

About the author

Michele Fadda is an Italian software developer with over 30 years of expertise in a range of sectors, including banking, healthcare, and open banking. He began his programming journey at 14 in Sassari and relocated to Milan in 1983, where he started his career in embedded systems software, later expanding into enterprise and mobile software development. Michele also contributed as a tech journalist from 1983 to 1997, focusing on digital electronics and programming. He is fluent in both Italian and English and holds an MBA from the Open University Business School, along with a diploma in business studies.

With a deep understanding of computing history, Michele has been at the forefront of software development since the Unix System V era. He has led IT projects for numerous Italian companies, mastering a variety of programming languages and, lately, specializing in iOS and Swift for mobile applications. Michele is particularly interested in cryptography and designing secure systems.

In addition to his professional achievements, Michele has a passion for electronic music, blending his technological expertise with a creative flair for sound. Since 2018, he has been working in the UK, working as an iOS developer. He is currently the CEO of FWLAB Limited and technical project and program manager at Eggon, an innovative Italian start-up.

I want to thank the Packt team and reviewers who helped me through this journey and made this book possible.

About the reviewer

Nimesh Neema is a passionate programmer who loves well-designed software. He is proficient with Apple developer technologies and has written apps for the iPhone, iPad, Mac, Apple Watch, and Apple TV. He has an excellent understanding of shell scripting, version control, and software engineering principles.

In a career spanning over 15 years, he has worked with teams of diverse sizes and backgrounds. He has experience writing utility, payment, gaming, hospitality, and low-level system apps.

He runs a software engineering consultancy, Perspicacious Solutions Private Limited, with clients from around the world. He engages in corporate training and speaking gigs. He is one of the highly-rated Apple development experts on `codementor.io`.

Table of Contents

3

Adding Interactivity to a SwiftUI View   65

Part 2: Scrollable Views

4

Iterating Views, Scroll Views, FocusState, Lists, and Scroll View Reader   87

5

The Art of Displaying Grids   105

Part 3: SwiftUI Navigation

6

Tab Bars and Modal View Presentation   129

7

All About Navigation   159

Part 4: Graphics and Animation

8

Creating Custom Graphics 191

9

An Introduction to Animations in SwiftUI 209

Part 5: App Architecture

10

App Architecture and SwiftUI Part I: Practical Tools 233

11

App Architecture and SwiftUI Part II – the Theory   255

Part 6: Beyond Basics

12

Persistence with Core Data   285

13

Modern Structured Concurrency   313

Preface

This book teaches you about SwiftUI, a multiplatform declarative user interface framework that can be used to program all Apple devices, currently including Mac, iPhone, iPad, Apple TV, Apple Watch, and Vision Pro.

Who this book is for

This book is aimed at iOS developers who want to expand their knowledge of adding SwiftUI to their bag of tools and want to progress further in their professional careers.

What this book covers

Chapter 1, Exploring the Environment – Xcode, Playgrounds, and SwiftUI, is an introduction to the software tools used when working with SwiftUI, the new exciting, efficient, and simple-to-use Apple framework for user interfaces.

Chapter 2, Adding Basic UI Elements and Designing Layouts, shows you how to properly refactor view code. Then, it describes how to combine basic views with stacks and control their visual layout.

Chapter 3, Adding Interactivity to a SwiftUI View, discusses the conversion from static to dynamic SwiftUI views, with a focus on responsive design, including taps and gestures. This chapter explores mechanisms to enable views to be made interactive. It covers topics such as view creation, interactivity enhancement, property wrappers, limitations of `@State`, bidirectional bindings, subviews, and the use of `@ObservableObject` and `@StateObject` classes.

Chapter 4, Iterating Views, Scroll Views, FocusState, Lists, and Scroll View Reader, focuses on showing lists in SwiftUI, through scrollable views such as scroll views or lists. It shows how to handle the visibility of the iOS system keyboard. It introduces `NavigationView` for view titles and covers iterating views, `@ViewBuilder`, scroll views, `@FocusState` for keyboard control, lists, and `ScrollViewReader` for element positioning within lists or scroll views.

Chapter 5, The Art of Displaying Grids, moves on to creating grid structures in SwiftUI. Topics covered include displaying grids in iOS, the grid view, lazy grids, using `GridItem` for layout control, conditional view formatting, and responding design to device orientation changes.

Chapter 6, Tab Bars and Modal View Presentation, focuses on using tab bars and modal view presentations in SwiftUI. It begins with the `TabView`, which is the most common way of moving between views in a small-scale iOS app. Topics covered include how to add a tab bar using `TabView` and `tabItem`, implementing custom tab bars, and an exhaustive investigation into modal views such as sheets, alerts, and popovers.

Chapter 7, All About Navigation, introduces the concept of navigation in SwiftUI. It starts with an overview of iOS navigation and then deals with programmatic and user-initiated navigation. It illustrates the changes with Swift 4 and iOS 16. Topics discussed are navigation across platforms, basic navigation with `NavigationView` and `NavigationLink`, `.navigationDestination`, user-controlled and split view navigation, programmatic navigation with `NavigationPath`, and saving/restoring the navigation stack in the JSON format.

Chapter 8, Creating Custom Graphics, shows you how to style apps by creating custom modifiers, diving into the use of core graphics inside the Canvas view, `CALayers` integration with SwiftUI. Then, the chapter goes further, illustrating how to use `CustomLayout`.

Chapter 9, An Introduction to Animations in SwiftUI, highlights SwiftUI animations, explaining their state-driven, reactive nature, made possible by SwiftUI's declarative syntax. It explains the built-in modifiers of animation, transition, and `scaleEffect`.

Chapter 10, App Architecture and SwiftUI Part I – the Practical Tools, dissects the impact that SwiftUI has had in restructuring the application architecture on Apple's operating systems. It introduces conceptual tools that allow a developer to segment an app into manageable components. This chapter focuses on ad hoc architecture rather than offering a one-size-fits-all solution. Key topics include diagrams, dependency inversion, clean architecture, decoupling techniques, state management, and iOS 17 changes on state bindings.

Chapter 11, App Architecture and SwiftUI Part II – the Theory, introduces modern application architecture, taking note of the specificity of the iOS context. It explains the concept of software architecture to give a theoretical understanding and criteria for evaluating well-designed architecture. Key topics include the principles of lightweight architecture, conflict resolution, defining good architecture, the importance of software patterns, the role of the architect, consulting experts, the difference between full-scale applications and examples, and the impact of Conway's law.

Chapter 12, Persistence with Core Data, focuses on defining persistence, explaining Core Data's structure, its integration with SwiftUI, and its practical use in Xcode. It touches on CloudKit for cloud-based data storage. Key topics include the Core Data's framework classes, Core Data with SwiftUI, project creation and migrations, the SQLite data file, and CloudKit.

Chapter 13, Modern Structured Concurrency, discusses concurrency in mobile application development nowadays, applied specifically to Swift. The chapter outlines the history of concurrency from traditional mechanisms, such as threads and callbacks, to Apple's modern structured concurrency approach. Its topics include `async/await`, tasks, task groups, asynchronous sequences and streams, actors, and integrating old-fashioned concurrency with modern structured concurrency.

Chapter 14, An Introduction to SwiftData, describes Apple's **ORM (Object Relational Mapping)** framework, SwiftData, which is set to replace Core Data in SwiftUI development. The topics covered include SwiftData versus Core Data, SwiftData's features, SwiftUI integration, data modeling, and the changes in binding.

Chapter 15, Consuming REST services in SwiftUI, explains HTTP, and REST as concepts and how to integrate REST services into SwiftUI applications for iOS apps that demand communication over the internet. Topics covered include HTTP requests made using `URLSession`, converting to and from JSON using Codable, watching UI changes with `ObservableObject` and `@Published`, avoiding man-in-the-middle attacks, and handling network errors.

Chapter 16, Exploring the Apple Vision Pro, introduces Apple Vision Pro, an advanced mixed-reality headset, and its importance for spatial computing. It describes the device's immersive three-dimensional interface. It also goes into the development tools for visionOS, starting development with visionOS, and the initial steps in visionOS development.

To get the most out of this book

It is assumed that you will be familiar with basic computer science and programming in the Swift programming language on Apple devices.

Software/hardware covered in the book	Operating system requirements
macOS	A recent macOS Version, at least Sonoma (14.2.1 or later), in order to follow examples based on Xcode 15.2 for the last chapters.
Xcode	Most examples will run on Xcode 14.3 or later except when indicated at the beginning of the chapter.
	The chapters on SwiftData and visionOS require Xcode 15.2 or later.
Physical devices	You can follow the examples for iOS and iPadOS by using the simulator; you don't need physical devices for learning.
	To run the code in this book on macOS, you will need macOS 14.2.

If you are using the digital version of this book, we advise you to type the code yourself or access the code from the book's GitHub repository (a link is available in the next section). Doing so will help you avoid any potential errors related to the copying and pasting of code.

You will need a developer's account only if you want to use physical devices. Xcode can be downloaded for free from the Mac App Store and won't require a developer's account in order to run your own applications on the simulator.

Download the example code files

You can download the example code files for this book from GitHub at `https://github.com/PacktPublishing/An-iOS-Developer-s-Guide-to-SwiftUI`. If there's an update to the code, it will be updated in the GitHub repository.

We also have other code bundles from our rich catalog of books and videos available at `https://github.com/PacktPublishing/`. Check them out!

Conventions used

There are a number of text conventions used throughout this book.

`Code in text`: Indicates code words in text, database table names, folder names, filenames, file extensions, pathnames, dummy URLs, user input, and Twitter handles. Here is an example: "In order to create explicit animations, you use the `.animation(_: value:)` modifier rather than the simpler `.withAnimation` closure."

A block of code is set as follows:

```
// if you are using Xcode 14.x you will need this syntax for the
preview functionality:

struct ContentView_Previews: PreviewProvider {
    static var previews: some View {
        ContentView()
    }
}
```

When we wish to draw your attention to a particular part of a code block, the relevant lines or items are set in bold:

```
[default]
// if you are using Xcode 15 or later, the preview can be simplified
as follows:
#Preview {
  ContentView()
}
```

Any command-line input or output is written as follows:

```
$ cd projectFolder
$ open .
```

Bold: Indicates a new term, an important word, or words that you see on screen. For instance, words in menus or dialog boxes appear in **bold**. Here is an example: "Select **Settings** from the **Xcode** menu."

> **Tips or important notes**
> Appear like this.

Get in touch

Feedback from our readers is always welcome.

General feedback: If you have questions about any aspect of this book, email us at `customercare@packtpub.com` and mention the book title in the subject of your message.

Errata: Although we have taken every care to ensure the accuracy of our content, mistakes do happen. If you have found a mistake in this book, we would be grateful if you would report this to us. Please visit `www.packtpub.com/support/errata` and fill in the form.

Piracy: If you come across any illegal copies of our works in any form on the internet, we would be grateful if you would provide us with the location address or website name. Please contact us at `copyright@packt.com` with a link to the material.

If you are interested in becoming an author: If there is a topic that you have expertise in and you are interested in either writing or contributing to a book, please visit `authors.packtpub.com`.

Share Your Thoughts

Once you've read *An iOS Developer's Guide to SwiftUI*, we'd love to hear your thoughts! Scan the QR code below to go straight to the Amazon review page for this book and share your feedback.

https://packt.link/r/1801813620

Your review is important to us and the tech community and will help us make sure we're delivering excellent quality content.

Download a free PDF copy of this book

Thanks for purchasing this book!

Do you like to read on the go but are unable to carry your print books everywhere?

Is your e-book purchase not compatible with the device of your choice?

Don't worry!, Now with every Packt book, you get a DRM-free PDF version of that book at no cost.

Read anywhere, any place, on any device. Search, copy, and paste code from your favorite technical books directly into your application.

The perks don't stop there, you can get exclusive access to discounts, newsletters, and great free content in your inbox daily

Follow these simple steps to get the benefits:

1. Scan the QR code or visit the following link:

https://packt.link/free-ebook/9781801813624

2. Submit your proof of purchase.
3. That's it! We'll send your free PDF and other benefits to your email directly.

Part 1: Simple Views

In this part, you will be introduced to SwiftUI, the multiplatform UI framework from Apple that allows developers to build user interfaces for all Apple devices. These chapters have been designed for iOS developers in such a way that they guide you through the main concepts of SwiftUI and its practical implementation, offering a concrete base to develop powerful and visually beautiful applications.

You will start to explore the fundamentals of SwiftUI and its declarative syntax to build an intuitive and efficient UI. We'll cover key concepts, such as views, modifiers, and state management, demonstrating how these components work together to build dynamic layouts.

You will learn to manage data well within SwiftUI, ensuring slick, dynamic user interfaces are produced through bindings, observable objects, and environment values.

This part will teach you how to work with animation and the gesture features of SwiftUI by applying them with a layer of polish and interactivity to your apps. You should reach the end of this section prepared with the knowledge and skills needed to begin using SwiftUI for your iOS development projects, making applications that are not only functional but also visually engaging.

This part contains the following chapters:

- *Chapter 1, Exploring the Environment – Xcode, Playgrounds, and SwiftUI*
- *Chapter 2, Adding Basic UI Elements and Designing Layouts*
- *Chapter 3, Adding Interactivity to a SwiftUI View*

1

Exploring the Environment – Xcode, Playgrounds, and SwiftUI

This chapter is an introduction to the tools used when working with SwiftUI, the new, exciting, efficient, and simple-to-use Apple framework for **user interfaces** (**UIs**). We're going to cover the following main topics in this chapter:

- Exploring Xcode and SwiftUI

- Creating a multi-platform SwiftUI project

- Using Swift Playgrounds to test fragments of code

- Adding tests

- The App submission process

By the end of this chapter, you will learn how to create a project from scratch. You will also learn how to create a project using the project templates and how to add tests and preview your SwiftUI views code.

> **Note**
> The opinions expressed in this book are solely those of the author and do not necessarily reflect the views or policies of his employers or other entities. Any reference to organizations, events, or individuals is purely fictional and intended for illustrative purposes only. Resemblance to any existing companies, events, or persons, living or deceased, is purely coincidental unless the specific name of an individual is mentioned.

Technical requirements

You will require a recent Apple computer to run the examples and code in this book. In general, the more RAM and more powerful your system, the better. This book has been tested on an Intel MacBook Pro running macOS 13.6 (Ventura) with 16 GB of RAM. It will work just as fine on a more recent Apple Silicon machine.

To follow this chapter and the rest of the book, you will be required to install Xcode version 15.0 or later.

If you want to run code on a physical device with Xcode 15.0, you will be able to use the async/await pattern in concurrent programming for devices running at least iOS 13. We suggest updating your device to iOS 17 or later to follow this book.

The complete projects and code samples for the examples discussed in the book can be found under the GitHub repository: `https://github.com/PacktPublishing/An-iOS-Developer-s-Guide-to-SwiftUI`.

Exploring SwiftUI with Xcode

In this section, we are going to look into the Xcode UI in the context of a SwiftUI project.

Xcode is quite a large topic by itself. We will focus on SwiftUI and explain enough about how Xcode usage differs in SwiftUI from UIKit to get you started, how to create a SwiftUI project, and add targets for various Apple platforms. Also, we will explain how to add tests to a project.

A brief tour of Xcode

Xcode is an **integrated development environment** (IDE) for developing any code on any device that Apple produces. Xcode is therefore a massive and complex app capable of supporting many different types of projects and technologies. Not all of these types of projects are relevant to SwiftUI, so we will limit ourselves to Swift as a language and SwiftUI as a UI framework. In the past, the only supported language for app development was Objective-C and the only supported UI framework was different for each device platform, notably UIKit for iOS and AppKit for macOS. Swift was introduced at a later stage, but before SwiftUI, the core architecture of the UI layer for Apple apps did not change, and actually, most of it was still dependent on frameworks developed internally in Objective-C. SwiftUI is the first "pure" Swift approach to UIs. We will focus on Swift and SwiftUI.

You can install Xcode from the Mac App Store, or if you have an Apple Developer account, you can choose to download a particular version of it from the download section of your developer account. It is a hefty download; it will take a while unless you have a high-speed internet connection.

After downloading and installing it, you will be asked to download additional components; permit it by clicking **Install**:

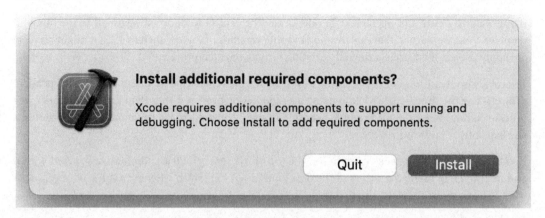

Figure 1.1 – Installing the additional Xcode components

Installing Xcode from the Mac App Store is the easiest way to get the most recent stable version. If you want to install a beta version or a previous specific version, you can download it from your developer's account download area. It will download an archived file with a .xip extension. Double-clicking on it will expand the archive to give the Xcode.app bundle. You might want to rename it if you're using different versions of Xcode on the same machine.

You may also want to install the current version from a .xip file if you don't have a good internet connection in order to overcome installation difficulties. However, please don't install multiple versions of Xcode unless you have an excellent reason to do it, as this might cause you some additional problems. When you open a project with an older version of Xcode, this might cause some obscure bugs when you forget to select the appropriate version of the command-line tools.

Luckily, with SwiftUI, several incompatibilities and difficult-to-diagnose bugs due to the corruption or slight incompatibilities among storyboard files are gone as you won't be working with storyboard files anymore, and the representation of views is done with declarative Swift code; it is just human-readable plain text. These problems and the difficulties of merging storyboard files, which were never intended to be edited by hand with a text editor, were particularly relevant when using storyboards in large teams, to the point that many development teams chose to give up on storyboard and resorted to programming views in code in UIKit for this precise reason.

It is advisable to install Xcode in the Applications folder for everyday use, like any regular app.

The Applications folder is where Xcode is usually installed when you download it from the App Store. In rare cases where you want to have more than one version of Xcode on the same machine, you might want to install some of the other versions in other folders (e.g., the Desktop folder).

Bear in mind that Apple keeps on adding features and project templates for various coding artifacts, so feel free to experiment and learn what different project creation options do.

If you want to delete a project, close Xcode, delete the project folder by dragging it to the bin, and reopen Xcode. Be warned that due to a bug in some versions of Xcode, such as 13.2, it might recreate an empty project if you delete the only existing recently created project.

You could also structure your project using workspaces, which could contain one or more interdependent projects. For the time being, stick to using a single Xcode project rather than an Xcode workspace unless you have a reason; for example, wanting to use a third-party package manager that requires you explicitly to use workspaces.

Xcode has a relatively extensive menu (on the top of the screen). Please familiarize yourself with it and use the **Help** menu item to read the developer documentation whenever you have a doubt or want to learn more about its functionality.

Xcode defaults with Xcode 15 are pretty good the way they are; for instance, you won't need to set it to display line numbers, as that is the default behavior.

You might want to change the Xcode default editor theme to something of your liking; some developers prefer to work with light text on a dark background. You can choose that by selecting the desired theme under the **Themes** tab in Xcode **Preferences**. I usually like the default white background as I feel that it is easier on the eyes, but it is a matter of personal preference. It would help if you personalized your editor in a way that suits you.

You will need to add your Apple Developer account under **Preferences** | **Accounts** if you have one. This will automatically allow Xcode to deal with your application certificates, which is the easiest way to work alone on your apps.

To be sure that the command-line interface for Xcode has been installed correctly, you should run the following command:

```
xcode-select -install
```

If you see a prompt asking you to accept the Xcode license agreement, accept it.

Also, Xcode may occasionally ask for your permission to access a folder or to perform a certain action; this will typically require your user password. You are normally supposed to be the administrator of your own machine in order to be able to develop with Xcode.

When you run Xcode, you will see a dialogue showing projects and playgrounds you have accessed recently if any along with the **Create New Project...**, **Clone Git Repository...**, and **Open Existing Project...**:

Figure 1.2 – Initial Xcode screen and menu

Now that we have gone through some basic information about Xcode, we will move on to the next section where we will see how a SwiftUI app starts in Xcode.

How the app starts

To get started, clone or download this book's project files from GitHub (the link to the GitHub repository is mentioned in the *Technical requirements* section), navigate to the CH1 | Ch1FirstProject folder, and open the project file named Ch1FirstProject.xcodeproj.

Once you open the project, you will notice that the AppDelegate project file has been replaced by an App file, which now contains just a struct implementing the App protocol and is marked with @main, signifying that it is the main entry point for the code execution of the app.

This struct creates WindowGroup from ContentView. According to the Apple documentation, WindowGroup is a container for your app's view hierarchy. It adapts to the supported platform supporting its peculiar capabilities (e.g., supporting more than one window (for iPadOS and macOS)). The WindowGroup supports the main app UI interface, except for document apps which require DocumentGroup instead.

The following screenshot shows the main Xcode UI:

Figure 1.3 – Locating the App file in a project

The following code segment shows the SwiftUI equivalent of the old `AppDelegate`:

```
import SwiftUI
@main
struct Ch1FirstProjectApp: App {
    var body: some Scene {
        WindowGroup {
            ContentView()
        }
    }
}
```

This is what developers normally refer to when they talk about the Composition Root in a SwiftUI app: the place where all the main components of the application get instantiated.

Click on the `ContentView` file in the Xcode Project navigator shown on the left. You will see that the UI of Xcode is by default subdivided into four main areas:

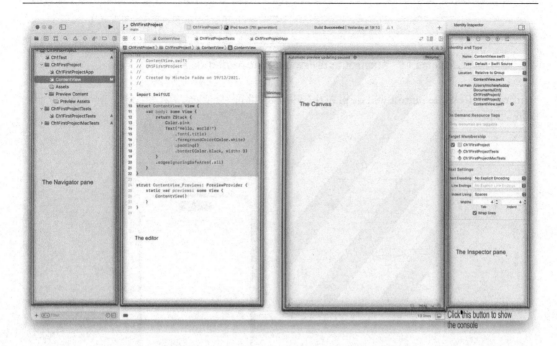

Figure 1.4 – Xcode interface, the four main areas

You are probably already somewhat familiar with it, but there are some differences in SwiftUI projects, due mostly to replacing the storyboards with the Canvas preview and project templates. The navigator area behaves as you would expect and allows you to select and open the various files in your project. Then the main editor is displayed, and next to it, the Canvas and the Inspector area.

Some panes, such as the debug area, are only displayed during debugging or if you open it manually, that is, by clicking the toggle button with a line used to open and close the panes. You can find this button on the right side at the bottom.

You won't need to open the Assistant Editor to display the storyboard associated with a view controller anymore, and the Canvas preview has superseded its functionality.

The Canvas will render the SwiftUI view corresponding to the edited view file.

By default, the first time the Canvas is displayed, its real-time rendering will be paused. You will initially see an empty Canvas with the **Automatic preview updating paused** warning, and you will need to hit the **Resume** button to make the Canvas render a preview of the view in real-time.

The following figure shows what this message looks like:

Automatic preview updating paused ⓘ   Resume

Figure 1.5 – Automatic preview updating paused, detail of the Canvas

Hitting the **Resume** button will display the view in all its `Hello, world!` Default glory, after some time:

Figure 1.6 – Running a preview in the Canvas

If nothing is displayed the first time, do not despair; exit Xcode and relaunch it. With Xcode 15, this bug occurring is unlikely, and it was quite common with previous releases, but you have been warned in case it happens.

The library is still available with the + button on top of the Canvas, which you will use to drag new UI elements. However, it is not a component library; UI elements are not components but rather code snippets that will produce the desired UI element or allow it to be modified using modifiers.

You can do it in two ways: directly editing the code representing the view or modifying the idea with a view inspector. You can also drag visual elements from the library to the preview; they will be rendered together with the corresponding code changes in the editor.

While you are editing a `View` Swift file, you can access the Attributes Inspector from the Inspector area on the right by selecting the three-slider menu. This will allow you to modify the current statement and see how the code generates that view changes in real-time, together with the effects of your edit changes.

Let's take a simple example:

1. Click on the **Add modifier** text pane at the bottom of the Inspector area.

    Start typing the first few characters of a modifier to find it; for example, start typing `fore` to find the **Foreground Color** option.

2. Add **Foreground Color** and set it to **.red**.

    You will notice that the `Hello World` text color changes to red.

Let's modify the previous code slightly, by switching `.padding()` with the `.foregroundColor(.red)` lines.

Now, let's have a look at the code more closely.

After importing the SwiftUI framework, you will see that there are two structs. One declares `Contentview`, which is of the opaque View type and the other declares `ContentView_Previews`.

Let's examine the first struct:

```
struct ContentView: View {
    var body: some View {
        Text("Hello, world!")
            .padding()
            .foregroundColor(.red)
    }
}
```

Notice the `some` keyword marking an opaque type conforming to `View`, which is satisfied by `Text` (which is one of the many different types of views supported by SwiftUI).

A `Text` in UIKit is called `Label`.

Notice that whenever you add a modifier, you add a function applied to a view and the function returns a modified view.

You start with a default `Text` view and process it with the `foregroundColor(.red)` function to change its color to red:

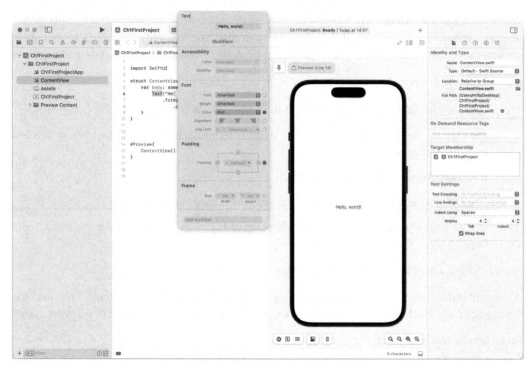

Figure 1.7 – Adding foreground color to Text

You can either edit the code or use the SwiftUI inspector that you can access with the right button, after selecting the corresponding View on the Code area.

You might wonder if this new SwiftUI's approach is computationally faster than UIKit's.

It really is as if SwiftUI views are now `struct` instances, a value type that is stored on the stack, without the need to count references for deallocation. Creating and modifying views is way faster this way than it was before with UIKit. UIKit instead uses objects (class instances, which are reference types) to represent views allocated on the heap.

To be even more precise, as a data type, SwiftUI views are not really "objects," but are more like "building instructions" recipes that SwiftUI uses to concretely create their representation displayed on the screen.

You will notice that the SwiftUI approach is purely declarative: you declare a view inside the closure of the body, then apply modifier after modifier, where each modifier is a function that operates on the previous version of the view and returns a modified version of it until your view looks the way you intended. You don't need to create support for autolayout, constraints, and so on.

This approach is more straightforward, and there is no need for autolayout to perform complex calculations, which amounts to solving a system of disequations with many variables for complex views in UIKit. That simplification also adds up in rendering speed and makes your life as a programmer simpler.

We will explain the available modifiers and the many different supported views in greater detail in the following chapters.

For now, let's observe the order in which you need to apply modifiers:

Changing the order of modifiers changes the way a view looks; for instance, try the following approach:

```
struct ContentView: View {
    var body: some View {
        Text("Hello, world!")
            .foregroundColor(.red)
            .padding()
            .border(Color.blue, width: 3)

    }
}
```

You can also try this approach:

```
struct ContentView2: View {
    var body: some View {
        Text("Hello, world!")
            .foregroundColor(.red)
            .border(Color.blue, width: 3)
            .padding()
    }
}
```

The first approach will result in the border being drawn after the Text view has been surrounded by padding; the second will draw padding (which will not be visible) after surrounding Text with a border without adding padding first. The graphical result is quite different. Think of a modifier like a black box that inputs a view and returns a modified version of that view. You normally chain many modifiers until you get the result you want.

Notice that you can use multiple previews to view the differences in results between two different approaches, as shown in the following screen screenshot:

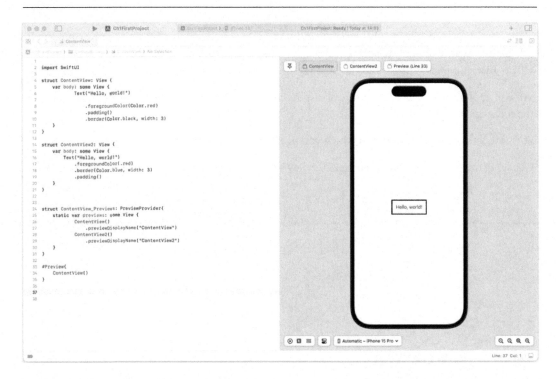

Figure 1.8 – A different order of the same modifiers results in different final result

In Xcode 15, you can use both the traditional `ContentView` preview or the new #Preview macro to show a preview. You can select different previews by clicking on their corresponding buttons at the top of the Canvas preview. You can use the `.previewDisplayName()` modifier to give a different name to a preview.

> **Note**
>
> In SwiftUI, you are not just selecting an option for an attribute that affects the whole view, but the order in which you apply the modifiers changes how the resulting view will look.

Suppose you want to change the background color to pink.

In SwiftUI, there isn't an attribute of a view; you can just set it to change the color of its background. Also, `Color` in SwiftUI is a view. You will need to add more than one view to obtain this desired effect.

Adding a `Color` view will result in this code, and it would have the same effect if you edited the view's code yourself:

```
struct ContentView: View {
```

```
    var body: some View {
        Vstack {
            Text("Hello, world!")
                .foregroundColor(.red)
                .padding()
            .border(Color.blue, width: 3)
            Color(red: 0.5, green: 0.5, blue:0.5)
        }
    }
}
```

Here's what to do to achieve the pink background:

1. Drag a **Color** view onto **Text** on the Preview inside the Canvas.

    Be sure that it is added before the existing `Text` with "add `Color` inside a VStack containing the existing Text." Right now, the color is not pink but a 50% default RGB grey.

2. Change `Color` to `Color.pink`.

    You can either edit it in code or select the color in the view Inspector. Also, the view geometry is not quite what we wanted; our color background and `Text` are displayed in different positions vertically as if they were inside a vertical stack view in UIKit. This is precisely the effect of a Vstack.

3. Change `VStack` into `ZStack` so that `Color` is not inserted before `Text` but behind it.

    There is still an area of the screen, the status bar, which was not covered in pink and has been left white.

4. Let's add an `edgesIgnoringSafeArea(.all)` modifier after the terminating bracket of `ZStack` so as to allow the `Color` view to cover the screen completely.

5. The color of `Text` is not particularly legible so let's change it to white with a font size of **Title** and correct the border so that it is displayed at some distance around it by changing the order of the padding modifier.

Note

You should learn early on to change the size of fonts semantically and educate your designers as well; users with different visual acuity will want to be able to set the preferred size of the fonts in their accessibility settings. Your designers should learn not to think just in terms of "pixel perfection" based on aesthetics alone but should strive to give the users the most customizable and more pleasurable user experience possible.

6.   Also, let's change the border color to black.

Your final code result should look like this:

```
struct ContentView: View {
    var body: some View {
        Zstack {
            Color.pink
            Text("Hello, world!")


                .foregroundColor(Color.white)
                .padding()
                .border(Color.black, width: 3)
        }
        .edgesIgnoringSafeArea(.all)
    }
}
```

Your preview should look like this:

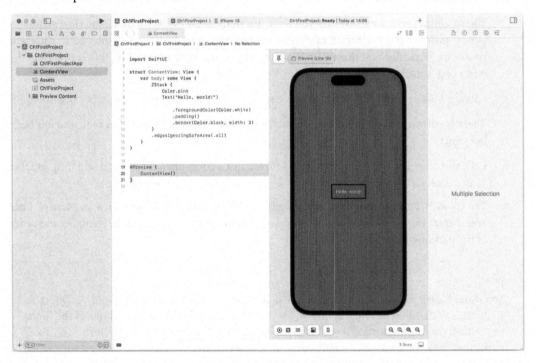

Figure 1.9 – Your final result should look like this one

HStack, VStack, and ZStack are containers, views capable of containing other views, thus allowing more than one view to be displayed at the same time.

HStack will display the views it contains on the horizontal axis. VStack will contain views spaced on the vertical axis. Finally, ZStack will allow views to be aligned on the Z axis as superimposed layers, allowing them to cover each other.

We will cover containers and more view types allowing you to code more complex UIs in more detail in the following chapters.

Notice that the signature of the body variable declared inside ContentView requires you to return some View, meaning that the return value is opaque: it just needs to be a view. Still, it is up to your code to decide which type of view it will be, which is convenient as you can substitute one for a different kind without changing the signature type. Stacks are containers, views that contain other views, allowing you to create some hierarchy of views while still conforming to the requirement of returning some view.

Views are allocated in memory on the Stack rather than on the Heap. The stack is where Swift places local variables that need to be accessed and disposed of quickly. Apple decided that it is better for a view not to be too complex on its own and limited the number of views that you can include inside VStack, HStack, or ZStack to 10.

Inserting more than 10 views inside any simple stack, prior to Xcode 15, was not supported.

If you need to add, for example, 12 views inside VStack, you could add two stacks, each containing a subset of your views, inside a third stack.

Nota bene: The return keyword is not required with Swift version 5.1 and above and is implied. At the time of the writing, the current version of Swift is 5.10.

If you want to add the return keyword, you could write the code as follows:

```
struct ContentView: View {
    var body: some View {
        return Zstack {
            Color.pink
            Text("Hello, world!")
                .foregroundColor(Color.white)
                .padding()
                .border(Color.black, width: 3)
        }
        .edgesIgnoringSafeArea(.all)
    }
}
```

This would work just fine. But note that `return` is not necessary, and Apple does not use it in their templates anymore. There are no official coding standards for Swift; however, developer teams typically prefer the shortest and more concise version of code, which is more "idiomatic" and preferable.

In this section, I introduced the first simple view modifiers, such as padding, `foregroundColor`, and borders. I also showed that changing the order of modifiers will change the end result, in terms of rendering a view. We finally introduced `VStack`, `HStack`, and `ZStack`.

In the next section, we will examine the creation of a SwiftUI project.

Your first SwiftUI project

In this section, we will look into the process of creating a new project supporting SwiftUI. We will first look into the easiest and quickest way to create a SwiftUI project. Then, we'll learn how to create a multi-platform project and at the end, there's also a multi-platform exercise for you to practice.

Creating a SwiftUI project

To create an app, start by clicking on **Create New Project…** on the initial **Welcome** Xcode screen. Be warned that this part is likely to change graphically and in terms of the options presented, with newer versions of Xcode.

I will teach you how to create a basic project with an app template or a multi-platform project from scratch, but we can't cover all the other options for all of the different kinds of projects Xcode can generate.

The following is the easiest and quickest way to create a basic project using an app template:

1.   Create an app for your desired platform by selecting **Create New Project…**:

Figure 1.10 – Create a new Xcode project

2. In the **Choose a template for your new project:** pane, select **App**:

Figure 1.11 – Choose the App template

3. You will have to select **Swift** as a programming language and choose the **SwiftUI** option rather than **Use storyboards** for the UI.

4. You can add a **Storage** option (Core Data or SwiftData) by selecting an option different from **None**. You can add tests from the start by ticking the **Include Tests** box.

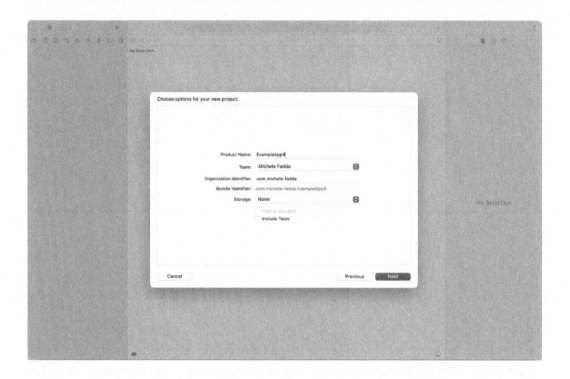

Figure 1.12 – Choosing options for the App template

> **Note**
>
> The method described previously is not the best approach as there is a definite advantage in developing multi-platforms from scratch. No matter what your desired platform is (iOS, iPadOS, macOS, watchOS or visionOS), you will want to have at least one or more macOS libraries for the shared business logic and networking layers, as you will want to run tests for the code-only parts of your app as unit tests and run those tests as fast as possible.
>
> You could create a simple app project, for example, for an iPhone-only app, by just accepting the defaults and creating an iOS-only target, but that would require tests to be run within the simulator.
>
> The simulator is a memory and resource-intensive app that will require a significant amount of time to get started. Running tests within it will slow them down by a factor of 6 to 10 times compared to the speed you would get by executing your tests within a Mac target.
>
> Running unit tests quickly is a definite advantage, and all properly structured apps should have modules for code unrelated to UI. There is no reason why this practice of creating libraries for non-UI code, even within a SwiftUI application, should not be common for any target platforms.

As an additional advantage of SwiftUI compared to UIKit, you will notice that the SwiftUI views are pretty similar or identical in terms of their coding across different platforms; they typically have the same syntax but differ in the way they are rendered with a UI representation that is appropriate for each platform.

For instance, a switch is rendered as a switch button on an iOS device, while this is rendered as a tick box on a Mac.

Unfortunately, SwiftUI is not a "develop once, run everywhere" framework, but rather the "you can use the same approach no matter what the platform" kind of UI framework, which is more convenient than the old UIKit for iOS and AppKit for the Mac.

The macOS interface has more components and is more complex, but typically a UI designed for a less capable device such as an iPhone will also work on a Mac and will require minimum adaptations.

When you create a project on Xcode for the first time, you will need to create a local GitHub repository for version management.

It is advisable, even if not required, to enter all the developer's git information in **Preferences | Version Management | Git of Xcode**.

Also, remember to set up your developer account by going to **Preferences | Accounts of Xcode**.

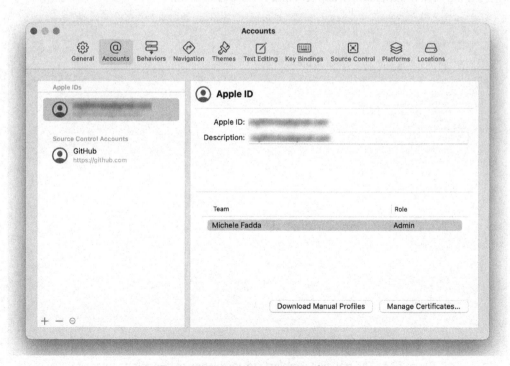

Figure 1.13 – Xcode account preferences

> **Note**
>
> Separating different concerns in different modules is a good practice, in general, as it helps structure an app architecture correctly and makes both testing and maintenance easier.
>
> As we are mostly exploring SwiftUI programming, we might decide to simplify things for clarity purposes and not always follow a layered architecture with our examples.
>
> But in a real-world app, that should never be the case, and you need to create and structure your project professionally from the start.

Creating a multi-platform project

In this section, we will show you an alternate approach for project creation, creating a multi-platform project by starting with an empty project. This is the quickest and easiest way to create a multi-platform project and is also the way to learn the most during the process. Then, you can add multiple targets as required: a macOS library, an iOS app, and so on.

Be aware that one of the meanings of "multi-platform" apps in Apple parlance is somewhat limited. Historically, a multi-platform app for iOS was intended as an app for "iPhone and iPad," to which Apple later added a **Catalyst** macOS app; now they call this target "Mac" (designed for iPad). Here's what a traditional multi-platform app template looks like in Xcode:

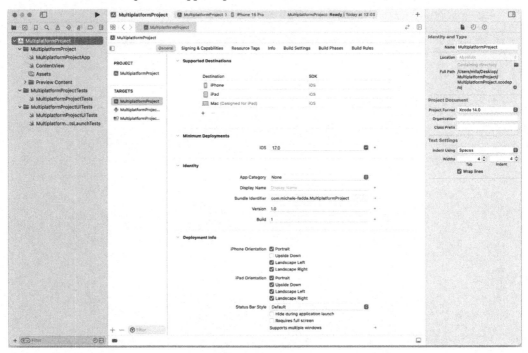

Figure 1.14 – The traditional project created by the multi-platform template

Catalyst is a framework allowing an app designed for iPad to be able to run on a Mac. We won't talk about this framework in more detail as it is beyond the scope of this book.

We mean a more general concept when we talk about a multi-platform project: it is a project with multiple targets for more than one platform. However, we will focus primarily on iOS and only cover SwiftUI-related aspects. Additional platforms you should consider are **tvOS** for Apple TV and **watchOS** for Apple Watch, whose development is greatly simplified as you don't need to dwell in specific UI frameworks for their development.

For a complex multi-platform project, you will need one app for every different platform and one or more frameworks for the non-UI part, plus the tests.

To start from scratch, you can create an empty project and add all the targets you will need separately later:

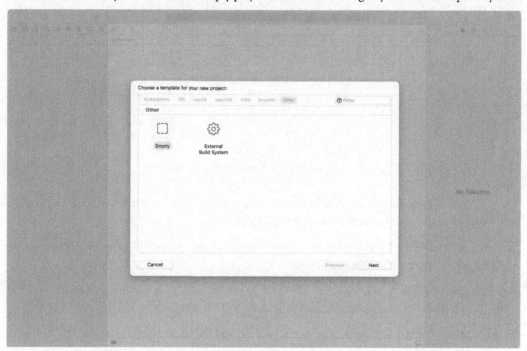

Figure 1.15 – The empty project template is a good starting point for a multi-platform project

Once we create an empty project, this is how it will look:

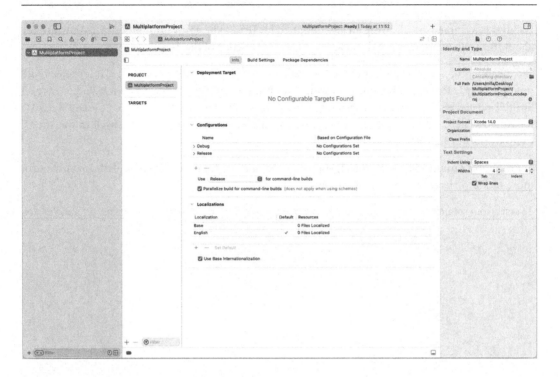

Figure 1.16 – An empty project after its creation

You will typically want to create a different app target as per each platform and add one or more "code-only" libraries and tests for each required platform.

You will need to add the Swift files shared across several different targets, to each one of these targets by using the + button in the **Targets** section.

You can select which target the new file belongs to either via Xcode's initial file creation dialog or by using the selection box on the right while the selected file content is shown in the main editor.

If you want a file shared across several targets, you can add the file to all the necessary targets in the identity inspector (first tab on the rightmost pane) by ticking on the appropriate boxes.

You can use a conditional compilation directive to allow for differences among several platforms by means of the `#if os()` directive.

Now, such a complex project will be unnecessary for our immediate purpose of teaching you the basics of SwiftUI. Still, this approach is best suited for a real-world complex app, in which you will want to reuse as much code as possible across different platforms.

A multi-platform exercise

Try running the same `Hello World` example view on several Apple platforms: iOS, macOS, tvOS, and watchOs.

Do you notice any differences? For some platforms, some UI elements are rendered differently.

In the next section, we will learn how to preview our views graphically and how to launch the simulator.

Previews and the simulator

Now, for the sake of simplicity, we will start again by creating a simple single-view project.

You can create a new project from the Xcode menu: **File** | **New** | **Project**.

You will see that Xcode will automatically create a simple project and create a view struct and a preview struct inside the `ContentView.swift` file.

The first struct inside this file describes a simple SwiftUI view (`Text`) and the second struct is used to pre-render it so that you can have an idea of the finished result without the need to launch the simulator.

You can have multiple previews, even for different devices simultaneously, but that depends heavily on the memory available on your system and has been somewhat error prone in the past.

You can give each preview a name, by using the `previewDisplayName` modifier on the content view in the preview, for example, name the currently rendered device **iPod**.

You can also change the desired rendered device in code using the `previewDevice` modifier on `ContenView`, like in the following code fragment:

```
struct ContentView_Previews: PreviewProvider {
    static var previews: some View {
        ContentView()
            .previewDevice("iPhone 11")
            .previewDisplayName("iphone 11")
    }
}
```

The rendering takes place on the Canvas, that is, on the right of the code describing the view. If the rendering is stopped, you can resume it with the **Resume** button or pressing *option + command + P* on the keyboard.

> **Note**
>
> From Xcode 15 onwards, you can abbreviate the previous preview to just the following syntax:
>
> ```
> #Preview {
>
>         ContentView()
>
> }
> ```

If the Canvas is not displayed, you will need to enable it via the **Editor** menu.

Also, in the **Editor** menu, you can decide whether you want to display a **Minimap** of your code, which can help you navigate through your code to an extent, especially if you have a large external monitor. If you are using a laptop, you may want to disable the **Minimap**.

Typically, the rendering is paused at startup, and you will need to restart it by clicking the **Resume** button to start rendering the preview in real-time. If that does not work due to an occasional Xcode bug, you will need to quit Xcode, reopen it, and reopen your project.

Be warned that Xcode and the simulator are large applications, so try not to open too many other apps simultaneously, especially if you are working on a complex app and have a limited amount of RAM.

You can also change the device used to pre-render the view in code and have a separate render for each different device, but according to my experience, that approach might not always be reliable due to bugs in Xcode.

If you select an element of the UI on the Canvas and hit *command* + left-click, your cursor will be transported to the code section responsible for that element in the **Editor**.

To see how the view will behave dynamically, you can press the play button on the preview (the triangle with the tip to the right inside a circle):

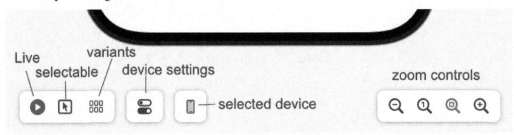

Figure 1.17 – The buttons on the Canvas panel

From left to right, these buttons on the bottom of the Canvas panel are as follows:

- **Live**: This renders the preview.
- **Selectable**: This allows selecting a UI element on the preview and highlights it on the Editor area at the same time.
- **Variants**: This allows us to see how the view will render on different variants of the preview. Pressing this button will present a menu allowing us to choose the following:
  - **Color scheme variants**: Light and dark
  - **Orientation variants**: Preview variants for rotated devices
- **Dynamic types variants**: This previews variants for different font sizes selected by the user.
- **Device settings**: Pressing this button will present a menu allowing us to change the main settings of the selected device shown in the preview. These changes include the color scheme (light/dark), orientation, and the dynamic type size.
- **Selected device**: This button will present a menu allowing us to change the device being simulated in the preview.
- On the right, we find the **zoom controls** affecting the preview: zoom out, zoom to 100%, zoom to fit, and zoom in.

To see what our complete app looks like, which presently displays the `Hello World` text at the center of the screen, we will run the simulator. Click the triangular play button on the top left panel of Xcode after selecting which device you want to simulate (hovering on the triangular play button will display the **Start the active scheme** ooltip).

This will start the simulator and run your app:

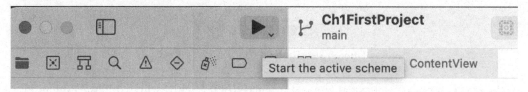

Figure 1.18 – Detail of the play button to run the app in the simulator

You can achieve the same result from the **Product | Run** menu or by pressing *command + R* on the keyboard.

You can also click the green play button on the Canvas, but that would start a dynamic rendering of the view including state changes on a separate window, and would not start the simulator. We will cover changing a view dynamically in *Chapter 3*.

You need to select a device to be able to simulate it. You can also choose to connect your physical device and run on that if you have a developer's account.

The simulator will be launched after your app has compiled. The preview rendering will be paused while the simulator is running.

You will probably want to get rid of the device bezels by deselecting **Show device bezels** in the **View** menu of the Simulator, as that will leave more space available on your computer screen. This is what it will look like:

Figure 1.19 – The simulator without bezels

In the next section, we will explain how to use playgrounds with SwiftUI and the limitations of this approach.

Playgrounds

Swift Playgrounds is an excellent way to test Swift code without creating an app or a complete project.

Unfortunately, Swift Playgrounds was developed for UIKit and does not completely support SwiftUI.

In Xcode, there is an option to create a `Playground` containing a view, but that will create a view with `ViewController` using UIKit, not SwiftUI, and that's not ideal for our purposes.

You can, however, start with an empty Playground and create your view in code with SwiftUI and then set it as the current view by using `PlaygroundPage.current.setLiveView(ContentView())`.

Your code will look like this:

```
import SwiftUI
import PlaygroundSupport
struct ContentView: View {
    var body: some View {
        Text("I love SwiftUI")


    }
}
PlaygroundPage.current.setLiveView(ContentView())
```

However, the support for SwiftUI in Swift Playgrounds is far from ideal, and not updated in real-time, meaning that you will need to re-run the playground via the play button continually whenever you need to change anything.

Swift Playgrounds also doesn't constantly render all the variations inside the Canvas preview you would get within a typical project within the **Editor** of an app project. Except for the most straightforward views, some views will not work correctly in Swift Playgrounds, and you are likely to encounter other problems dealing with complex views.

Your playground should look like the following screenshot:

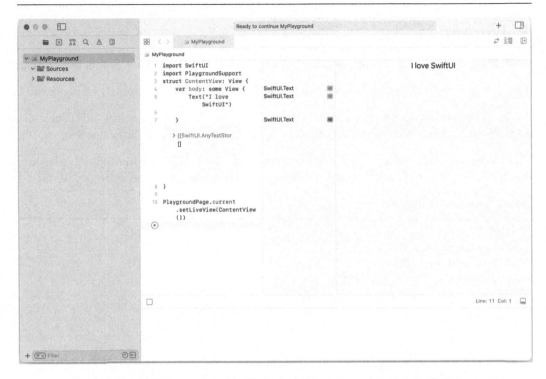

Figure 1.20 – Swift Playgrounds is of limited usefulness in prototyping SwiftUI views

That said, Swift Playgrounds is primarily helpful for rapidly prototyping non-UI-related code.

In the next section, we will explain how to add tests to an existing project.

Adding tests to a project

If you have a simple project structure, it is often easier to add your tests at the project creation. You can achieve this by ticking the **Include tests** checkbox as shown in the following screenshot:

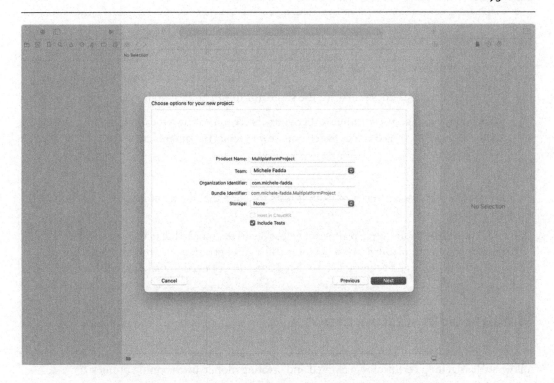

Figure 1.21 – Creating tests while creating the project is often easier

If, while creating your project, you did not select the option to create tests during its creation, you can add tests to an existing project by navigating to the project and hitting the + button in the **Targets** section.

Choose the platform you want to add tests for iOS and add unit tests.

You will want to run tests on both macOS and iOS by adding both targets.

Try running an elementary test, such as the following, on both macOS and iOS:

```
func testExample() throws {
        XCTAssert(2+2 == 4, "result != 4")
}
```

The testExample() function should be added to a test class belonging to your desired platform target. This test itself has no particular meaning, its purpose is just to make sure that the test target compiles correctly, and your project is capable of running tests.

You should add this function to the test class generated automatically.

Now, here's a simple exercise for you to try out:

- How many seconds does it take for the simulator to run and for your tests to start on iOS?

- Can you try to measure a simple test of your choice, repeating a loop a million times on both iOS and macOS? Which one is faster, and how much is the difference?

> **Note**
>
> You should always strive to run your unit tests for code that does not involve the UI under macOS rather than iOS.
>
> SwiftUI is present for all Apple platforms; before SwiftUI, you needed to deal with different UI frameworks for each platform. However, it is still a good practice to ensure that your business logic, network code, and other non-UI-related code do not need to include SwiftUI.

The app submission process

When submitting iOS and macOS applications to the Apple App Store, there are a number of steps to follow, such as getting certificates generated and creating mobile provisioning profiles.

You will need to use both the Apple Developer website and Xcode.

Certificates identify you as the developer of your apps and ensure the security and integrity of your apps. Different certificates will be required for development and distribution.

Certificates

There are two main types of certificates that are relevant to app development:

- **Development certificate**: This is used to authorize the installation of applications on physical devices while developing the application.

- **Distribution certificate**: This is required for application distribution in the App Store or ad hoc (on selected specific devices, the latter usually for testing purposes).

  Additional certificates can be needed for specific purposes, for example, enabling push messages.

The following steps are required to create certificates:

- **Certificate Signing Request (CSR)**: First, create a CSR on Mac using the Keychain Access app. This basically involves opening Keychain Access, selecting **Certificate Assistant**, and then selecting **Request a Certificate from a Certificate Authority**, following the prompts.

- **Developer ID Certificates**: In the developer center, go to **Certificates, Identifiers & Profiles** and click on **Certificates**, then click the + button to add a new certificate. Choose the appropriate certificate type (**Developer ID Application** or **Developer ID Installer** for macOS apps) and follow the instructions to upload your CSR and generate the certificate.

  Once the certificate has been generated and countersigned by Apple, you should install it using the Keychain App on macOS, normally in the login keychain. The system keychain is associated with the development machine, not the developer, and it requires applications to have admin credentials to access the certificates. The drawback of using the login keychain is that only you will have access to it on your own machine.

Mobile provisioning profiles

Provisioning profiles link the App ID in your app to a particular development team, and they also identify devices authorized to run the app. They are used both in development and distribution:

- **Development provisioning profile**: This is a profile necessary to execute and test an application in development. The profile contains a development certificate, devices, and an App ID.

- **Distribution provisioning profile**: This is a profile necessary to distribute an app through the App Store. This profile includes a distribution certificate and an App ID. The App ID uniquely identifies your app in the App Store.

The following are the steps you will need to follow to create provisioning profiles:

1. You will create and manage provisioning profiles in the **Certificates, Identifiers & Profiles** section of the Apple Developer portal.
2. Select **Provisioning Profiles** and choose to create either a development or distribution profile according to your needs.
3. During the creation process, choose the App ID for your application and the certificates to be used in it.

After creation, download the profile and install it in Xcode.

Note

Xcode also provides an automatic management function of certificates and provisioning profiles, making it much easier for beginner developers. When this mode is activated, Xcode manages the development and distribution certificates required, as well as the provisioning profiles, so you won't need to manually create and maintain these through the Apple Developer website.

To enable the automatic management of certificates and profiles in Xcode, simply follow these steps:

1. Open your app project in Xcode.

2. If the Project Navigator is hidden, reveal the project settings by selecting **Show project settings** from the **View** menu in Xcode.

3. Select your target and proceed to the **Signing & Capabilities** tab.

4. Check the **Automatically manage signing** option box.

5. Choose your team from the drop-down list. Xcode will proceed to exchange data with the Apple Developer website, and it will create and download the certificates and provisioning profiles.

For large development teams, the manual management of certificates is preferred. For individual developers, the automatic management of signing is normally easier and more convenient.

This automatic process simplifies app development and submission, minimizing the steps needed for managing certificates and provisioning profiles. It ensures that the app's signing certificates and provisioning profiles are current.

The application submission process

Now that all certificates and provisioning profiles are in place, you can get your application ready for submission:

1. *Prepare app metadata*: Set the name, description, screenshots, and other app metadata in **App Store Connect**, using this URL: `https://appstoreconnect.apple.com`.

2. *Archive and upload the app*: Archive your app using Xcode and then upload the build to App Store Connect. Open the project in Xcode and follow these steps:

    I.   Open the scheme for the app to archive and set it to a generic iOS device.

    II.   Choose **Product | Archive** from the Xcode menu. This will build the app and create an archive.

    III. After the archive has been created, the Xcode Organizer will open, with the new archive selected. Within the Organizer, you can verify the archive for potential problems before uploading it to App Store Connect by using the Validation function on the Organizer. After the validation, the archive can be uploaded directly to App Store Connect using the **Upload to App Store** button.

3. *Submit for review*: Before uploading your build and submitting your app for review from the App Store Connect, it is advisable to ensure that it complies with the App Store Review Guidelines, which you can find at this URL: `https://developer.apple.com/app-store/review/guidelines/`

4. *Testing on physical devices using TestFlight*: Sending your app to testers via App Store Connect is facilitated through TestFlight, which allows you to invite users to test your app before its official release on the App Store. This process allows you to gather feedback and identify issues. More information about TestFlight can be found here: `https://developer.apple.com/testflight/`.

    Here are the steps you need to follow to send your app to testers using TestFlight:

    I.   Upload your app to App Store Connect, ensuring it adheres to the Review Guidelines and is ready for testing.

    II.   Go to the **My Apps** section in App Store Connect and select your app.

    III. Click on the **TestFlight** tab, where you'll see sections for both internal and external testers. You can potentially invite up to 10,000 external testers using just an email address. Note: No Apple account ID is required for external testers.

    IV.   For internal testing, you will be able to add only up to 25 team members, with roles such as Admin, Legal, or App Manager, who will be allowed to test on up to 30 devices using TestFlight.

    V.   Apple will review the beta version of your app; this process can take several days, before external testers will be allowed to begin testing.

    VI.   Once approved, testers will receive an email invitation to test the app. They will be invited to install the TestFlight app and access the beta version of your app through this app.

    VII. TestFlight offers the opportunity to evaluate the app's functionality, performance, and user experience with a wider audience before it is released to the public.

5. *Release*: After approval, you can use App Store Connect to release your app on the App Store, either immediately or at a scheduled release date.

This procedure will ensure that apps are securely identified, authorized to run on physical user devices, and comply with Apple guidelines for distribution in the App Store. Refer to the official Apple Developer Documentation about certificates and look at the **Manage your signing certificates** section of Xcode's **Help** for a more complete guide.

Summary

We have just covered some initial ground.

You should now be able to create your projects and add several target platforms to them.

You have been given a brief introduction about using Xcode to create and modify a simple text view, and you should be able to preview, modify, and run your first very simple app with static text and a color background.

You have seen the basics of project creation; you know how to modify a project to add tests or support for another platform on your own.

You know the limits and advantages of Swift Playgrounds rather than previews and can solve the most common Xcode problems you face as a SwiftUI beginner.

In the next chapter, we will explore SwiftUI views and their modifiers in greater detail, and we will create more complex screens.

2

Adding Basic UI Elements and Designing Layouts

In this chapter, we will start by learning how to improve your SwiftUI views code by structuring it into more manageable and understandable chunks. Then, we will proceed to explain more basic views and how to compose them together with stacks, to create more complex and interesting views containing more UI elements and adjusting the geometry of their placement.

In this chapter we're going to cover the following main topics:

- Reusing views code
- Digging deeper into stacks
- Using `GeometryReader`

Technical requirements

The code used in this chapter can be found at `https://github.com/PacktPublishing/An-iOS-Developer-s-Guide-to-SwiftUI` under the folder `CH2`

Reusing views code

In this section, we will learn a refactoring technique for SwiftUI views: extracting subviews.

You can structure your code any way you want, but if you allow your code to contain many duplicates for the same functionality, you will end up having to replace and correct multiple instances of the same fragments of code whenever you change anything. This is both boring and prone to error, and it involves having to work more in order to achieve little.

We want to show you an important "trick" that allows you to better structure your code. As you build larger and more intricate UI screens and apps, you will often notice that the same elements and groups of views will need to appear identical in several places inside the same app.

Of course, rewriting all of them from scratch every time and inside a content view would eventually create a giant, messy blob of difficult-to-understand code.

Let's examine for instance a very simple view containing VStack, which contains different Text views.

You could simply write it this way:

```
VStack {
                Text("Title")
                    .font(.largeTitle)
                    .fontWeight(.heavy)
                    .foregroundColor(Color.red)
                Text("subtitle")
                    .font(.headline)
                    .fontWeight(.bold)
                Text("This is a rather longish description on multiple
lines of text")
}
.padding()
```

Next, let's add VStack to ContentView and another Text view just beneath VStack containing Title, Subtitle, and Description.

You can start with the default created "Hello World" and modify it so that it looks like the following screen capture:

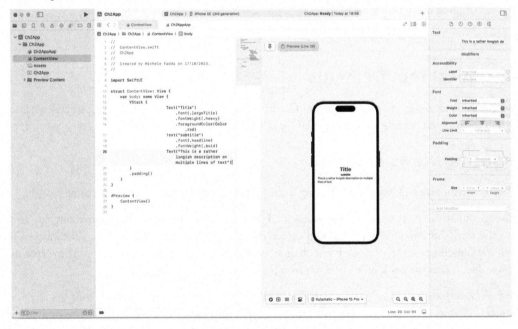

Figure 2.1 – Example of an unstructured code for the creation of a view in SwiftUI

This code will work, but writing everything manually is not the most efficient way. Let's suppose you need the exact same `VStack` with the same three `Text` views within another screen.

Partitioning and reusing code sensibly so that the code is easier to maintain and understand is not exactly a new principle and SwiftUI makes no exception.

You can write by hand a struct that will generate the common repeated view where needed and assign it a good easy-to-understand name, and just invoke it in the places where the refactored view is needed.

However, there is a better way to do this, rather than doing everything by hand and achieving the same result automatically.

Start by pressing the *Command* key and clicking on either the code or the preview (while it's visible), and then select **Extract Subview** from the context menu.

Figure 2.2 – Extracting a view (command-click after selecting the subview to extract)

The end result will be the following:

```
import SwiftUI

struct ContentView: View {

    var body: some View {
        VStack {
            ExtractedView()
        }

    }
}

struct ContentView_Previews: PreviewProvider {
    static var previews: some View {
        ContentView()
    }
}
struct ExtractedView: View {
    var body: some View {
        VStack {
            Text("Title")
                .font(.largeTitle)
                .fontWeight(.heavy)
                .foregroundColor(Color.red)
            Text("subtitle")
                .font(.headline)
                .fontWeight(.bold)
            Text("This is a rather longish description on multiple
lines of text")
        }
    }
}
```

As you can see, Xcode has named the extracted view to `ExtractedView`. Let's rename it to something more descriptive and useful, for instance, `ScreenHeader`, by right-clicking on `ExtractedView` and selecting the **Refactor** | **Rename** option.

You can see the finished product in the following screen capture:

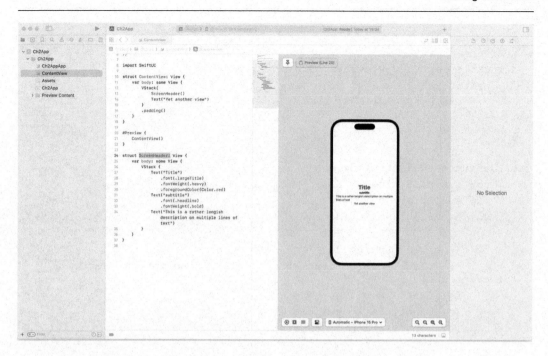

Figure 2.3 – Extracted and renamed view

If you compare the refactored code with our unstructured initial approach, it is now much clearer and easier to read. However, this is not yet finished, as only the text of the strings is fixed, and we want to be able to customize it to different content on different screens. This part we are going to do by hand.

You only need to add `init` to the extracted view and allow parameters to be passed at its instantiation.

The final code is the following:

```
import SwiftUI

struct ContentView: View {

    var body: some View {

        VStack {
            ScreenHeader("Hello",subtitle: "Example", description:
"This is the refactored view as an example for the beginning of
chapter two")
            Text("Yet Another view")
        }

    }
```

```
}

struct ContentView_Previews: PreviewProvider {
    static var previews: some View {
        ContentView()
    }
}

struct ScreenHeader: View {
    var title: String
    var subtitle: String
    var description: String

    init(_ title: String,
            subtitle: String = "subtitle", description: String =
"description") {
        self.title = title
        self.subtitle = subtitle
        self.description = description
    }
    var body: some View {

        VStack {
            Text(title)
                .font(.largeTitle)
                .fontWeight(.heavy)
                .foregroundColor(Color.red)
            Text(subtitle)
                .font(.headline)
                .fontWeight(.bold)
            Text(description)
        }
        .padding()
    }
}
```

As an exercise, add a few parameters with default values to `init` of the `ScreenHeader` struct, allowing you to be able to change colors and fonts when you instantiate the view.

In the next section, we will learn more about the `Text` view.

More about Text

There is a lot more to add to the humble `Text` view, which we will now examine in more detail. This view is among the most important building blocks in SwiftUI.

`Text` is a struct that takes a `String`, or `Date` and `DateStyle` as input and returns a view that displays that string.

It is worth remembering that you can further process the string you pass as a parameter for its constructor; for example, you can format `Date` on the go with `formatted()`:

```
Text(Date.now.formatted())
```

You can also add value interpolation to the string passed to the `Text` constructor if you need to visualize a numerical value.

You can modify the appearance of `Text` using modifiers.

Here are some of the most common modifiers for `Text` as examples:

```
Text("The Divine Comedy")
    .font(.system(size:12, weight: .light, design: .serif))
    .italic()

let myAttributedString = try! AttributedString(
    markdown: "_The Divine Comedy_ by *Dante Alighieri*")

var body: some View {
    Text(myAttributedString)
        .font(.system(size: 13, weight: .medium, design: .monospaced))
}
```

Notice that you can also apply styling to portions of a string by creating `Text` from `AttributedString`, which allows you to enter Markdown to style portions of the text. You can find more information about the Markdown format here: `https://www.markdownguide.org`.

You can freely mix string attributes with SwiftUI modifiers, but the string attributes (e.g., those specified with the Markdown notation) will have priority.

`Text` will always just use the exact space it needs to display its contents unless you modify its frame, for example, with a `.frame` modifier. It will normally try to "hug" its contents (if you want to reason similarly to how the old autolayout constraints worked).

If you want to visualize the actual occupied space by a view, you can add a border modifier to it like the following:

```
Text(myAttributedString)
                .font(.system(size: 13, weight: .medium, design:
.monospaced))
                .border(Color.red, width: 2)
```

You can also remove it immediately afterward if the border is not actually needed.

You can use `line` modifiers such as `lineLimit`, `allowsTightening`, `minimumScaleFactor`, and `truncationMode` to handle how the text will be displayed if there is not enough space to display the content string inside the text: accordingly, `Text`'s behavior will allow single or multiple lines, shrinking, shrinking up to a minimum size, truncating.

So, you get the same kind of text formatting power you were accustomed to with UIKit.

SwiftUI Text has another important feature that affects localization.

Localization is the process of allowing users speaking different languages to see the text of apps shown in their languages. This process used to require more manual work on the developer's side.

Now, Apple has made localization simpler by adopting a modality called **implicit localization** by default. Let's say your app is localized (i.e., you have added more than one language to the project), and you initialize a `Text` with an explicit string literal like so:

```
Text("Carbonara")
```

The `Carbonara` string will be considered localized and iOS will search for its text as a key in the default localization table in the main bundle.

That is, you can now avoid doing anything to mark your strings as localized in your code.

If, instead, you want to deliberately bypass localization, you must use the `Text` constructor with the `verbatim` parameter:

```
Text(verbatim: "Carbonara")
```

This will display the `Carbonara` string independently from the user's locale.

> **Note**
>
> If you use a string variable as an argument for the `init` of `Text`, the string contained in the variable won't normally be localized unless you explicitly use the `LocalizedStringKey()` function to convert the string to a localization key before invoking the default constructor of `Text`.

In this section, we learned about styling and the localization of Text in SwiftUI.

We will now proceed to learn about how to control empty space in our designs.

Managing "empty" space, or the distance among other visual elements, is as important as color and typography in visual design. We need to be able to control that to a great extent while designing a screen.

Managing space in SwiftUI

Nobody likes to look at views that are just crammed together without any space between them. In visual design, empty space is just as important and is used to give "air" and "breathing space" to the content.

Many modifiers in SwiftUI implement the View protocol and accept an input view returning another modified view.

The space-controlling modifiers are among the most commonly used modifiers and can be used with all kinds of SwiftUI views. We will go over these commonly used modifiers in this section and also learn how they work.

> **Note**
>
> For your convenience, Xcode offers a list containing all the views and modifiers that you can use, allowing you to drag and drop them onto the canvas or the code panels. Just click the **Library** button to display this list.

The commonly used modifiers used to change the balance between content and the surrounding space around the content do so by affecting **Frame**, **Alignment**, and **Padding**. We will be covering padding in the next section and the alignment and frame modifiers immediately afterward.

The padding modifier

padding is a modifier that adds "padding" (i.e., the empty space between the view's content and its frame). If you only pass a number as a parameter to its initializer, that number will determine the size in pixels of the padding that will be applied on all four sides of the view. If you pass Text to a padding(8) modifier, you will get another view that will contain that text surrounded by an empty space of eight pixels around all four sides.

If you instead pass an EdgeInsets value to the initializer of padding or multiple Edge values, you can specify how much padding has to be added on each of the sides of the view.

If you look it up, padding's declaration is as follows:

```
func padding(_ edges: Edge.Set = .all, _ length: CGFloat? = nil) ->
some View
```

edges are the set of edges to pad for the view. The default is all.

A single `Edge` is an enum, and its possible values are self-explanatory: `.top`, `.bottom`, `.leading`, and `.trailing`.

`Edge` is declared as a `@frozen` enum, meaning it is guaranteed not to get any new values in the future when new versions of Apple operating systems are introduced.

`length` is a value in typographical points meant to pad a view on the specified edges. If you don't set this parameter, it will default to an appropriate value, depending on the development platform.

The following code example shows the difference between padded and unpadded `Text`:

```
VStack {
    Text("Text with no padding.")
        .border(.blue)
    Text("Text padded by 30 points on the bottom and leading edges.")
        .padding([.bottom, .leading], 30)
        .border(.red)
}
```

In the next section, we will be going over the `.frame` modifier.

The .frame modifier

`.frame` is a view modifier, and its declaration is as follows:

```
func frame(width: CGFloat? = nil, height: CGFloat? = nil, alignment:
Alignment = .center) -> some View
```

The following are the `init` parameters of `.frame`:

- `width` constrains the resulting view to a fixed width. It defaults to `nil`. If `width` is `nil`, the resulting view will behave as the view this modifier processes in terms of its horizontal size.

- `height` constrains the resulting view to a fixed width. It defaults to `nil`. If `height` is `nil`, the resulting view will behave as the view this modifier processes in terms of its vertical size.

- `alignment` allows the view to change the alignment inside the resulting frame. The alignment defaults to `.center`.

> **Note**
>
> With `.frame`, most alignment values have no effect when the size of the frame is precisely the same as that of the view being modified.
>
> If you specify only one parameter between `width` and `height`, the resulting view will be constrained only in the dimension of the parameter you specify and will have its standard behavior in the other dimension.

One of the allowed forms of the `.frame` init is the following, which contains an `alignment` parameter:

```
frame(width: CGGloat?, height: CGFloat, alignment: Alignment)
```

> **Note**
>
> We can't really detail all possible variations and parameters of all modifiers.
>
> In order to familiarise yourself with all the possible variations and uses of a keyword such as `frame`, you should consult the Apple developer documentation at the following link: `https://developer.apple.com/documentation/swiftui`.

In order to get information on a keyword from Xcode, you can just hover on a keyword and hit the **Option** button; alternatively, you can select the keyword you want information about, and then hit the button with a circled **?** in the inspector pane:

Figure 2.4 – Getting help on a keyword in Xcode

The .alignment modifier

The `.alignment` modifier in SwiftUI lets you control the alignment of child views within their parent. The modifier is particularly useful when dealing with container views such as `VStack`, `HStack`, or `ZStack`. It takes a parameter of type Alignment.

The possible values for the Alignment enum are self-explanatory:

`.topLeading`	`.top`	`.topTrailing`
`.leading`	`.center`	`.trailing`
`.bottomLeading`	`.bottom`	`.bottomTrailing`

A single `Edge` is an enum with the values `.top`, `.bottom`, `.leading`, and `.trailing`.

For instance, you could select to pad 20 points, only on `.bottom` and `.left` by using the following:

```
.padding([.bottom, .left], 20)
```

The next screen capture shows an example of using the `padding` modifier on `Text`.

Figure 2.5 – Example of selecting edges in .padding

Nota bene: The process of choosing `edges` functions uniformly for numerous SwiftUI modifiers

In the next code example, you will see how to use all possible Alignment values:

```
import SwiftUI

struct ContentView: View {
    let colors: [Color] = [.red, .blue, .green, .yellow, .orange,
.brown, .pink, .gray, .black]
    var shuffledColors: [Color] { colors.shuffled() }
```

```
    var body: some View {
        let randomizedColors = shuffledColors
        return ScrollView {
            VStack(spacing: 20) {
                alignmentBox(.leading, color: randomizedColors[0],
text: "Leading")
                alignmentBox(.center, color: randomizedColors[1],
text: "Center")
                alignmentBox(.trailing, color: randomizedColors[2],
text: "Trailing")
                alignmentBox(.top, color: randomizedColors[3], text:
"Top")
                alignmentBox(.bottom, color: randomizedColors[4],
text: "Bottom")
                alignmentBox(.topLeading, color: randomizedColors[5],
text: "TopLeading")
                alignmentBox(.topTrailing, color: randomizedColors[6],
text: "TopTrailing")
                alignmentBox(.bottomLeading, color:
randomizedColors[7], text: "BottomLeading")
                alignmentBox(.bottomTrailing, color:
randomizedColors[8], text: "BottomTrailing")
            }
            .padding()
        }
    }

    func alignmentBox(_ alignment: Alignment, color: Color, text:
String) -> some View {
        Text(text)
            .frame(width: 300, height: 60, alignment: alignment)
            .background(color)
            .foregroundColor(.white)
            .cornerRadius(10)
    }
}

struct ContentView_Previews: PreviewProvider {
    static var previews: some View {
        ContentView()
    }
}
```

You can see the result in the next screenshot:

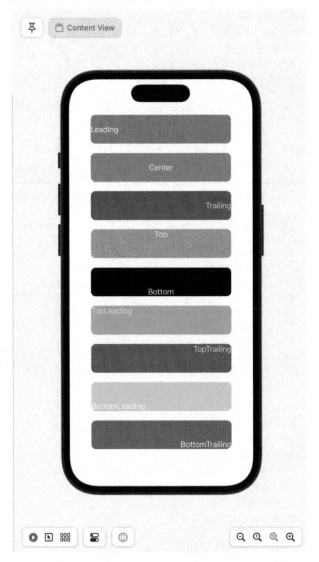

Figure 2.6 – All the possible alignment values

Next up is the `Spacer`.

The Spacer

Suppose you want to separate your views on VStack and send one of them to the top. How can you do it? One way is by filling the available blank space with a filler view, which will take all the remaining available space by itself.

Color is such an expansive view, but suppose you want to fill the space with an empty view, one without any content, not even a different Color. One such SwiftUI view, which is normally empty and takes all available remaining space in its container by itself, is Spacer.

Contrary to Text, which is a "hugging" view, Spacer is an expansive view; it normally fills up all the available space across the available dimension (vertical for vertical stacks and horizontal for horizontal stacks).

Spacers are just views and can be modified like any other views; for instance, you can add .background to them, or specify their frame.

If you want to constrain your Spacer modifier to a fixed height, you just add a .frame modifier to it, specifying only the height parameter like so:

```
VStack {
            Text("First Label")
            Spacer()
                .frame(height: 50)
            Text("Second Label")
        }
        .border(Color.blue, width: 1)
```

The preceding code will create VStack containing two Text views, separated at least by 50 points. Spacer will, however, get all the remaining space if more than 50 points are available. If you want it to be exactly 50 points, you can add a second Spacer View after the second Text label. This last Spacer would get all the remaining space for itself.

If you want to partition the space differently, you can use multiple instances of Spacer without constraining them with a frame modifier.

Each of these instances will get an equal share of the remaining space available.

For example, in order to put a String at one-third of the available vertical space, you can use `VStack` containing three instances of `Spacer`, one before the Text (which will inflate to one-third of the available vertical space remaining after the vertical frame size of the Text) and two more after it so that each one of them will take one-third of the available vertical space. Here's a code example:

```
import SwiftUI

struct ContentView: View {
    var body: some View {
        VStack {
            Spacer()
            Text("one third of the way")
            Spacer()
            Spacer()

        }
        .padding()
    }
}

struct ContentView_Previews: PreviewProvider {
    static var previews: some View {
        ContentView()
    }
}
```

The result is shown in the next screen capture:

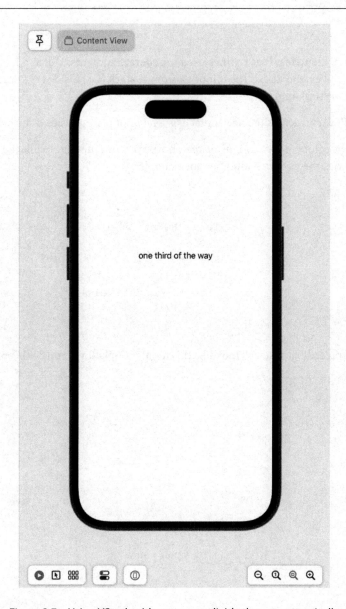

Figure 2.7 – Using VStack with spacers to divide the screen vertically

In the next section, we will move to the Divider.

The Divider

Dividers are visual elements, that is, lines used to separate contents. When a `Divider` is placed inside a stack, it will extend across the minor axis of the stack (i.e., inside `HStack`, the divider will be displayed as a vertical line).

A `Divider` will extend across the horizontal axis when not placed inside a stack.

You can change the color of `Divider` using the `.background` modifier, while the size of `Divider` can be changed with the `.frame` modifier, for example:

```
VStack {
            Divider()
            Text("First Label")
            Divider()
            Spacer()
            Divider()
            Text("Second Label")
            Divider()
}
```

The result of the preceding code will look like this for a multiplatform app, with a preview on a Mac:

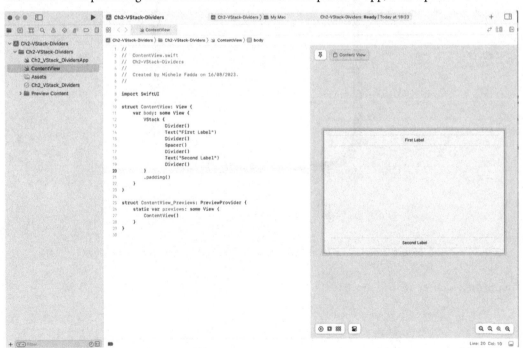

Figure 2.8 – Using Spacer to partition space across a view

We have examined how we can use empty space in our screens and how to constrain that empty space geometrically, for the purpose of creating a visually pleasing screen layout.

In the next section, we will examine stacks in more detail.

Digging deeper into stacks

Stacks are an important part of SwiftUI and historically, the simplest stacks were among the first introduced features of the framework. With stacks, you can solve most of the commonly encountered layout issues, allowing you to recreate the commonly used screens in most applications. In this section, you will learn more about the various types of stacks available in SwiftUI and their differences, including the advantages and disadvantages of similar ones.

Overview of stacks

Stacks allow composing different views together. They basically serve the same purpose as stack views in UIKit. By grouping views vertically and horizontally, you can create much more complex views. Autolayout and its constraints are no longer needed to create views that will adapt to all screen sizes. You can achieve the same results by means of stacks. The simplest versions of stacks that we have already met are `VStack`, `HStack`, and `ZStack`.

`VStack` lays out the contained views across the vertical axis, `HStack` does the same horizontally, while `ZStack` allows views to cover each other across the third dimension (like a stack of cards, for instance).

Nota bene: You can specify the spacing of `VStack` by passing it as a parameter at initialization time.

These three versions of a stack have a few common aspects:

- Each instance of a simple stack can contain at most 10 other views (this limit was removed with Swift 5.9 in Xcode 15)
- All simple stacks pre-allocate all the contained child subviews in memory all at once, even if their children are not displayed together at the same time. This strategy of memory allocation is called **eager**. Eager allocation is very simple but consumes too much memory even for the most powerful devices for very large datasets. Besides being inefficient, it also becomes too slow and sluggish for large datasets.

If you need to display a very large number of subviews and scroll among them, then simple stacks are not the right choice.

> **Note**
> In order to be able to scroll a view, in SwiftUI you can embed the view inside `ScrollView`. You can change the behavior of `ScrollView` by using its `init` parameters.

If you need to scroll large sets of data, SwiftUI offers **lazy stacks**, which are roughly equivalent to the eager ones, but instead would allocate views in memory only as these subviews are needed for display. Therefore, these lazy containers are able to handle much more complex views, contain many more subviews, and are more responsive for "real" heavy-duty apps.

The lazy "equivalent" of `VStack` and `HStack` are `LazyVStack` and `LazyHStack`. They are not exactly a Plug and Play exact replacement for their eager counterparts as their behavior is a little different visually.

Simple stacks "hug" across their minor axis (e.g., `VStack` will have its children take the minimum space possible horizontally).

Lazy stacks instead are expansive across their minor axis (e.g., `LazyVStack` will expand to all the available space horizontally, without regard for its "hugging" subviews (such as `Text` or `Image`, for example)).

Here's an example: change `ContentView.swift` to the following:

```swift
import SwiftUI
struct ContentView: View {

    var body: some View {

        VStack {
            Example()
        }
    }
}


struct ContentView_Previews: PreviewProvider {
    static var previews: some View {
        ContentView()
    }
}


struct Example: View {
    var body: some View {
        LazyVStack {
                Text("LazyVStack First Label")
                Spacer()
                Text("LazyVStack Second Label")
        }
        .border(Color.blue, width: 2)
        VStack {
                Text("VStack First Label")
```

```
                Spacer()
                Text("VStack Second Label")
                Spacer()
            }
            .border(Color.red, width: 2)
            Spacer()
        }
    }
```

The preceding code will result in very different layout behavior:

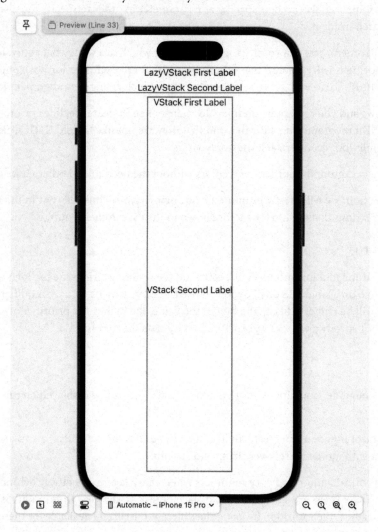

Figure 2.9 – The different layout behavior of LazyVStack and VStack

In the next sections, we will examine the horizontal counterparts of the vertical stacks we have just examined, beginning with `HStack`.

HStack

`HStack` stands for **horizontal stack**. Like its vertical counterpart, it is a container that will "hug" its contents (trying to minimize its occupied space) and will display its contents on the same horizontal line. It also has a limitation of a maximum of 10 child views. If you need more than 10 subviews, you can add them inside multiple nested `HStack` instances.

The `HStack` initializer also accepts spacing as a parameter in order to specify the distance between adjacent children inside it.

In terms of alignment, you can specify top and bottom, which are somewhat equivalent to leading and trailing for `VStack`, but add two other options that are exclusive for horizontal containers: `firtsTextBaseline` and `lastTextBaseline`, which change the alignment for text.

Stacks are views and you can apply modifiers to change their appearance, like any other view. If you come from UIKit programming, bear in mind that they are not like the old `UIStackView`, which were "non-rendering" geometrical layout-only views.

They can have backgrounds, borders, and colors without the need to add other views to them.

In the next section, we will briefly examine **layout priority**, which is relevant to the layout of text, when we have strings that are too long to be shown to the user in their entirety.

Layout priority

When you are using multiple instances of `Text`, and the resulting strings are too long to be displayed at the same time on a single `HStack`, you can use the `layoutPriority` modifier to determine which `Text` will be truncated last. The higher the value, the higher the priority not to truncate the text. If you don't specify a value, `layoutPriority` defaults to zero.

ZStack

`ZStack` is a "hugging" container view that allows its children to be displayed on top of each other, in "depth."

`ZStack` is one of how you can create multiple layers, besides the `.background` and `.overlay` modifiers, but with more control over sizing and spacing.

The `.background` and `.overlay` modifiers will create a layer respectively behind or in front of another view. These layers are stacked on top of each other and the view they modify is like a stack of cards. You can adjust their position by using the different initializers available for these views, which can accept alignment and offsets.

Nota bene: You can stack multiple instances of `.overlay` and `.background`, which can be useful if you want to compose the resulting screen using transparencies, as each of these will be treated as an additional layer.

If you want a container view such as `ZStack` to expand to all available space in a device, you have to use a `.ignoreSafeArea(.all)` modifier at its end, so that it will also be forced to occupy the safe area, which is the same as what you would have done with UIKit.

You could use `.ignoreSafeArea`, passing only a set of edges, for special cases, such as resizing automatically when a keyboard is shown on a mobile device.

When using `.ignoresSafeArea()`, be sure to check that no important text is pushed out of the visible area on the device (e.g., on the top). Generally, it is a better idea to use `.ignoreSafeArea` only for the individual views that actually need to be expanded outside the safe area inside `ZStack` (e.g., `Color` or `Image` used as a background, rather than setting it for the whole `ZStack`).

Use `ZStack` whenever you need to layer views (e.g., placing text on top of images).

As with other layer modifiers, you can specify the alignment and offset with `ZStack` at init time. Here's an example for you:

```
ZStack {
            Color.blue
                .ignoresSafeArea()
            VStack{
                Text ("This is behind")
                Text ("This is behind")
                Text ("This is behind")
                Text ("This is behind")
                Text ("This is behind")
                Text ("This is behind")
                Text ("This is behind")
                Text ("This is behind")
                Text ("This is behind")
                Spacer()
            }
            Image(systemName: "icloud.fill")
                .resizable()
                .frame(minWidth: 300, idealWidth: 300, maxWidth: 300,
 minHeight: 300, idealHeight: 300, maxHeight: 300, alignment: .center)
                .foregroundColor(.pink)

            Text("This text is in front of the image")
                .bold()
                .foregroundColor(.white)
        }
```

The preceding code will result in this screen:

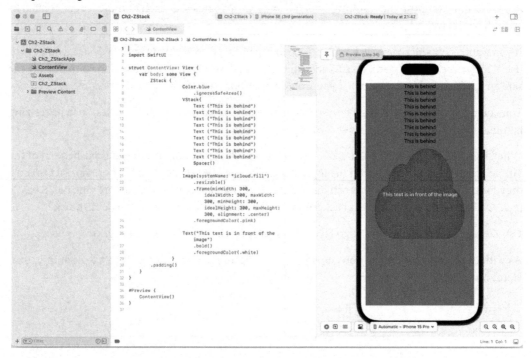

Figure 2.10 – Using ZStack to superimpose views as layers

In the next section, we will explain how to access programmatically geometrical information about a view and how to achieve precise positioning, not achievable with Spacer, using GeometryReader.

GeometryReader

When you can't achieve the proportions of views you wanted with Spacer, or if you need to know the exact dimensions of a view, it is time to use GeometryReader.

GeometryReader is similar to an expansive container view in the sense that it is a view and you can add child subviews to it.

You can then access properties such as height, width, and safe insets and use these to compute the parameters of the views inside GeometryReader so that these are displayed correctly on all devices.

By default, `GeometryReader` children are aligned in the top-left corner (`.leadingTop`).

Child subviews of `GeometryReader` will be placed on top of each other, like in `ZStack`.

`ZStack`, however, provides alignment options, while `GeometryReader` does not.

`GeometryReader` provides a way to read and constrain (among other things) coordinates, sizes, and aspect ratios of its subviews.

`GeometryReader` works by using a closure that takes a 'proxy' as its input parameter. This proxy helps figure out the size and other spatial details of the elements it contains.

For example, if you wanted to know the exact size occupied by `VStack`, you could surround it with `GeometryReader`:

```swift
import SwiftUI

struct ContentView: View {
    var body: some View {
        GeometryReader { geometry in
            VStack(spacing:20) {
                Text("Horizontal size: \(geometry.size.width)")
                Text("Vertical size: \(geometry.size.height)")

            }
            .padding()
            .border(Color.blue,width: 1)
        }
    }
}
#Preview {
    ContentView()
}
```

The result will be like the following screen capture:

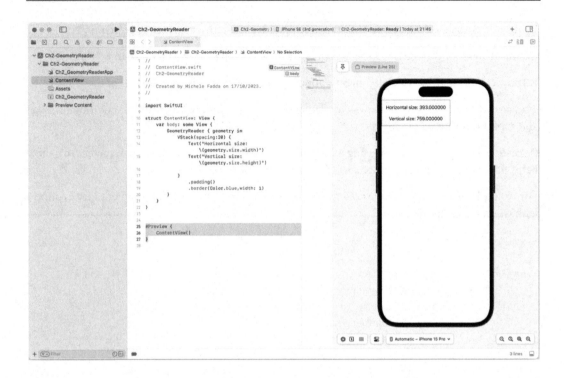

Figure 2.11 – Using GeometryReader to get the exact size of a view

However, `GeometryReader` cannot only "read" the coordinates and sizes of a view, but can also be used to position a subview precisely inside itself.

Let's say you edit `ContentView.swift` so that it matches the following example:

```
import SwiftUI

struct ContentView: View {
    var body: some View {
        GeometryReader { geometry in
            Color.blue.ignoresSafeArea()

            Text("Center top") .position(x:geometry.size.width/2,y:
geometry.size.height/30)
            Text("Center one fifth height") .position(x:geometry.size.
width/2,y: geometry.size.height/5)
            Image(systemName: "folder")
                .position(x:geometry.size.width/3,y: geometry.size.
height/2)
            Text("Center bottom") .position(x:geometry.size.width/2,y:
```

```
geometry.size.height-30)
            }
        .foregroundColor(.white)
    }
}


#Preview {
        ContentView()
}
```

The result will look like this:

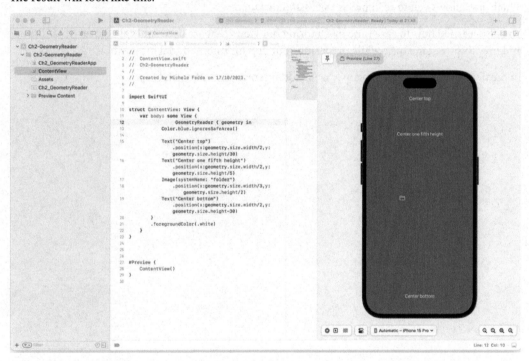

Figure 2.12 – With GeometryReader we can precisely control the position of its subviews

In this section, we examined the GeometryReader container, which allows us to have views that behave like superimposable layers, in a similar way to ZStack. However, GeometryReader allows us to determine distances and measurements precisely and also allows us to "read back" geometrical information such as sizes and position coordinates from the visual elements it contains.

Summary

In this chapter, we went into more detail about layouts in SwiftUI, introducing more of the available tools for screen layout design.

We explained the advantages and disadvantages of lazy rather than eager stacks, allowing you to choose appropriately.

We then showed you how to partition the space available to subviews within a stack using spacers, dividers, and modifiers. If you want to precisely control the geometry layout of stacks, and if spacers and dividers are not enough for the degree of precision you need, you can use `GeometryReader`, which also allows you to read precise sizes and distances.

You also learned how to save time by factoring out views that are used multiple times across the app and how to save some time while preparing your app for international localization.

In the next chapter, we will explain how to add interactivity to SwiftUI views.

3
Adding Interactivity to a SwiftUI View

So far, we have explored how to create complex views in SwiftUI by adding more elements, but all these views have been static; that is, they don't respond to user interaction such as tap events. This limitation would be just acceptable if we only needed to draw pretty pixels on a user's mobile screen, but we normally want those pretty pixels to respond dynamically to the user's interactions and be "responsive." By user interaction, we mean whatever gestures the user may perform in order to control the UI (e.g., tapping on a button, pinches, sliding, etc.).

In SwiftUI, views are created by means of structs, which are normally immutable. So, how can we make these views respond to user actions and change their appearance in real-time? In SwiftUI, views are not objects with delegate methods that will get invoked when a user action takes place, as they are in UIKit; rather, SwiftUI views get rapidly re-created whenever a change takes place.

In this chapter, we are going to deal with user interaction by covering the following topics:

- Passing values at view creation
- Adding interactivity within a view: a button and `@State`
- **Property wrappers** in Swift
- Limitations of `@State`
- Bidirectional binding of `TextField`, toggles, and `Picker`
- Subviews and `@Binding`
- The `@ObservableObject`, and `@StateObject` classes

By the end of the chapter, you will have learned to create simple views capable of responding to user interaction, using some common UI elements.

Technical requirements

All the code files related to this chapter can be found at `https://github.com/PacktPublishing/An-iOS-Developer-s-Guide-to-SwiftUI/`.

Passing values at view creation

In this section, we will learn about the simplest way of changing a view content programmatically by passing values at view creation.

You can actually change the values of variables contained in a `View` struct while you are instantiating it, as shown in the following example:

```
import SwiftUI
struct PassByValue: View {
    var name = "Michael"
    var body: some View {
        VStack(spacing:25) {
            Text("My Name is:")
                .font(.headline)
                .fontWeight(.light)
                .padding()
            Text("\(name)")
                .font(.title)
                .fontWeight(.medium)
                .padding()
            Spacer()
            Text("Although the default name is Michael, it gets
replaced on invocation")
                .foregroundColor(.red)
            Spacer()

        }
    }
}

struct PassByValue_Previews: PreviewProvider {
    static var previews: some View {
        PassByValue(name:"Peter")
    }
}
```

The result of the previous code example is the following:

Figure 3.1 – Passing a parameter to a View

> **Note**
> The `var` declaration must be accessible from the scope where you instantiate your view in order to allow this parameter passing to be achievable; otherwise, `var` should be declared `public`.

Yet, passing values at the view's instantiation won't solve the problem of making the view responsive because while this allows us to further customize a view while we are creating it, the view will still be immutable and static afterward.

In the next section, we will show you how to respond to user interaction and change the view after it has been created.

Responding to a button tap

In this section, we will begin making a view responsive by examining the simplest case; that is, building a view that needs to respond to a simple user event, a button tap, and changing the view appearance in response.

Let's start by trying to write the first thing that would intuitively come to mind; let's change a variable's value and have the view respond to that value change, as shown in the following code example:

```swift
import SwiftUI

struct MyViewStruct: View {
    var name = "Mary"
    var body: some View {

        VStack(spacing: 20) {
            Text("Variables in structs are immutable")
                .fontWeight(.heavy)
            Text("Name: "+name)
            Button(action: {
                print("The button was pressed")
                // self.name = "John"
            } ) {
                Text("Press this button")
            }
            .padding()
            .border(Color.red, width: 1)
        }
    }
}

struct ContentView: View {
    var body: some View {
        MyViewStruct()
    }
}

struct ContentView_Previews: PreviewProvider {
    static var previews: some View {
        ContentView()
    }
}
```

If you copy the preceding fragment of code, replacing your `ContentView.swift` file content after creating a standard simple iOS application with the project template, you will notice that whenever you hit the **Hit this button** button, a line with the **The button was pressed** text will be printed to the console. However, do try to uncomment the line by deleting the double slash at the beginning of the line:

```
// self.name = "John"
```

From the previous example, the program won't even compile, as Xcode will emit the **Cannot assign to property: 'self' is immutable** error, reminding us that the struct we have declared and its contents are immutable.

For the program to work, we have to prepend `@State` before the `var name` declaration.

If we do that, the first time we press the button, the view will display **John** instead of **Mary**. The result of the code example is in the following figure; you will need to execute the program in the simulator to see it working.

Figure 3.2 – Dynamically changing a label

What is happening? What is the @State magic?

Well, @State is a property wrapper; we will explain property wrappers in the next section.

Property wrappers

In Swift, property wrappers are program entities with names starting with @.

Property wrappers are "logic" code fragments, which are executed whenever set or get is executed on that property. In our case, a property or an attribute is, to keep things simple, just a fancy name for a variable within our struct.

So, whenever you "do" something to that variable, the corresponding property wrapper will be invoked.

In the case of @State, which is a property wrapper defined by Apple, it tells the following SwiftUI a few things about the view struct:

- It tells SwiftUI that the value should be persisted and not reset to its initial value whenever the view gets redrawn
- It tells SwiftUI that a property's value is allowed to change
- It tells SwiftUI to redraw that corresponding view whenever the @State property changes

The following figure shows you a conceptual flowchart on how SwiftUI uses the @State wrapper to redraw a view.

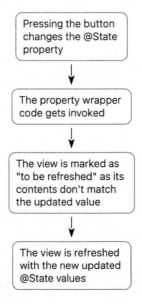

Figure 3.3 – @State conceptual flowchart

We don't need to know how `@State` is implemented by Apple; however, now that you know that this "trick" is possible, you may want to be able to build your own property wrappers.

The `@propertyWrapper` keyword creates a property wrapper that you can use to add behaviors to your own properties.

For example, you could use the following example to automatically capitalize strings (you could run this example in a Swift Playground):

```
import Foundation
@propertyWrapper
struct Capitalised {
    private var value = ""
    var wrappedValue: String {
        get { return value }
        set { value = String(newValue.capitalized) }
    }
}

class Person {
    @Capitalised var name: String
    @Capitalised var surname: String

    init(name:String, surname: String) {
        self.name = name
        self.surname = surname
    }
}

var employee = Person(name:"john", surname: "smith")

print (employee.name)
print (employee.surname)
```

In the following section, we will show when `@State` is applicable and when it is not.

Limitations of @State

So far, so good. If you keep on experimenting with `@State`, you will quickly realize that by itself, `@State` alone is not a complete solution to our problems.

The two main limitations of `@State` are as follows:

- The flow communication of `@State` is just "one way;" that is, it allows a view to respond to changes that occur outside that view, but, for instance, it won't allow us to report changes from within that view elsewhere in our program, which is what you normally expect from `TextField` instances and other common user inputs

- It is limited to a single view, meaning it won't work for more complex views that contain many multiple subviews

Let's tackle these limitations step by step. The first limitation is easy to overcome, as it won't allow a user to change it; you need to mark a value that you want to be "read back" into the view after a user changes it, by prepending it with $.

This is called "binding" the value, and it allows the view to update the value instead of just responding to the value changing.

As an example, let's ask the user for their name, and use that value to greet the user, as shown in the following example:

```
import SwiftUI
struct TextFieldExample: View {
    @State var name = "Michele"
    var body: some View {
        VStack (spacing:25) {
            Text("Changing the string in the textfield will
immediately update the Text output")
                    .padding()
            TextField("Enter your name here:",text: $name)
                .textFieldStyle(.roundedBorder)
                .padding(.horizontal)
            Spacer()
            Text("Hello, \(name)!")
                .font(.callout)
                .fontWeight(.semibold)
                .foregroundColor(.blue)
            Spacer()
        }
    }
}
```

```
struct TextFieldExample_Previews: PreviewProvider {
    static var previews: some View {
        TextFieldExample()
    }

}
```

The following figure shows you the result of the preceding code:

Figure 3.4 – Previewing TextField with bidirectional binding

As soon as you tap a letter inside the TextField, the Text containing the salutation to the user gets immediately updated.

There are many different UI elements that can respond to user interaction; in the next section, we will examine the toggle switch.

Changing a view appearance dynamically using modifiers

In this subsection, we will use another common UI interface element, a toggle switch, to drive changes in a view appearance dynamically, in response to its state changes.

The following code example shows how a Boolean flag is shared between the view and a toggle inside that view:

```
import SwiftUI
struct ToggleExample: View {
    @State private var toggleState = false
    var body: some View {
        ZStack {
            Color(toggleState ? .lightGray : .orange)
                .ignoresSafeArea()
            VStack(spacing: 20) {
                Text("in this example, we use a toggle with a binding
variable.")
                Spacer()
                Toggle(isOn: $toggleState) {
                    Text("This toggle state is: \(toggleState ? "ON" :
"OFF")")                    }                            .padding(.horizontal)
                Spacer()
                Text("This text box appearance is also affected when
the toggle is switched on or off")
                    .fontWeight(toggleState ? .semibold : .light)
                    .multilineTextAlignment(toggleState ? .trailing :
.leading)
                    .padding()
                    .background(toggleState ? Color.yellow : Color.
pink)

                Spacer()
                Text("Actually, the whole view gets redrawn when we
switch the toggle")
                Text("We can use modifiers to change the appearance
dynamically based on state variables")
                    .font(.body)
                    .padding()


            }
        }
    }
}
```

```
struct ToggleExample_Preview: PreviewProvider {
    static var previews: some View {
        ToggleExample()
    }
}
```

The toggle's `isOn` attribute is bound to the `var toggleState` Boolean state. That is, when the `isOn` attribute changes, the `toggleState` variable will change accordingly.

`toggleState` is used with a ternary logical operator to modify parameters and modifiers of other `Text` and `Color` variables within the view so that when the variable changes according to the user switching the toggle switch on or off, the text will change its font, background color, and alignment. We can change how a view looks this way, and now we can do it in real time, not just at the view creation.

Note

A ternary operator in Swift is a concise way to perform a conditional check and choose between two values based on the result of that check. It's a compact version of an `if-else` statement. The ternary operator takes three operands:

1) A condition to check.

2) A value to use if the condition is true.

3) A value to use if the condition is false.

The format is as follows: `condition ? valueIfTrue : valueIfFalse`.

It evaluates the condition, and if it's `true`, the value specified before the colon (`:`) is chosen, otherwise, the value specified after the colon is selected. This is quicker to determine a value based on a condition than having to write a full `if-else` block. However, while in most cases it enhances readability, overcomplicated or nested ternary operations can be difficult to understand.

The following figure shows the effect of these appearance adjustments taking place in real time in response to the `toggleState` state variable changing its value:

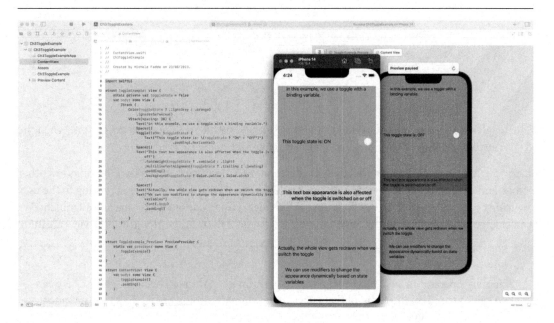

Figure 3.5 – In this example, we used toggle with a binding variable

> **Note**
>
> Notice the change of perspective in SwiftUI compared to UIKit. In SwiftUI, a view is not "an object" and does not have delegates that will respond to user changes by invoking methods.
>
> Rather, it is the changing data that drives different ways for the view to be represented, and the whole view gets redrawn if its data changes.
>
> It is the data driving how the view looks, and not vice versa. You cannot "tell" the UI elements to perform "actions." You change the data bound to UI elements, and the UI elements will change their appearance, provided that you define their data structures to respond to these changes.

In this section, we have just begun to add user interaction to our views. In the next section, we will dig into more complex views using lists and tables.

Bidirectional binding with Picker

In this section, we will use `Picker` and a bound state variable to allow the user to choose one color from a group of five choices. Take a look at the following example:

```
import SwiftUI

struct StateWithPicker: View {
```

```
    private let colors = ["White", "Red", "Blue", "Green", "Black"]
    @State private var color = "White"
    var body: some View {          VStack(spacing: 15) {
        Spacer()
        Text("Choose your color by name")
        Picker("Name", selection: $color)
{                   ForEach(colors, id: \.self) { name
in                      Text("\(name)")                    }
        }
        .padding(.horizontal)
        Button("Click here to reset your choice")
{                   color = "White"
        }.font(.title3)
        Spacer()

        Text("Selected color: \(color)")
            .padding()
        Spacer()
    }
    .font(.title)
    }
}

struct Previews_ContentView_Previews: PreviewProvider {
    static var previews: some View {
        StateWithPicker()
    }
}
```

Notice that the binding to `Picker` is completely bidirectional: the button press will reset the selected color to `White`, and this will update the selection shown by `Picker` as well.

`Text` is instead bound in "read-only mode" (as text labels are not normally capable of editing their own content).

The following image shows `Picker` in action within the simulator:

Figure 3.6 – Picker inside the simulator

In the next section, we will complete our description of `@Binding`, `@ObservableObject`, and `@StateObject`.

Final notes on Subviews and @Binding, Classes, and @ObservableObject

There are a few more things worth noticing while examining bindings: you cannot bind a UI element to more than just one variable, and that variable needs to be defined in just one place.

This means that we cannot bind the same element to several different variables, but just one. This avoids inconsistencies and ambiguities.

You are allowed to use the same `@State` variable for many different views and purposes. For instance, we used a single variable to change the background color, alignment, font, and so on.

You can, of course, have as many state variables as you need, within a view for the many UI elements contained in that view.

You can (and should) group together conveniently many different state variables within the same `struct` and use the attributes of `struct` to bind to UI elements.

You will need to bind with $ in front of the struct name:

```
$structName.structAttribute
```

However, binding with `@State` will not work correctly if you need to pass data bidirectionally between a parent view and its children's views. The children's views will receive the changes to the `@State` variable from their parent view, but the parent view will not get updated when the children's views submit their own changes back.

If you have subviews that need to receive updates from their parent view, and vice versa, the variables need to be declared as `@State` inside the parent view and using the `@Binding` property binding within the children subviews.

This will allow the children to receive changes from the parent, and the parent to receive back changes from the children views.

An example of subviews binding is the following piece of code:

```
import SwiftUI
struct PersonData {
    var name: String
    var surname: String
    var phone: String
}

struct EditNameView: View {
    @Binding var person: PersonData
    var body: some View {
        VStack(spacing: 20) {
            Group {
                TextField("Name", text: $person.name)
                    .textFieldStyle(.roundedBorder)
                TextField("Surname",
                        text: $person.surname).textFieldStyle(.
roundedBorder)
                TextField("Phone number",text: $person.phone)
```

```
                        .textFieldStyle(RoundedBorderTextFieldStyle())
                }
            .padding(.horizontal)


        }
        .navigationTitle("Subview (Edit)")
    }
}

struct ParentView: View {
    @State var person = PersonData(name: "John", surname: "Smith",
phone: "555-12345"
    )
    var body: some View {
        NavigationView {
            VStack(spacing: 25) {
            Spacer()
            Text("Current user profile")
                    .foregroundColor(.black)
            Text("\(person.name) \(person.surname)")
                .font(.title)
                .fontWeight(.semibold)
                .foregroundColor(.gray)
            Text("\(person.phone)")
                    .font(.title2)
                    .fontWeight(.semibold)
                    .foregroundColor(.gray)

            NavigationLink(destination: EditNameView(person: $person))
{
                    Text("Edit user")
                }
            Spacer()
        }
        .font(.title)
        .navigationTitle("User profile")
        .font(.headline)
        .foregroundColor(.blue)
        }
    }
}
```

```
struct ParentView_Previews: PreviewProvider {
    static var previews: some View {
        ParentView()
        EditNameView(person: Binding.constant(PersonData(name:"Jacob",
surname:"Miller",              phone: 5555-444444)))
    }
}
```

The preview of the Parent View in its initial state is the following one:

Figure 3.7 – Preview of ParentView

You can see the result in the simulator in the following screenshot:

Figure 3.8 – Subview that allows the user to edit values in a child view

Notice that we passed a `Binding.constant.PersonData` constructor with dummy values in order to get the preview to display our child view with fake data, like the following:

```
EditNameView(person: Binding.constant(PersonData(name:"Jacob",
surname:"Miller",
phone:"5555-444444")))
```

Finally, the bindings we have discussed so far only work correctly if the data you are binding are value types: Structs, Enums, and primitive types such as Strings, Int, Bool, Tuple, and so on.

The bindings we have used this far for structs will not work correctly for reference types, (e.g., classes).

If you try, you will notice that, once again, you will be only creating one-way bindings, and you won't be able to affect the view if you change the class data inside it.

If you need to bind a class as your data, you should instead be using the `@ObservableObject` property binding instead, and `@StateObject` to avoid it being deallocated when the view where it gets allocated first is refreshed. Do not worry; we will dive down deeper into that in the following chapters.

Summary

In this chapter, we examined the problem of adding user responsiveness to the views we create in SwiftUI and Apple's solution, which uses `@State` variables bindings for view structs, giving examples for `Button`, `TextField`, and `Picker`.

We stated the purpose and limits of struct view bindings.

We also examined the problem of bidirectional data bindings across views and dependent child views, including how to mock data in previews of child views.

In the next chapter, we will start learning about advanced layouts with scroll views, controlling focus, iterating lists, and `ScrollViewReader`.

Part 2: Scrollable Views

In this part, we will start by walking through using the various scrollable interfaces in SwiftUI – ScrollView and List – to display lists and ensure the iOS system keyboard is managed effectively. You'll learn to incorporate `NavigationView` to enchance view titles, navigate through different views with @`ViewBuilder`, understand the intricacies of ScrollView, manage keyboard interactions with @`FocusState`, and employ `ScrollViewReader` to accurately position elements within lists and scroll views.

You will then begin your journey toward mastering grid layouts in SwiftUI, utilizing the various grids available in SwiftUI for layout management, both eager and lazy, applying conditional formatting to your views, and adapting your designs to accommodate device orientation changes.

This part contains the following chapters:

- *Chapter 4, Exploring Lists, Scroll Views, and Navigation*
- *Chapter 5, The Art of Displaying Grids*

4

Iterating Views, Scroll Views, FocusState, Lists, and Scroll View Reader

In this chapter, we will look at how to display lists in SwiftUI, in particular, views that have scrollable contents, either with scroll views or lists. We will also add a bit more functionality to our text fields by allowing the system keyboard to be shown or hidden on iOS. We will briefly touch on the topic of `NavigationView`, in order to display the titles of views.

In this chapter, we are going to cover the following main topics:

- Iterating views
- Hiding or showing the keyboard in a form using `@FocusState`
- `@SwiftUIBuilder` and the limit of only 10 views
- Controlling scrolling programmatically using `ScrollViewReader`

Technical requirements

You will find the code related to this chapter here: `https://github.com/PacktPublishing/An-iOS-Developer-s-Guide-to-SwiftUI/`, under the Ch4 folder.

Iterating views

In this section, I will describe how you can display multiple views, as you previously would have done in UIKit using `UITableViews` and `UICollectionViews`.

In UIKit, you would have, for the purpose of visualizing tables and grids, created derived classes inheriting from `UITableViewControllers` and `UICollectionViewControllers`. To control their appearance and behavior, you would have used properties and delegate methods.

In SwiftUI, you have several ways to achieve this result. The first is iterating, that is, repeating views with a loop. You can achieve this with the specialized view called `ForEach`. `ForEach` does not have the limitation of 10 maximum views that affect views entered manually.

For example, the following fragment of code will create a form containing 90 subviews:

```
Form {
        ForEach (0..<90) { number in
            Text ("Hello #\(number)")
        }
}
```

`Form` is a view normally used to contain input fields, but of course, we can use it with other UI elements as well. You are not limited to just `Text` and TextField, which you would normally associate with a text input form. You can place practically all possible SwiftUI views inside a `Form`. Notice that the `Form` will scroll in the vertical direction. To iterate multiple instances of the same type of view, notice how we use `ForEach` with a closure.

Closures

A closure is a self-contained block of functionality, without the need to create a named function, that can be passed around and used in your code. Closures can capture and store references to any constants and variables from the context in which they are defined, which is known as "closing over" those constants and variables, or "capturing values from the context." You can read more about closures at `https://docs.swift.org/swift-book/documentation/the-swift-programming-language/closures/`.

There are multiple ways to declare closures in Swift. The following is an example of a simple closure:

```
let add: (Int, Int) -> Int = { (a, b) in
return a + b
}
```

The most commonly used closure in SwiftUI is the trailing closure. If you need to pass a closure as a final argument to a function as a closure, you can simply write the following:

```
functionThatAcceptsaClosure(firstParameter: someValue) {
    // this is the closure body
}
```

As the `ForEach` view accepts a closure as a parameter, it is possible to use its abbreviated form and refer to its parameter using the short form, `$0`. For this purpose, you can use `List` instead of `Form`; the result will be visually identical (but forms are preferred for elements of the UI used for user input). Here is an example using `List`:

```
List {
        ForEach (0..<90) {
            Text("Goodbye #\($0)")
        }
}
```

An example of using both `Form` and `List` on the same screen is shown in the following code segment, which splits a VStack in two between `Form` and `List`:

```
import SwiftUI

struct ContentView: View {
    var body: some View {
        VStack {
            Form {
                ForEach (0..<90) { number in
                    Text("Hello #\(number)")
                }
            }
            List {
                ForEach (0..<90) {
                    Text("Goodbye #\($0)")
                }
            }
        }

        .padding()
    }
}

struct ContentView_Previews: PreviewProvider {
    static var previews: some View {
        ContentView()
    }
}
```

The result is the following screenshot:

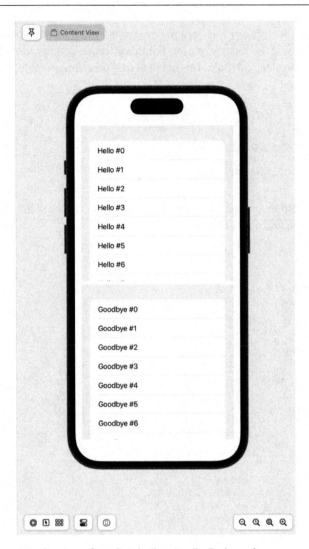

Figure 4.1 – Preview of two lists built using ForEach on the same screen

Please observe that the result looks visually similar to a `ListView` in UIKit.

`ForEach`, besides this simple example, is normally used to iterate through collections. It expects `RandomAccessCollection` of some data type, which can be user-defined, for example, a struct. The collection elements must either conform to the `Identifiable` protocol or supply an `id` parameter to the `ForEach` initializer.

Here is a more complex example involving an array. In order to give each cell a unique ID, we have used the `UUID()` function, which produces a **Universally Unique Identifier** (**UUID**). UUIDs are 128-bit-long numbers, normally used to provide a unique identifier for UI elements or in a network communication protocol. When they are created, UUIDs are assigned random values, the theory being that two UUIDs being identical by chance is, in practice, a statistical impossibility. If you need to convert a UUID to a string, call the `string()` method on a UUID:

```swift
import SwiftUI

private struct Person: Identifiable {
    let name: String
    let surname: String
    var id: UUID { UUID() }
}

private let people: [Person] = [
    Person(name: "John", surname: "Ross"),
    Person (name: "Jinny", surname: "White"),
    Person (name: "Susan", surname: "Brown"),
    Person (name: "Mike", surname: "Sander"),
    Person (name: "Tina", surname: "Russel"),
    Person (name: "Jonathan", surname: "Sparrow")
]


struct ContentView: View {
    var body: some View {
        List{
            ForEach(people) { person in

                HStack{
                    Text(person.name)
                    Text(person.surname)

                }
            }
        }
    }
}

struct ContentView_Previews: PreviewProvider {
    static var previews: some View {
        ContentView()
    }
}
```

The result of the previous code example is the following:

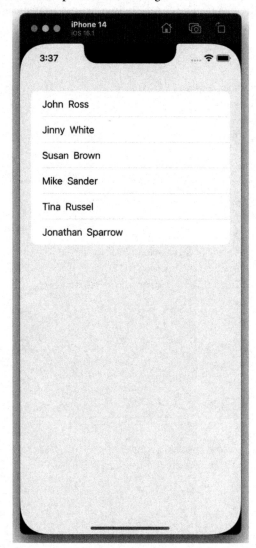

Figure 4.2 – An array shown as a list in the simulator

Now let's complete the screen by adding NavigationView.

NavigationView, as in UIKit, displays the screen title in large font at the top of the screen (in the navigation bar).

In order to do so, all you have to do is enclose your view in a `NavigationView`. In order to give `NavigationView` a title, just use the `.navigationTitle` modifier.

Notice that you might think about adding this modifier to the end of `NavigationView`, but instead, you need to add it to the view contained within `NavigationView`, in our case, the `List`. This is because `NavigationView` can potentially show many views as its content. Attaching the title to one of these views allows the title to change according to the individual view currently displayed.

Here is the example code:

```
import SwiftUI

struct ContentView: View {
    var body: some View {
        NavigationView {
            List {
                ForEach(people) { person in
                    HStack {
                        Text(person.name)
                        Text(person.surname)
                    }
                }
            }
            .navigationTitle("People list")
        }
    }
}
struct ContentView_Previews: PreviewProvider {
    static var previews: some View {
        ContentView()
    }
}
```

Instead of a form, we have used a list; we have iterated through the multiple instances of an `HStack` containing the name and surname of the `Person` struct, again with `ForEach`. As you can see, on iOS, there is no visible difference from using a `Form`. Be warned that potentially, different UI elements can be represented differently on different mobile devices, for example, on an iPad rather than an iPhone, on a Mac, or AppleTV.

In the following screenshot, you can see the result:

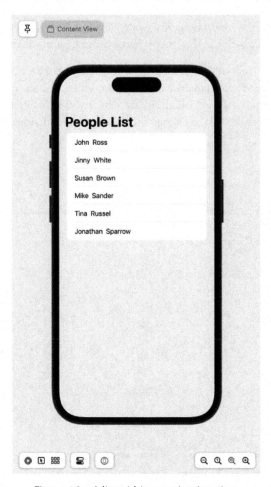

Figure 4.3 – A list within a navigation view

In the following section, we will learn how to make the system keyboard appear when you tap on an item view.

Hiding or showing the keyboard in a form using @ FocusState

You may notice that if you add `TextField`, you will be able to enter some text. Once you tap inside the `TextField`, the system keyboard will appear. The system keyboard won't "go away" by itself on an iPhone. So, you may be wondering how to remove it programmatically. For the keyboard to disappear when you tap outside the TextField, add a `@FocusState private var textFieldIsFocused: Bool` property to your `ContentView`. The TextField is said to be "focused" when it is accepting input from the user and "unfocused" when it is not. We can attach the `.focused` modifier to the

TextField so that the TextField receives the focus; it displays the keyboard and hides it again when it loses focus. You can also force a TextField to go out of focus, thus making the keyboard disappear, by setting the @FocusState variable to false.

In order to attach our @FocusState   textFieldIsFocused variable to a TextField, you just need to add a .focused($textFieldIsFocused) modifier. The following code fragment is an example that involves using a TextField coupled to @State (email) and @FocusedState (emailFieldIsFocused):

```swift
import SwiftUI

func validate(email: String) {
    print(email)
}

struct ContentView: View {
    @State private var email: String = ""
    @FocusState private var emailFieldIsFocused: Bool

    var body: some View {
        TextField(
            "email address",
            text: $email
        )
        .textFieldStyle(.roundedBorder)
        .focused($emailFieldIsFocused)
        .onSubmit {
            validate(email: email)
        }
        .textInputAutocapitalization(.never)
        .disableAutocorrection(true)
        .border(.secondary)
        Text(email)
            .foregroundColor(emailFieldIsFocused ? .blue : .gray)
    }
}

struct ContentView_Previews: PreviewProvider {
    static var previews: some View {
        ContentView()
    }
}
```

The result is shown in the following screenshot:

Figure 4.4 – A text field with focus handling (non-focused)

The Text view that copies the user-editable string within the text field switches from blue to gray depending on the TextField having focus. If you are using the simulator, the IO/Keyboard/Show simulator menu will show the keyboard rather than simulating it using your Mac keyboard.

In the next section, we will introduce scroll views.

Scroll views

ScrollView, as the name suggests, is a view that displays its content within a scrollable region, and can scroll both horizontally and vertically. The ScrollView responds to the user action gestures that depend on the platform, and it reacts by adjusting what portion of the scrollable content is available.

`ScrollView` is a view that can either scroll in a single direction, horizontally or vertically or allow scrolling in both directions at the same time. An important limitation of the SwiftUI `ScrollView` compared to its equivalent in UIKit, `UIScrollView`, is that `ScrollView` does not provide zoom functionality. You cannot use the pinch gesture with two fingers to zoom in or out of a SwiftUI `ScrollView`.

An effective way to add back the zoom functionality is actually embedding a UIKit `UIScrollView`, using the `UIViewRepresentable` protocol.

We will examine the `UIViewRepresentable` protocol later in this book when we describe the integration between SwiftUI and UIKit.

Also, please remember that in SwiftUI, views are just structs, so views providing similar functionality do not belong to an inheritance hierarchy; in UIKit, `UITableView` derives from `UIScrollView`. In SwiftUI, `List`, `Form`, and `ScrollView` support some similar functionality but are not related (and they cannot be, as structs do not support inheritance).

We could, however, use the same approach with `ForEach`, but this time with the text views contained in a `Stack`. Choose an `HStack` if you want the view to scroll horizontally and a `VStack` if you want to scroll vertically.

The first parameter of the `ScrollView` initializer is the axis set; if you need to be able to scroll both horizontally and vertically, set it to `[.horizontal, .vertical]`.

The following code fragment demonstrates a horizontally scrollable list of `Text` instances.

```
import SwiftUI

struct ContentView: View {
    var body: some View {
        VStack {
            Text("A horizontal ScrollView")
                .font(.title)
            ScrollView([.horizontal], showsIndicators: false) {
                HStack(alignment: .center) {
                    ForEach(0..<100) {
                        Text("[Column \($0)]")
                            .background(Color.yellow)
                    }
                }
            }
        }
    }
}
```

```
struct ContentView_Previews: PreviewProvider {
    static var previews: some View {
        ContentView()
    }
}
```

Notice the differences—the content view "pulls in", i.e.: shrinks to the minimum space possible, no delimiter or cell is shown, and the whole structure does not look visually similar to a UIKit `UITableView`.

In our case, we have decided to create a horizontally scrollable `ScrollView` that does not show the scrollable indicators because it contains `showIndicators:false` in its initializer.

The following screenshot shows the resulting preview within Xcode:

Figure 4.5 – A horizontal ScrollView

In this section, we have seen how to add views to a `ScrollView`, that `ScrollView` can be used even in cases when you don't want a look similar to a UIKit `UITableView`, and that `ScrollView` can be used to build horizontal scrollers.

In the next section, we will dig a little deeper into how stacks are actually implemented in SwiftUI.

@SwiftUIBuilder and the limit of only 10 views

In this section, we will explain why we have a limit of just 10 child views, for example, on HStacks and VStacks.

Nota Bene: This limit of 10 views existed prior to Xcode 15, as `@ViewBuilder` used `TupleView`. From Xcode 15 onwards, this limitation has been removed.

The `@SwiftUiBuilder` attribute is a result builder that allows the creation of child views for a SwiftUI view without the need for return keywords.

You are already using `@ViewBuilder`; internally, the definition of the `protocol View` internal to the SwiftUI framework is the following:

```
Public protocol View {
    Associatedtype Body:  View
 @ViewBuilder var body: Self.Body { get }
}
```

There is no need to add the preceding code yourself, as this is a part of the SwiftUI code.

The effect of this protocol declaration is that you can write your SwiftUI body the way you have seen so far, that is, omitting the return. Take the following example:

```
struct ContentView: View {
    var body: some View {
            Text("Example")
        }
}
```

`@ViewBuilder` is defined this way inside SwiftUI:

```
@available(iOS 13.0, OSX 10.15, tvOS 13.0, watchOS 6.0, *)
extension ViewBuilder {
    public static func buildBlock<C0, C1>(_ c0: C0, _ c1: C1) ->
TupleView<(C0, C1)> where C0 : View, C1 : View
}
```

`@ViewBuilder` contains a static `buildBlock` method that receives two views and returns a `TupleView` function of generic views conforming to the `View` protocol.

`@ViewBuilder` also has similar definitions for up to 10 different views.

This is the underlying reason why `@Stackbuilder` and the views built with it, for example, HStacks and VStacks, can only contain up to exactly 10 different views.

We can use @ViewBuilder directly ourselves, inside initializers, definitions of methods, or in front of properties.

By using the @Stackbuilder result builder, it is possible to create more compact code and improve readability, or we can create our version of a view, kind of like a custom UI component.

In this section, we have explained the otherwise apparently "mysterious" limit of 10 views within stacks. In the next section, we will examine using ScrollViewReader to implement programmatic scroll.

Controlling scrolling programmatically using ScrollViewReader

In this section, we will see how to make ScrollView move to a specific position within its displayed content.

This result can be achieved by embedding ScrollViewReader inside ScrollView.

ScrollViewReader has a scrollTo() method, which can make the content of ScrollView scroll to the position of the anchors of any of the views inside ScrollView.

In the following code example, we will see how to scroll to the position of an arbitrary view inside ScrollView:

```swift
import SwiftUI

struct ContentView: View {
    let myColors: [Color] = [.red,.orange, .yellow,.green,.blue ]

    var body: some View {
        ScrollView {
            ScrollViewReader { value in
                Button("Scroll to end") {
                    withAnimation{
                        value.scrollTo(49, anchor: .top)
                    }
                }
            }
            .padding()
            .border(Color.blue)
            .padding()
```

```
                    ForEach(0..<50) { i in
                        Text("Position \(i)")
                            .font(.callout)
                            .frame(width: 200, height: 70)
                            .background(myColors[i % myColors.count])
                            .id(i)
                            .border(Color.black)
                    }
                    .padding()
                    Button("Scroll to top") {
                        withAnimation{
                            value.scrollTo(1, anchor: .bottom)
                        }
                    }
                    .padding()
                    .border(Color.blue)
                }
            }
            .frame(height: 550)
    }
}


struct ContentView_Previews: PreviewProvider {
    static var previews: some View {
        ContentView()
    }
}
```

Notice that we have embedded the `scrollTo()` method within a `withAnimation` closure.

The scroll view will scroll smoothly, with a default animation effect to its destination view. For `ScrollViewReader` to be able to identify which view to scroll to, the `scrollTo` method must receive the ID, that is, the unique identifier, of the target view.

The following screenshot illustrates the result of this example:

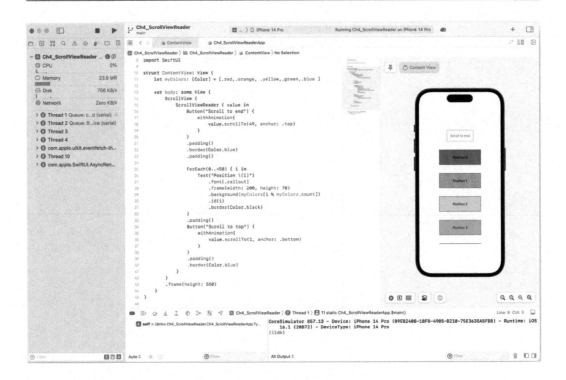

Figure 4.6 – Scrolling to an arbitrary position inside ScrollView with ScrollViewReader

In this example, we are just displaying numbers; therefore, the numerical position of the view and its ID conveniently have the same value. In practice, we could have used another suitable ID, for example, a string or a UUID if that is included, for example, with data read from a web service.

The `scrollTo()` method works equally well within lists and forms; remember to add an ID to each of the target views.

Take the following example:

```
struct ContentView2: View {
    var body: some View {

        ScrollViewReader { j in
            Form {
                Text("TOP")
                .id(100)

                ForEach(1..<30) { index in
                    Text("row\(index)")
                    .id(index)
```

```
                }
                Button(action: {
                    j.scrollTo(100)
                }) {
                    Text("Scroll to top")
                }
            }
        }
    }
}
```

The result this time is shown in the following preview:

Figure 4.7 – The result of tapping on Scroll to top button

Summary

In this chapter, we continued our exploration of SwiftUI's UI elements. We showed how to display lists of items, allowing views to scroll to the position of elements within a list. We also showed how to make the keyboard appear and disappear. We also shed some light on how SwiftUI actually composes views in containers such as stacks. We also learned how `@ViewBuilder` works. Finally, we introduced `ScrollViewReader`, which is used to scroll to a specified position inside scrollable content in SwiftUI, programmatically.

In the next chapter, we will talk about grids and dig deeper into navigation.

5

The Art of Displaying Grids

This chapter will discuss how you can create grid structures in your SwiftUI applications.

We won't cover supporting iOS 13; that would require the *old* approach with nested stacks. The old approach would have created a grid by using horizontal stacks, each representing a row inside a vertical stack. You could also do the opposite, but this would be less common. As SwiftUI evolved, we can now represent orthogonal grids directly, instead of having to compose them. Grids are among the most important ways to structure content in iOS and are essential in other Apple platforms as well.

In this chapter, we are going to show you how by covering these main topics:

- Displaying grids in iOS
- The grid view
- Lazy grids
- Using GridItem to control the lazy grid layout
- Conditional formatting of a view
- Reacting to device rotation

At the end of this chapter, you will be able to decide whether to use eager or lazy grids, knowing the pros and cons of each approach, and being aware of several ways you can lay them out.

Technical requirements

You will find the code related to this chapter at `https://github.com/PacktPublishing/An-iOS-Developer-s-Guide-to-SwiftUI`, under the `CH5` folder.

Displaying grids in iOS

You already know how to display grids in SwiftUI in the simplest way possible, and in the only way this was achievable with the first versions of SwiftUI. Of course, you can place a horizontal stack containing a row inside a vertical stack or you could place multiple `HStack` instances inside `List`.

This is more or less the same, historically, as what happened with UIKit before the introduction of `UICollectionView`, you had to simulate them with `UITableViewCell` and `UITableViewController` or use `UITableView` yourself directly (usually not recommended).

If you wanted it to scroll horizontally a `UITableView`, you could do a crazy trick by rotating `UITableView` by 90 degrees or (better) program `UIScrollView` to instantiate its contents on the fly, taking memory allocation into your own hands. It was possible, but it was not a walk in the park. And we won't include an example here, because that is a bad practice you should carefully avoid learning and practicing.

Bear in mind that at that time, **Automatic Reference Counting (ARC)**, automating memory deallocation, did not exist yet in iOS and macOS, and you needed to deallocate, very precisely, everything you had created only once, and one tiny mistake would have meant your precious program would crash mercilessly, maybe after a few minutes of usage, or if you were really unlucky, unpredictably, after many hours.

This approach of creating a grid composed of other user interface elements in UIKit was problematic and error-prone, besides being hard work. In the first iterations of SwiftUI, this was the same: It was inefficient, required lots of work, and was more challenging to get right.

> **Note**
> When programming for Apple, if you find yourself putting in excessive effort to accomplish a task, you are likely approaching it in a way that is overly complicated and not supported by the system.

Nowadays, in modern SwiftUI, if you want to display a grid, you can choose between grids and lazy grids.

The Grid view

Besides stacks, SwiftUI defines a container view called `Grid` to lay out child views in a grid. An example of a grid would be a checkerboard, where each square tile would be a grid item. Everything you can achieve with lists and tables, you can also achieve with a grid, as a list is just a grid where you happen to have a single item per row (instead of many!).

Apple's definition of `Grid` is, "*a container view that arranges views in a two-dimensional layout*".

To be more precise, a `Grid` view shows its contents in multiple orthogonal rows and columns and is an *eager* container. It is eager because it allocates all memory necessary at once.

According to Apple documentation, the `Grid` is declared as follows:

```
@frozen struct Grid<Content> where Content : View
```

The `Grid` initializer is as follows:

```
Grid(alignment: Alignment, horizontalSpacing:
CGFloat,  verticalSpacing: CGFloat, content: <a closure> )
```

This initializer will create a `Grid` view defining its grid-like layout at the same time.

The `Alignment` argument specifies the alignment of the grid content in the same way we have already described for other simpler views.

Bear in mind that, exactly as it happened with UIKit, most grids can be approximated with lists, and all lists are just a corner case of a grid, particularly if the row contains multiple items, such as an icon followed by a text description on the right.

Visually and functionally speaking, there is no difference in what you can achieve with grids, if you use them to approximate lists. The main difference between the two approaches is historical, and grids are the most powerful approach between the two.

You should use lists only if it is clear from the beginning that you will deal with rows in a relatively simple way. In all other cases, you may save effort by considering grids first.

Alignment is a struct that contains a `HorizontalAlignment` guide and a `VerticalHorizontal` guide.

The default alignment of a grid is `center`.

The `horizontalSpacing` and `verticalSpacing` arguments define the space in points between cells as a `CGFloat`, while the `content` argument provides the content closure defining the grid.

You need to place more instances of `GridRow`, one for each row, as in the following example:

```
import SwiftUI
struct GridDemo: View {
    var body: some View {
        Grid() {
```

```
                    GridRow {
                        Text("[R1, C1]")
                        Text("[R1, C2]")
                    }

                    GridRow {
                        Text("[R2, C1]")
                        Text("[R2, C2]")
                    }
                    GridRow {
                        Text("[R3, C1]")
                        Text("[R3, C2]")
                    }
                }
            }
        }

struct ContentView: View {
    var body: some View {
        Vstack {
            GridDemo()
            Text("A Grid containing GridRows")
                .foregroundColor(.secondary)
        }
        .padding()
    }
}

struct ContentView_Previews: PreviewProvider {
    static var previews: some View {
        ContentView()
    }
}
```

The following screenshot shows the result of this fragment of code in the **Preview** pane:

Figure 5.1 – A simple grid with multiple GridRow instances

According to Apple, `Grid` and `GridRow` instances behave like a collection of `HStack` instances inside `VStack`. However, the grid handles row and column creation as a single operation, applying alignment and spacing to cells, rather than to rows first, and then to a column of unrelated rows.

SF font support in iOS

When we need some quick and easy sample images to show some images in our brand-new grid, we can use San Francisco system images. San Francisco is the system font of modern iOS apps, and it includes specially designed icons that you can freely use – lots of them!

SF Symbols is a library of over 4,000 symbols you can use in your app designs if you need icons supported by a mobile Apple operating system. It is very convenient, and it is free. Search on Google for the most recent **SF Symbols App** for Apple developers.

At the time of writing this book, this app called SF Symbols, is now in its fourth release, SF Symbols 5, but this revision will change as Apple keeps adding new symbols to the library. The installer of SF Symbols will install both the app and the font so that you can use the font in your design documents. The SF Symbols app is indispensable, as otherwise, you won't be able to navigate through so many different symbols in a meaningful way and find the system image you need.

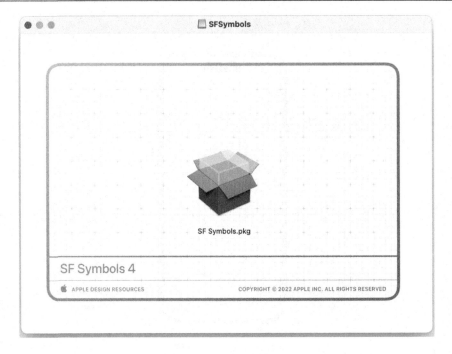

Figure 5.2 – SF Symbols installer

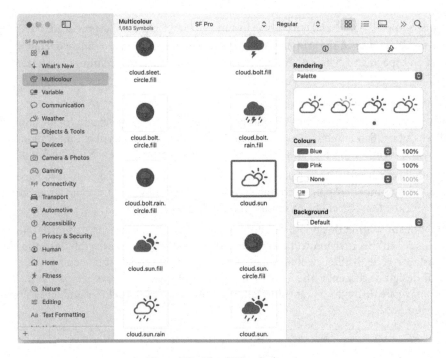

Figure 5.3 – The SF Symbols app

Creating a simple static grid

The following fragment of code would create a system image corresponding to the **pencil.circle.fill** icon, using modifiers to change the background to blue, displaying it within a square with rounded corners (choose `cornerRadius` equal to half the width, and you will get a circle, with blue background).

Note that if you want the image to adapt automatically to user preferences in terms of font size, don't add the frame modifier:

```
Image(systemName:"pencil.circle.fil")
           .frame(width: 20, height: 20)
           .background(Color.blue)
           .cornerRadius(5)
```

The names of the images tend to be self-explanatory. In most cases, there is a variant that lacks the fill and another one where the image is filled.

In some recent versions of Apple operating systems, such as iOS 16, you will find some symbols that have multicolored versions.

For multicolored system images, the image will change depending on how you set the accent and primary color. The following code example shows how to display a static grid of three rows (on an iPhone) containing system images. As the `Divider` view takes all the available space horizontally, the cells on a row are spread horizontally across the available space:

```
import SwiftUI


struct ContentView: View {
    var body: some View {
        VStack{
            Grid {
                GridRow {
                    Image(systemName: "umbrella")
                    Image(systemName: "cloud")
                    Image(systemName: "heart")
                }
                Divider()
                GridRow {
                    Image(systemName: "hand.wave")
                    Image(systemName: "arrow.left")
                    Image(systemName: "arrow.left")
                }
                Divider()
                GridRow {
```

```
                      Image(systemName: "arrow.down")
                      Image(systemName: "arrow.up")
                      Image(systemName: "arrow.right")
                  }
              }
              .foregroundColor(.red)
            Text("A Grid with Dividers and images")
                .foregroundColor(.secondary)
          }
          .padding()
      }
  }
}
struct ContentView_Previews: PreviewProvider {
    static var previews: some View {
        ContentView()
    }
}
```

Here we are using a static grid, and inside that static grid, we are instantiating system images – the ones supplied by the San Francisco font.

Due to `Grid` being an eager container, the total memory necessary for displaying a whole static grid is allocated all at once, without regard for whether the grid elements need to be displayed simultaneously. This approach is practical only to display a grid containing a minimal number of elements.

The only real advantage of static grids is their predictability in terms of their geometry: their look can be predicted and designed precisely at design time, there won't be unpredictably loaded elements, uncertainties with dimensions of elements, and so on.

Here are a few interesting things about static (or eager grids) in terms of controlling their look:

- We can make a cell refrain from making the grid have more space than the cells on other rows require by specifying the `.gridCellUnsizedAxes()` modifier, which has as a parameter an `Axis.Set` value. `Axis.Set` can contain `.horizontal`, `.vertical`, or both `[.horizontal, .vertical]`.

- The `alignment` parameter affects all the cells in the grid unless it is overridden by one of the Row alignment parameters.

- You can also specify row alignment by passing `VerticalAlignment` to the `alignment` parameter in the constructor of the row. The row's vertical alignment will have priority over the vertical component of the global alignment of the whole grid.

- Besides specifying vertical row alignment, you can specify horizontal column alignment by using the `gridColumnAlignment` parameter. When you set the `gridColumnAlignment` parameter, each cell within the specified column will align its content according to the chosen alignment value. For example, if you choose `.center`, all the items in that column will be centered horizontally within their respective cells.

- A single column cell may also span over several columns by specifying the `.gridCellColumns(count:)` parameter.

- You can ask SwiftUI to consider an arbitrary point belonging to the grid element rather than the geometrical center of a cell while setting up the grid by specifying `.gridCellAnchor()`, for example, `gridCellAnchor(.init(x:0.25, y:0.0)` would shift this cell by 25% to the right.

In the following code example, we will show you what you can achieve in controlling alignment, column spanning, and sizing of cells in a grid. The result is visually appalling, but our purpose is to illustrate a technique:

```
import SwiftUI

struct ContentView: View {
    var body: some View {
        Grid(alignment: .topLeading, horizontalSpacing: 8.0,
verticalSpacing: 8.0) {
            GridRow {
                GradientCell(color: .blue, width: 70, height: 75)

                GradientCell(color: .brown, width: 70, height: 75)
                    .gridColumnAlignment(.trailing)

                GradientCell(color: .orange, width: 70, height: 120)
            }

            GridRow(alignment: .bottom) {
                GradientCell(color: .blue, width: 70, height: 75)
                GradientCell(color: .yellow, width: 70, height: 75)
                GradientCell(color: .red, width: 70, height: 120)
            }
            GridRow {
                GradientCell(color: .green, width: 120, height: 80)
                GradientCell(color: .yellow, width: 120, height: 75)
                GradientCell(color: .orange, width: 70, height: 50)
            }

            GridRow {
```

```
                    RoundedRectangle(cornerRadius: 8.0)
                        .fill(.red.gradient)
                        .frame(height: 80.0)
                        .gridCellUnsizedAxes(.horizontal)

                    GradientCell(color: .yellow, width: 120, height: 80)
                    GradientCell(color: .orange, width: 70, height: 80)
            }
            GridRow(alignment: .bottom) {
                    RoundedRectangle(cornerRadius: 8.0).fill(Color(.blue).
gradient)
                            .frame(width: 120.0, height: 100.0)

                    RoundedRectangle(cornerRadius: 8.0).fill(Color(.cyan).
gradient)
                            .frame(width: 50.0, height: 100.0)

                    RoundedRectangle(cornerRadius: 8.0).fill(Color(.
darkGray).gradient)
                            .frame(width: 50.0, height: 50.0)
                }
            GridRow(alignment: .bottom) {
                    RoundedRectangle(cornerRadius: 8.0).fill(Color(.blue).
gradient)
                            .frame(width: 120.0, height: 50.0)

                    RoundedRectangle(cornerRadius: 8.0).fill(Color(.cyan).
gradient)
                            .frame(height: 50.0)

                    RoundedRectangle(cornerRadius: 8.0).fill(Color(.
darkGray).gradient)
                            .frame(width: 50.0, height: 50.0)
                }
            GridRow(alignment: .bottom) {
                    RoundedRectangle(cornerRadius: 8.0).fill(Color(.blue).
gradient)
                            .frame( height: 50.0).gridCellColumns(2)
```

```
                    RoundedRectangle(cornerRadius: 8.0).fill(Color(.
    darkGray).gradient)
                         .frame(width: 50.0, height: 50.0)
                }
        }
    }

    struct GradientCell: View {
        let color: Color
        let width: CGFloat
        let height: CGFloat

        var body: some View {
            RoundedRectangle(cornerRadius: 8.0)
                .fill(color.gradient)
                .frame(width: width, height: height)
        }
    }
}
struct ContentView_Previews: PreviewProvider {
    static var previews: some View {
        ContentView()
    }
}
```

Please make sure to read the Apple documentation as Apple keeps adding to this list, and in future versions of SwiftUI, you are likely to find more interesting parameters and modifiers.

Notice that the grid won't scroll on its own. You need to embed a grid inside `ScrollView` if you want it to scroll.

The column count is determined by the row containing more cells. The grid will rearrange all the other rows accordingly by adding empty cells to the rows that don't contain enough elements.

The width of a column is determined by the widest cell among all rows, while the tallest cell in a row determines the height of the whole row.

Performance-wise, the layout of an eager grid costs less than the layout of a lazy grid, but a lazy grid will start to perform better, given that there are enough elements to be displayed. You should switch to a lazy grid only if you have a measurable performance or memory allocation advantage.

The result of the last code example is shown in the next figure:

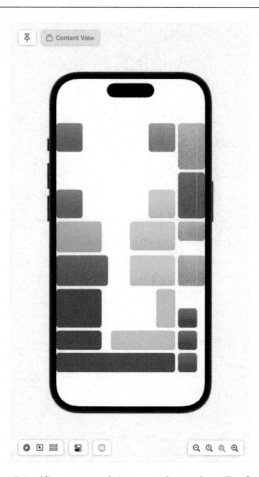

Figure 5.4 – Alignment and size control over the cells of a grid

In the next section, we will introduce lazy grids, which allow us to deal with a large number of items efficiently, in terms of memory allocation and performance (and are less likely to stutter and lag, in terms of user responsiveness).

Lazy grids

If you need a way to display larger grids containing a vast number of elements, you need lazy grids. Lazy grids come in two varieties: `LazyHGrid` (horizontal) or `LazyVGrid` (vertical), depending on which direction you want to scroll. In order for the grid to scroll, you will need to place the grid inside `ScrollView`:

```
import SwiftUI
```

```
struct ContentView: View {
    var body: some View {
        ScrollView {
                LazyVGrid(columns: [GridItem(.
flexible()),GridItem(.flexible()),GridItem(.flexible()),GridItem(.
flexible()),]) {
                        ForEach(1...300, id: \.self) { I in
                            RoundedRectangle(cornerRadius: 10)
                                .fill(Color.cyan)
                                .frame(width: 60, height: 60)
                    }
                }
        }
        .padding()
    }
}

struct ContentView_Previews: PreviewProvider {
    static var previews: some View {
        ContentView()
    }
}
```

> **What to do if you get the mysterious "missing scene" error**
>
> "`Info.plist` contained no UIScene configuration dictionary (looking for configuration named "no name")." While launching an app, you have just created on the simulator with **Xcode 14.2**, add the `Scene Configuration` key under **Application Scene Manifest**, under the project's **Settings | Info | Custom iOS Target** properties. There is no need to add anything else; the defaults will already be populated correctly.
>
> We mention this as we met this error while working on this topic. This Xcode bug was eventually solved by Xcode 15, but it has been around for quite a while, and if you are using an Intel Mac you are likely to encounter this problem, so we thought it might be helpful to point out its solution.

The result of the previous example code will look like the following screenshot:

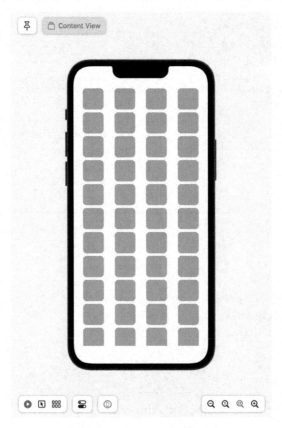

Figure 5.5 – A simple LazyVGrid

In the previous example, LazyVGrid receives, in a columns parameter, an array of GridItem, one per column, and each GridItem is configured with flexible().

Let's look at a possible way to slightly improve the previous example's appearance and make it more elegant, instead of passing four GridItem instances as column parameters to LazyVGrid, as we just did and as is shown in the following code fragment:

```
[GridItem(.flexible()),GridItem(.flexible()),GridItem(.
flexible()),GridItem(.flexible())]
```

We can instead pass a repeating Array initializer, like the following one:

```
Array(repeating: GridItem(.flexible()) count:4 )
```

However, that improvement would look nicer but is only *syntactic sugar*, meaning that the explicit syntax will produce precisely the same code. Using four explicit `GridItem` instances makes it easier to control each column separately in case you need to change its layout behavior separately. In the next section, we are going to talk about `GridItem`.

Using GridItem to control the layout of LazyVGrid

`GridItem` controls how the corresponding column of a grid (for `LazyVGrid`) or row (for `LaxyHGrid`) will behave in terms of the layout.

The option we used in the previous section was `.flexible()`. It means that the corresponding column will take up as much space as is available.

However, `GridItem` has many more options, which include the following:

- `.adaptive(minimum:maximum:)`: This option creates a grid item that can take up a varying number of columns, depending on the available space.

  Note that you can also use `.infinity` instead of a number for the minimum or maximum values of `GridItem(.adaptive(minimum: CGFloat, maximum: CGFloat))` to tell SwiftUI that the row or column can grow or shrink indefinitely.

- `.fixed(size:)`: This option creates a grid item with a fixed size.

- `.absolute(size:)`: This option creates a grid item with an absolute size.

  The difference between .fixed and .absolute is that .fixed is specified in *typographical points* (iOS) or in *pixels* (macOS). The resulting geometrical size will be the same on all devices and screens. In iOS, one point will be one physical pixel on a 1X screen, two physical pixels on a 2X screen, and three physical pixels on a 3X screen.

- `.absolute`: This option is specified in logical units, meaning that in iOS, a value of *1* will correspond precisely to one physical pixel on a 1X device, one physical pixel on a 2X device, and one physical pixel on a 3X device.

- `.fractionalWidth(place:)`: This option creates a grid item that takes up a fraction of the available width. This is useful if you want to partition the available width according to some precise percentage of the total that isn't easily obtainable by other means.

- `.fractionalHeight(place:)`: Like the previous option, this one creates a grid item that takes up a fraction of the available height.

- `.fractionalWidth(minimum:maximum:)`: This option creates a grid item that is a fraction of the available width, with a minimum and maximum size.
- `.fractionalHeight(minimum:maximum:)`: Like the previous option, this one specifies the height fraction, with a minimum and a maximum.

As an exercise, try changing the code in the example in the previous section, by changing the options of the individual grid items corresponding to each column using our list of possible options. What happens?

Scrolling horizontally and sizing the grid automatically

The following example shows how you can modify the previous example by substituting ContentView, so that you can scroll horizontally by setting the `.horizontal` parameter in the ScrollView instantiation. As we have used `.adaptive` in GridItem, we don't need to explicitly state how many rows or columns we want.

This will be determined automatically, given a minimum size of 100 points, and will change according to the device.

Notice that while LazyVGrid requires you to specify columns, LazyHGrid predictably requires rows. The next example will show LazyHGrid in action:

```swift
import SwiftUI

struct ContentView: View {
    var body: some View {
        ScrollView(.horizontal) {
            LazyHGrid(rows: [GridItem(.adaptive(minimum:
100))], alignment: .top) {
                ForEach(1...300, id: \.self) { I in
                    RoundedRectangle(cornerRadius: 10)
                        .fill(Color.cyan)
                        .frame(width: 60, height: 60)
                }
            }
        }
        .padding()
    }
}
```

The result is shown in the next screenshot:

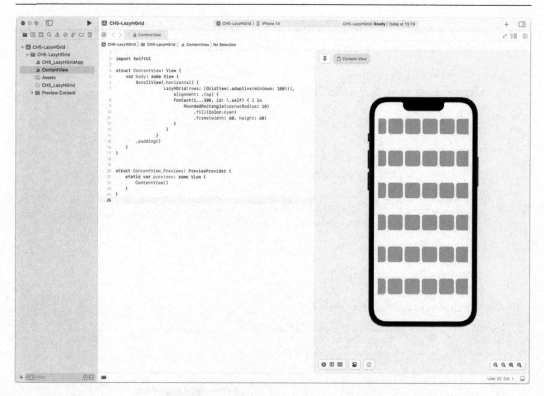

Figure 5.6 – A horizontal scrolling LazyHGrid

Conditional formatting of a view

This technique does not apply specifically to grids, but it is actually useful for all kinds of SwiftUI views.

Suppose you want to change, conditionally, the look of a view at runtime based on the content of a variable.

You might want to display different information, change the color, or add a shadow.

To do this, you can try one of these three approaches:

- Use an if-else clause
- Use a **ternary** operator
- Use an extension of View, creating your own modifier

You can use an `if-else` clause within the code of your view, driving it, for example, with an `@State` variable, as shown in the following code fragment:

```
struct ContentView: View {
    @State private var shouldBePink: Bool = true

    var body: some View {
        if shouldBePink {
            Text("I am now Pink!")
                .foregroundColor(.pink)
        } else {
            Text("I default to Blue")
                .foregroundColor(.blue)
        }
    }
}
```

The result is shown in the next screenshot:

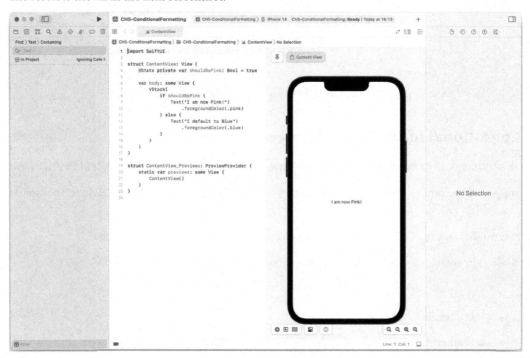

Figure 5.7 – Conditional formatting of a view

You now have to use an `if-else` clause explicitly, to decide what to display if the condition is `true`, and what to display if the condition is `false`. The disadvantage is duplicating code If your view needs to present similar elements in both cases.

You can sometimes improve this approach by using a ternary operator. It is less verbose, as it usually fits on just one line of code and can be cleaner. It is useful if, for example, you just want to change one modifier, as shown in the following example:

```
struct ContentView: View {
    @State private var shouldBePink: Bool = true

    var body: some View {
        shouldBePink ? Text("I am now Pink!").foregroundColor(.pink) :
Text("I default to Blue").foregroundColor(.blue)
    }
}
```

I won't show you a screenshot, as it will be exactly like the previous example. However, if you want to apply your modifier only if the `@State` variable is true, there is a much better approach, and this is writing a `View` extension.

Just add the following extension and `ContentView`, deleting the previous one:

```
extension View {
    @ViewBuilder func `if`<Content: View>(_ logicValue: Bool,
modifier: (Self) -> Content) -> some View {
        if logicValue {
            modifier(self)
        } else {
            self
        }
    }
}

struct ContentView: View {
    @State private var shouldAddShadow: Bool = true

    var body: some View {
        Text("Hi There!")
            .if(logicValue: shouldAddShadow){ view in
                view.shadow(color: .black, radius: 5, x: 5.0, y: 5.0)
            }
    }
}
```

The result is shown in the next screenshot:

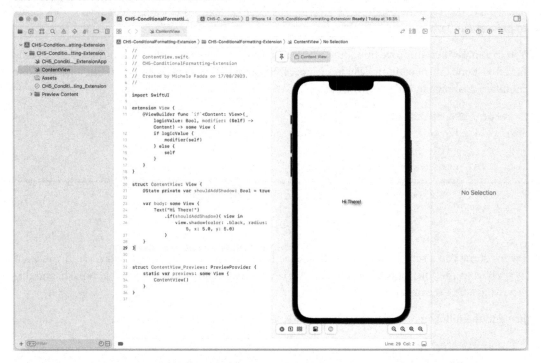

Figure 5.8 – Conditional formatting with an extension

Notice that we have used @ViewBuilder directly, injecting it with a modifier.

As we can see in this example, a modifier is just a closure that returns an opaque type of view.

Reacting to device rotation

SwiftUI does not have a built-in way of detecting device rotation and displaying different information depending on device orientation. However, it is possible to subscribe to the notification for the event using UIDevice.orientationDidChangeNotification, and to decode the device orientation when we receive the system notification.

We create our own view modifier that listens to this event and have it call a function when this happens. As a parameter to this function, we will include the UIDeviceOrientation value, because we need to be able to react differently to different orientations. In our example, we will decode all possible values for the orientation and visualize a different text in each case.

The following example illustrates this technique:

```swift
import SwiftUI
struct RotationModifier: ViewModifier {
    let action: (UIDeviceOrientation) -> Void

    func body(content: Content) -> some View {
        content
            .onAppear()
            .onReceive(NotificationCenter.default.publisher(for:
UIDevice.orientationDidChangeNotification)) { _ in
                action(UIDevice.current.orientation)
            }
    }
}
extension View {
    func onRotate(perform action: @escaping (UIDeviceOrientation) ->
Void) -> some View {
        self.modifier(RotationModifier(action: action))
    }
}



struct ContentView: View {
    @State private var orientation = UIDeviceOrientation.unknown

    var body: some View {
        VStack {
            switch orientation {
            case .faceDown:
                Text("Face Down")
            case .unknown:
                Text("unknown")
            case .portrait:
                Text("Portrait")
            case .portraitUpsideDown:
                Text("Portrait Upside Down")
            case .landscapeLeft:
                Text("Landscape Left")
            case .landscapeRight:
                Text("Landscape Right")
            case .faceUp:
                Text("Face Up")
            @unknown default:
```

```
                    Text("unknown position")
                }

            Text("I am showing device orientation").foregroundColor(.
    secondary)

        }
        .onRotate { newOrientation in
            orientation = newOrientation
        }
    }
}

struct ContentView_Previews: PreviewProvider {
    static var previews: some View {
        ContentView()
    }
}
```

Summary

In this chapter, we have learned how to display grids in SwiftUI, including details allowing us to customize how their cells are displayed, which approach to choose, whether to use eager grids or lazy ones, and why. We have seen how to structure grids in a precisely defined size for their cells, how to change the alignment and size of columns or individual cells, and how to let SwiftUI layout grids automatically for us.

At the end of the chapter, we added a few useful techniques that allow us finer control of how we want to change the visualization of SwiftUI views in general.

In the next chapter, we will examine the tab bar and take a deep view of the modal presentation.

Part 3: SwiftUI Navigation

This part introduces you to implementing tab bars and modal view presentations in SwiftUI. You'll enhance your understanding of using `TabView` to navigate between views in compact iOS applications, integrating a tab bar with `TabView` and `tabItem`, crafting custom tab bars, and engaging deeply with modal views, including sheets, alerts, and popovers. The exploration continues into the realm of navigation within SwiftUI, starting with foundational concepts of iOS navigation and advancing to both programmatic and user-driven navigation strategies. With updates in Swift 4 and iOS 16 in mind, this part covers navigation across platforms, from the basics of `NavigationView` and `NavigationLink`, using `.navigationDestination` to define navigation paths, to managing user-controlled and split-view navigations. It also includes insights into programmatic navigation with `NavigationPath` and techniques for storing and restoring the navigation stack in the JSON format.

This part contains the following chapters:

- *Chapter 6, Tab Bars and Modal View Presentation*
- *Chapter 7, All About Navigation*

Tab Bars and
Modal View Presentation

In this chapter, we will focus on tab bars and presenting views modally in SwiftUI.

We will begin by discussing how to implement tab bars using the standard UI elements, then we will examine recreating the equivalent of a tab bar that would require heavy customization and could not be obtained normally, such as a tab bar with the selection buttons on the top of the screen. Finally, we will examine the modal view presentation in depth.

In this chapter, we're going to cover the following main topics:

- Implementing tab bars with `TabView` and `tabItem`
- Implementing a customized tab bar
- All about modal views, including sheets, alerts, and popovers

By the end of this chapter, you will know all about tab bars and the many ways to present modal views.

Technical requirements

You will find the code related to this chapter at `https://github.com/PacktPublishing/An-iOS-Developer-s-Guide-to-SwiftUI`, under the CH6 folder.

Creating a standard tab bar

Follow these steps to create a standard tab bar:

1. We can start a new iOS project by using the usual iOS **App** template.
2. Then, we can add a new view to the project and name it `HomeView`.
3. To let `ContentView` use this `HomeView` view, we can substitute this view as the content of the default `ContentView`.

4.　Finally, we populate the `HomeView.swift` file with the following code.

We start by creating five views, which will be individually switched as the content of `TabView`:

```
import SwiftUI
struct ViewA:
    View {
    var body: some View {
            Text("This is View 1")
                .fontWeight(.bold)
                .font(.title)
                .foregroundColor(.blue)
                .padding(.all)
                .border(Color.black, width: 1)
        }
    }

struct ViewB:
    View {
    var body: some View {
        Text("This is View 2")
            .fontWeight(.bold)
            .font(.title)
            .foregroundColor(.red)
            .padding(.all)
            .border(Color.black, width: 1)
            }
}

struct ViewC:
    View {
    var body: some View {
        Text("This is View 3")
            .fontWeight(.bold)
            .font(.title)
            .foregroundColor(.brown)
            .padding(.all)
            .border(Color.black, width: 1)
        }
}

struct ViewD:
    View {
    var body: some View {
        Text("This is View 4")
```

```
                    .fontWeight(.bold)
                    .font(.title)
                    .foregroundColor(.purple)
                    .padding(.all)
                    .border(Color.black, width: 1)
        }
}

struct ViewE:
        View {
        var body: some View {
              Text("This is View 5")
                    .fontWeight(.bold)
                    .font(.title)
                    .foregroundColor(.teal)
                    .padding(.all)
                    .border(Color.black, width: 1)
        }
}
```

HomeView is the main view of our simple app and it contains TabView. Each of the four views is placed inside it, each one with a corresponding .tabItem modifier representing the view's selection tab, as shown in the following code block:

```
struct HomeView: View {
    var body: some View {
        TabView{
            ViewA().tabItem{
                Label("Menu 1", systemImage: "square")
            }
            ViewB().tabItem{
                Label("Menu 2", systemImage: "circle")
            }
            ViewC().tabItem{
                Label("Menu 3", systemImage: "triangle")
            }
            ViewD().tabItem{
                Label("Menu 4", systemImage: "hexagon")
            }
            ViewE().tabItem{
                Label("Menu 5", systemImage: "moon")
            }
```

```
            }
        }
    }

struct HomeView_Previews: PreviewProvider {
    static var previews: some View {
        HomeView()
    }
}
```

By selecting the corresponding tab, the related view will be displayed, as you can expect from a tab bar.

The following figure shows the final result of the previous code example:

Figure 6.1 – A simple tab bar

As you can see, the recipe for creating a tab bar in SwiftUI is simple. You need to have structs that create the views you will need inside the tab bar view. In our example, we used simple Text views just to show that, if you run this app, these views will be switched as you press the corresponding tab bar menu items. We used the same file for all these views to simplify things, as this is just an example. In an actual application, you will generally want a separate file for each view.

You then need to add all these views inside `TabView`, and finally, add the `.TabItem(title: image:)` modifier to each one of them.

The two parameters of the `.TabItem` modifier specifies the title and the icon to be used.

That's done! Navigation doesn't get any easier than this.

`.TabItem` is hard to beat and is typically the preferred solution if you have a simple app on an iPhone with a maximum of five different screens the user can switch between with just a tap.

`TabView` offers very little in terms of customization. You will obtain a tab bar with an "Apple" look and feel. You don't have a way to display the icons and titles in different colors, for instance.

However, this UI element will be adapted without any effort on your side to different Apple devices, translating its function to the "visual language" of the device.

SwiftUI is platform-independent and adapts the user interaction depending on the device, choosing a representation that makes sense. The following figure shows how a tab bar appears on an Apple TV:

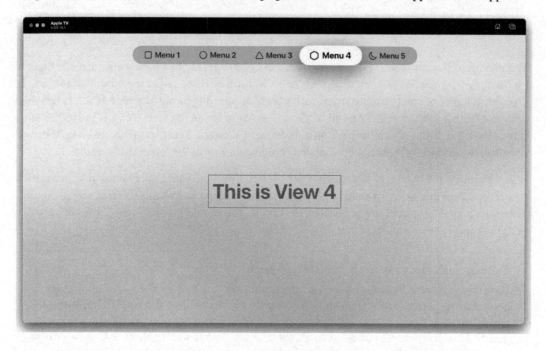

Figure 6.2 – A tab bar on an Apple TV

The following figure shows how a tab bar appears on macOS:

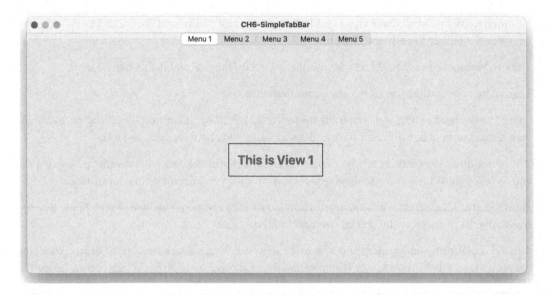

Figure 6.3 – How macOS shows the tab bar

This intelligent UI translation to the appropriate visual language is unfortunately not currently the case for `TabView` on the iPad. On an iPad, `TabView` will still be displayed at the bottom of the screen, probably because of compatibility issues with poorly designed apps of the past, but this is less than desirable from a user experience point of view. Users tend to see the screen of an iPad in the same way as they usually see a web browser on a desktop; in Western countries, when reading, they will prioritize the important information from left to right, starting at the top of the screen.

Also, tapping on the bottom of the screen is not the best thing you can think of in terms of navigation on a large screen device, as it would imply too far a movement to be within reach of a single thumb. Therefore, even if it is technically available as an option, you should probably ignore the tab bar when designing applications for iPad.

> **Good user interaction design is based on research**
>
> If you want more information on user interaction that you can apply to your app design, a good starting point is reading about user research. Besides reading the **Apple User Interface Guidelines** (`https://developer.apple.com/design/human-interface-guidelines/guidelines/overview/`), at the time of writing this book, the very best resource you can find on the internet is the blog belonging to the *Nielsen Norman Group*, in the section for the *Mobile and Tablet Research Reports*: `https://www.nngroup.com/reports/topic/mobile-and-tablet-design/`.

To specify a different view specific to a particular type of device at runtime, you can use the value of `UIDevice.current.userInterfaceIdiom` to distinguish between different visual languages specific to different devices and recognize the type of device your app is currently running on. This system variable will contain an `enum` value that, at runtime, can have one of these values:

- `.unspecified` – The UI is not specified
- `.phone` – The interface is designed for an iPhone
- `.pad` – The interface is designed for an iPad, including a Mac
- `.tv` – The interface is designed for Apple TV
- `.carPlay` – The interface is designed for a car
- `.mac` – The interface is Mac-specific

In the past, SwiftUI just supported the iPhone and iPad; nowadays, it supports many more different "visual languages," and you can expect this number to grow in the future.

Again, the tendency is to let SwiftUI adapt to the optimal display of the interface in a way that depends on the device in use. In general, you should never aim for a "pixel-perfect" match between your design and the graphical design of a visual artist, but you should let the operating system take care of most of the heavy lifting.

If you want to have absolute control over the result, this is a bad practice. If you do so, you will often sacrifice essential parts of the user experience, such as letting the users customize their preferred font sizes, and your design will match the graphical artist's only on one specific screen size on a specific device.

You don't know yet what resolutions will be available on what precise models of devices next year, and you should try to design your apps so that they can adapt without being constrained to specific, precise numbers of pixels.

Also, graphical design is part of the overall user experience; if your screen is too cluttered or too complex, it will take more time to be rendered. In particular, be wary of using too many gradients, corner rounding, and layering on too many elements all at once. This will make your screen more expensive to redraw and will end up limiting performance if you are scrolling very quickly, for instance.

Apple is trying to introduce extreme performance when it comes to screen refresh, reaching 120 images per second on selected models. This is because this creates a delightful user experience; the user doesn't even notice this at a conscious level but ends up loving the interaction with a system that responds without any perceptual lag.

You may think that using a very ornate style will produce a better experience, especially if you or your graphical designer have a typography culture and prefer to "sculpt" every shadow of each graphical element. While this complexity will add to your graphical expression and help guide the user through subtle cues about what is essential information on a screen, if you add too much visual complexity, performance will suffer.

And it doesn't matter whether SwiftUI is normally about 10 times faster than UIKit. At the end of the day, if the GPU of a mobile phone or an iPad needs to perform 42 different passes to render a screen that needs to scroll, you can expect less than stellar performance, even on quite powerful modern devices, despite SwiftUI being spectacularly good at rendering UIs very efficiently.

In the next section, we will explain how to create, from scratch, a UI resembling a tab bar.

Creating custom tab bars

Sometimes, you must implement your take on a tab bar because what you want cannot be created with the standard one; for example, you want something that resembles a tab bar but has custom graphical requirements and is in a different position on the screen. In this section, you will also learn that going for a custom approach requires much more work than the "standard Apple way" of doing things, besides having other drawbacks.

For our customized tab bar, we want it to have round corners, to be drawn in a frame, with a shadow, and to show the title in a different bright color, say in red and in bold, when a tab is selected. We also want it to sit at the top of the user screen rather than at the bottom.

To begin, it is essential to establish the necessary information for presenting a tab, which includes an image representing the non-selected state, an image representing the selected state, and a title. For the sake of simplicity, we will limit the usage to system images and utilize a struct that consists of three `String` values, as illustrated in the following code snippet:

```
struct ItemValue {
    let image: String
    let selectedImage: String
    let title: String
}
```

Then, we are going to need a view capable of displaying our own take on `tabItem`, in both selected and normal mode. We will call this view `MyTabItemView`, which will accept two parameters: an `ItemValue` parameter and the `selected` Boolean flag.

Depending on the `selected` flag, the proper system image will be chosen, and the title will be shown either in light or bold, with the selected title also colored in red for good measure.

Create a new SwiftUI view. Go to the Xcode menu and then navigate to **File | New | File...**. Under **iOS**, select **SwiftUI View under User Interface**. In the **Save As** dialog box, save the file as `MyTabItemView.swift`. Type the following code as shown:

```
struct MyTabItemView: View {
    let itemContent: ItemValue
    let selected: Bool
```

```
    var body: some View {
        VStack {
            Image(systemName: selected ? itemContent.selectedImage :
itemContent.image)
                .resizable()
                .aspectRatio(contentMode: .fit)
                .frame(width: 40, height: 40)
            Spacer().frame(height: 6)

            Text(itemContent.title)
                .fontWeight(selected ? .bold : .light )
                .foregroundColor(selected ? .red : .gray)
                .font(.system(size: 16))
        }
    }
}

struct TabItemView_Previews: PreviewProvider {
    static var previews: some View {
        MyTabItemView(itemContent: ItemValue(image: "moon",
selectedImage: "moon.fill", title: "Moon"), selected: true)
    }
}
```

Then, we are going to need a view to contain all the buttons in our imitation of `TabView`; let's call it `MyTabView`. Create another new SwiftUI `View` file named `MyTabView.swift` and add the following code:

```
import SwiftUI

struct MyTabView: View {

    let items: [ItemValue]
    var height: CGFloat = 72
    var width: CGFloat = UIScreen.main.bounds.width - 28
    @Binding var selectedIndex: Int

    var body: some View {
        HStack {
            Spacer()
            ForEach(items.indices, id: \.self) { index in
                let item = items[index]
                Button {
                    self.selectedIndex = index
```

```
                } label: {
                    let isSelected = selectedIndex == index
                    MyTabItemView(itemContent: item, selected:
isSelected)
                }
                Spacer()
            }
        }
        .frame(width: width, height: height)
        .background(Color.white)
        .cornerRadius(8)
        .shadow(radius: 3, x: 1, y: 2)
    }
}

struct TabBottomView_Previews: PreviewProvider {
    static var previews: some View {
        MyTabView(
            items: [
                ItemValue(image: "star", selectedImage: "star.fill",
title: "Star"),
                ItemValue(image: "triangle", selectedImage: "triangle.
fill", title: "Triangle"),
                ItemValue(image: "circle", selectedImage: "circle.fill",
title: "Circle"),ItemValue(image: "square", selectedImage: "square.
fill", title: "Square")],
                selectedIndex: .constant(0))


    }
}
```

In the previous code fragment, we keep track of the selected tab using `selectedIndex`. A tab view knows that it has been selected if its index is the same as `selectedIndex`. As we want `selectedIndex` to be accessible externally from this view, we declare it as `@Binding`.

Also, notice the use of `.constant(0)` as a way to simulate a value for a binding value in our preview.

Then, we want to use an enum to represent the different values of our tabs, and to be able to use it in a loop, we make it conform to the `CaseIterable` protocol:

```
enum Tabs: Int, CaseIterable {
    case moon = 0
    case star
    case triangle
    case square
```

```
      var tabItem: ItemValue {
          switch self {
          case .moon:
              return ItemValue(image: "moon", selectedImage: "moon.
fill", title: "Moon")
          case .star:
              return ItemValue(image: "star", selectedImage: "star.
fill", title: "Star")
           case .triangle:
              return ItemValue(image: "triangle", selectedImage:
"triangle.fill", title: "Triangle")
          case .square:
              return ItemValue(image: "square", selectedImage: "square.
fill", title: "Square")


          }
      }
}
```

Furthermore, we need four different views to be selected: one to contain the selection mechanism and the selected view, and one that is that selection mechanism. Let's call the first `CustomTabView` and the second `HomeTabView`. The four views to be selected, in our example, will show their name. In a real app, they can be whatever you want. Our `HomeTabView` view will cycle through all the values of the enum tabs, using the `@ViewBuilder tabView()` function to produce its contained views. You will want to use this approach, using `@ViewBuilder` when you want to produce multiple child views via a single closure or function call. The following code fragment shows how to build all the contained views: `StarView`, `MoonView`, `TriangleView`, and `SquareView` (they are just `Text` views with modifiers, each displaying its own name). They all share the same layout with padding, rounded corners, background material, and a shadow.

Create another new SwiftUI `View` file named `HomeTabView.swift` and add the following code:

```
import SwiftUI
struct StarView: View {
    var body: some View {
        Text("This is a Star")
            .padding(.all)
            .background(.regularMaterial)
            .cornerRadius(8.0)
            .shadow(color: .gray,radius: 5,x: 2.0,y: 2)
    }
}

struct MoonView: View {
    var body: some View {
```

```
            Text("This is a Moon")
                .padding(.all)
                .cornerRadius(8.0)
                .background(.regularMaterial)
                .shadow(color: .gray,radius: 5,x: 2.0,y: 2)
    }
}

struct TriangleView: View {
    var body: some View {
        Text("This is a Triangle")
            .padding(.all)
            .cornerRadius(8.0)
            .background(.regularMaterial)
            .shadow(color: .gray,radius: 5,x: 2.0,y: 2)
    }
}

struct SquareView: View {
    var body: some View {
        Text("This is a Square")
            .padding(.all)
            .cornerRadius(8.0)
            .background(.regularMaterial)
            .shadow(color: .gray,radius: 5,x: 2.0,y: 2)
    }
}

struct CustomTabView<Content: View>: View {

    let tabs: [ItemValue]
    @Binding var selectedIndex: Int
    @ViewBuilder let content: (Int) -> Content

    var body: some View {
        ZStack {
            TabView(selection: $selectedIndex) {
                ForEach(tabs.indices, id: \.self) { index in
                    content(index)
                        .tag(index)
                }
            }
            VStack {
```

```
                        MyTabView(items: tabs, selectedIndex: $selectedIndex)
                        Spacer()
                    }
                    .padding(.bottom, 8)
            }
        }
}

struct HomeTabView: View {
    @State var selectedIndex: Int = 0

    var body: some View {
        CustomTabView(tabs: Tabs.allCases.map({ $0.tabItem }),
selectedIndex: $selectedIndex) { index in
            let type = Tabs(rawValue: index) ?? .star
            tabView(type: type)
        }
    }

    @ViewBuilder
    func tabView(type: Tabs) -> some View {
        switch type {
        case .star:
            StarView()
        case .moon:
            MoonView()
        case .triangle:
            TriangleView()
        case .square:
            SquareView()
        }
    }
}

struct MainTabView_Previews: PreviewProvider {
    static var previews: some View {
        HomeTabView()
    }
}
```

The following points explain the preceding code block:

- CustomTabView is a struct that takes a view (Content: View) as a generic argument. It has the following properties:

  - tabs: An array of ItemValue, which describes each tab

  - selectedIndex: A @State Int that keeps track of the currently selected tab index

  - content: A view builder closure that takes an Int (the index of the selected tab) and returns Content

  - In body, it uses TabView and a custom tab view (MyTabView) in a ZStack to lay out the tabs

- HomeTabView is the main view of the app. It has a selectedIndex @State variable that tracks the currently selected tab.

- HomeTabView uses CustomTabView and sets its tabs with Tabs.allCases.map({ $0.tabItem }).

- Tabs is an enum that describes each tab and has a computed tabItem property of the ItemValue type.

- The @ViewBuilder func tabView(type: Tabs) -> some View function switches depending on the Tabs enum to determine which of the previously defined views (StarView, MoonView, etc.) is to be displayed.

To finish, we need to add HomeTabView to our default scene, WindowGroup, so that it is the view displayed at the application start. We can delete the ContentView view created by the Xcode wizard, as this is not necessary anymore:

```
import SwiftUI
@main
struct CH6_CustomTabBarApp: App {
    var body: some Scene {
        WindowGroup {
            HomeTabView()
        }
    }
}
```

The result is shown in the simulator in the following figure:

Figure 6.4 – Our custom tab bar at the top of the screen

We can conclude that often customizing existing interface elements just for esthetics can be fun but involves much more work. In our intentionally simple case, this effort was over an order of magnitude higher than just using the native UI elements provided by Apple. Be warned that precisely matching the original component's capabilities and functionality is also difficult. In our case, we sacrificed compatibility and ease of use with Apple TV and future Apple devices to display our titles in red and position the tab bar at the top of the screen in iOS.

Users may already be familiar with the existing UI elements unless using your customized versions is immediately understandable by a user. So, whenever you decide to implement your own modified version of an existing UI element, you should question yourself and consider whether that time would be better spent producing more value for your user by implementing more actual features.

Besides, if your customization effort goes too deep, it might be based on some mechanism that Apple will want to change in the next versions of iOS.

If you stick to Apple UI recommendations, if Apple decides to change the look and feel of apps in the next version of the operating system, your app will adapt, often without any modifications required on your side.

When this does not happen automatically, you may want to let your app perform differently under different conditions – namely, different versions of the compiler (which practically means different versions of Xcode) or different versions of the iOS operating system. In the next section, we will teach you how to adapt source code to different versions of the OS at compile time.

Adapting your code to different versions of the operating system

> **Conditional compilation rather than runtime check in Swift**
>
> If you want to adapt your code so that it is produced only for a certain version of the compiler or operating system, you can use conditional compilation. In the following example, different versions of the code will be compiled, depending on the version of Swift.
>
> You can also check for a specific version of an operating system, both at compile time and at runtime. If you don't want to link to the wrong version of an API, be sure to use conditional compilation.

An example of conditional compilation depending on the compiler is the following code fragment:

```
#if compiler(>=5.5)
    return self.previewCGImageRepresentation()
    #else
      return    self.previewCGImageRepresentation()?.
takeUnretainedValue()
#endif
```

The previous code fragment provides a different implementation of the preview image representation, depending on the compiler version. The inappropriate version would not be even linked, and this will avoid producing an error if the compiler version does not support that functionality.

If, instead, you want to compile different code depending on the supported API for different versions of the operating systems, you can use `if #available`, as in the following code fragment:

```
struct ContentView: View {
    var body: some View {
    Group {
            if #available(iOS 14.0, *) {
                ScrollView {
                    AnyView(LazyVStack { content.padding(.horizontal,
15) })
                }
            } else {
                List { content }
```

```
            }
        }
    }
}
```

In the previous code example, ContentView will contain a Group-based view hierarchy or a simple List, depending on the version of iOS being equal to or above 14.0.

In the next section, we will examine modal views in detail.

The hitchhiker's guide to modal navigation

In this section, we will examine, in detail, how to display modal views. A modal view is a view that appears on top of the currently displayed view and that prevents interaction with the underlying view. The modal view is used to capture user input or display additional information without navigating away from the current screen. Once a modal view appears, it needs to be dismissed before interaction is possible with the rest of the application.

Showing a modal sheet

Sheets are used to display a view on top of another one, and they can be dismissed by dragging them down or programmatically. You need a Boolean that controls whether the sheet is presented, and the sheet view can be attached to the main view using the .sheet(isPresented:) modifier.

An example of a modal sheet is the following code:

```
import SwiftUI

struct SheetView: View {
    @Environment(\.dismiss) var dismiss

    var body: some View {
        Button("Dismiss") {
            dismiss()
        }
        .font(.title)
        .foregroundColor(.red)
        .frame(minWidth: 120,minHeight: 90)
        .background(.regularMaterial)
        .cornerRadius(8.0)
    }
}
```

```
struct ContentView: View {
    @State var showingSheet = false

    var body: some View {
        Button("Show") {
            showingSheet.toggle()
        }.font(.title)
            .foregroundColor(.black)
            .frame(minWidth: 120,minHeight: 90)
            .background(.regularMaterial)
            .cornerRadius(8.0)
        .sheet(isPresented: $showingSheet) {
            SheetView()
        }
        .background(Color(.systemYellow))
    }
}

struct ContentView_Previews: PreviewProvider {
    static var previews: some View {
        ContentView()
    }
}
```

SheetView is a struct that defines a view that will be displayed as a modal sheet.

dismiss is an environment variable (one that can be accessed throughout the screen hierarchy) that provides a Boolean for dismissing the modal sheet.

body contains a red **Dismiss** button with set dimensions and rounded corners. When pressed, this button invokes the dismiss() method, which closes the modal sheet.

The @State property (showingSheet) is used to control the presentation of the sheet. It is initialized to false, meaning the sheet is not shown initially.

The .sheet modifier listens to changes in the showingSheet variable. When this variable is set to true, SheetView is presented as a modal sheet. When showingSheet is set to false, the modal sheet is dismissed.

The result is shown in the following figure:

Figure 6.5 – Presenting a modal sheet in SwiftUI for iOS 15

If you need to support previous versions of iOS, you can use the technique shown in the following example, which works with iOS 14:

```
import SwiftUI

struct MainView: View {
    @State private var showSheet = false

    var body: some View {
        Button("Show Sheet") {
            showSheet = true
```

```swift
            }
            .sheet(isPresented: $showSheet,
                   onDismiss: { print("dismissed!") },
                   content: { MySheet() })
    }
}

struct MySheet: View {
    @Environment(\.presentationMode) var presentationMode
    var body: some View {
        VStack {
        Text("This is my new Sheet")
            .onAppear {
                print("Showing")
            }
        }
    }
}

struct ContentView: View {
    var body: some View {
        MainView()
        .padding()
    }
}

struct ContentView_Previews: PreviewProvider {
    static var previews: some View {
        ContentView()
    }
}
```

In the preceding code block, we have to use the now deprecated `.presentationMode` and use the `@Environment` property wrapper to create a global binding. As we don't supply a button for the dismissal, to dismiss the modal sheet, you can drag it down.

Note
The closure on `.onAppear` will be invoked any time a view is presented on the screen.

If you want your modal sheet to cover a view entirely and not be dismissible by dragging, you can use the .fullScreenCover modifier, as in the following example:

```swift
import SwiftUI

struct FullScreenModalView: View {
    @Environment(\.dismiss) var dismiss

    var body: some View {
        ZStack {
            Color
                .yellow
                .edgesIgnoringSafeArea(.all)
            Spacer()
            Button("Dismiss") {
                dismiss()
            }
            .padding()
            .border(.blue,width: 2)
        }
    }
}

struct ContentView: View {
    @State private var isPresented = false

    var body: some View {
        Button("Show") {
            isPresented.toggle()
        }
        .foregroundColor(.white)
        .padding()
        .background(.blue)
        .clipped(antialiased: true)
        .border(.blue, width: 2)
        .cornerRadius(8)
        .fullScreenCover(isPresented: $isPresented, content:
FullScreenModalView.init)
    }
}
```

```
struct ContentView_Previews: PreviewProvider {
    static var previews: some View {
        ContentView()
    }
}
```

The previous example shows a button in `ContentView` that, when pressed, presents a full-screen modal view, named `FullScreenModalView`.

The `.fullScreenCover` modifier listens to the `isPresented` state variable. When this becomes `true`, `FullScreenModalView` is presented modally in full screen.

Note that `.fullScreenCover()` is not implemented in macOS.

In the next section, we will learn how to show an alert.

Showing alerts

Suppose you need to show alerts to the user. In that case, the approach is similar to that used for sheets: you need a Boolean to decide whether the alert is shown, and then you attach the `alert()` modifier to the main view and include all the buttons you need inside the alert. Any button will dismiss the alert when tapped, so an empty action will be sufficient if you need just a simple dismissal.

The following code example shows how to display an alert on iOS 15:

```
import SwiftUI

struct ContentView: View {
    @State private var showingAlert = false

    var body: some View {
        VStack{
            Text("The button shows an Alert")
            Divider()
            Button("Show") {
                showingAlert = true
            }
            .alert("The Alert is showing", isPresented: $showingAlert)
            {
                Button("OK", role: .cancel) { }
            }
        }
    }
}
```

```
struct ContentView_Previews: PreviewProvider {
    static var previews: some View {
        ContentView()
    }
}
```

You can add as many buttons as you need; if you don't add any, the system will add an **OK** button for you. The result is shown in the next figure:

Figure 6.6 – Showing an alert

In iOS 14, you should instead use the now deprecated `Alert` struct, as shown in the following code fragment:

```
Alert(
    title: Text("Alert title"),
    message: Text("this is the alert message"),
    dismissButton: .default(Text("OK"))
)
```

In the next section, we will discuss a way to present an alternative to sheets that, traditionally on iOS, is commonly used for iPads, as these have quite a lot of screen estate.

The popover

The popover was originally an iPad-only view presented modally and originates from the point where it is invoked, generally on a button. The popover was normally presented as a translucent view, with a triangle pointing at the "origin" from which the popover "expanded" as an animation.

Popovers can also be used on the iPhone, which is not even recent news. From your perspective, these are just another UI tool to use appropriately to design an appropriate user experience. If you have buttons you need to associate with the informational display of a modal view, which is smaller than the original view, then the popover is the tool of choice on the iPad. On iPhone, however, the popover will be presented normally as a modal sheet.

According to Apple, the popover is declared as follows:

```
func popover<Content>(
    isPresented: Binding<Bool>,
    attachmentAnchor: PopoverAttachmentAnchor = .rect(.bounds),
    arrowEdge: Edge = .top, @ViewBuilder content: @escaping () ->
Content
) -> some View where Content : View
```

The `popover` function in SwiftUI is a view modifier that displays a popover. It takes four main parameters:

- `isPresented`: A binding variable to control the visibility of the popover.
- `attachmentAnchor`: Specifies where the popover anchors. It defaults to the bounds of the target view.
- `arrowEdge`: Indicates the edge where the popover's arrow points. It defaults to the top edge.
- `content`: A closure that generates the content inside the popover.

`popover` returns a modified view that shows the popover whenever `isPresented` is set to `true`.

> **Note**
>
> It is often helpful to browse the documentation on Apple's developers' website: `https://developer.apple.com/documentation/swiftui`.
>
> This is one way to determine whether some iOS or other Apple operating system-related programming mechanism has been updated or deprecated. Inserting the precise URL for the popover wouldn't make much sense, as this information is bound to change.
>
> However, you should check by searching this website whenever you have a question about a particular feature of an Apple framework. Due to the complexity of SwiftUI, you should peruse this website quite often.

Here's an example of using a popover:

```swift
import SwiftUI

struct ViewWithAPopover: View {
    @State private var isShowingPopover = false

    var body: some View {
        Button("Show Popover") {
            self.isShowingPopover = true
        }
        .popover(isPresented: $isShowingPopover) {
            Text("This Text is the Popover content")
                .padding()
        }
    }
}

struct ContentView: View {
    var body: some View {
        VStack {
            ViewWithAPopover()
                .padding()
            Text("pushing the button will show a Popover")
        }
        .padding()
    }
}

struct ContentView_Previews: PreviewProvider {
```

```
        static var previews: some View {
            ContentView()
        }
    }
```

`ViewWithAPopover` creates a button with the label **Show Popover**. The `isShowingPopover` variable controls whether the popover should be displayed or not. When the button is pressed, it sets `isShowingPopover` to `true`, causing the popover to appear.

The `@State` Boolean `isShowingPopover` variable is bound to the parameter of the `.popover` modifier, and the contents in the modifier's closure are displayed inside the popover. Refer to Apple's documentation if you need further customization of a popover's appearance.

The result of the previous code example is shown in the next figure:

Figure 6.7 – A popover on an iPhone

For an iPad, the result of pressing the button is shown in the following figure, and it is very similar to what you would have obtained with UIKit:

Figure 6.8 – A popover on an iPad

For an iPhone, you will get the very same behavior and appearance as a modal sheet.

In the next section, we will show how to limit the covering of a modal screen to a part of the screen using detents.

Presentation detents

The .presentationDetents modifier allows you to present a modal sheet extending only partially to cover the screen, in steps you can specify.

If you don't specify any detent, the default is going to be .large. You can specify standard "stops" where the modal sheet will stop from covering the whole screen– for example, .medium (half screen) or .large (full length) – use an array of floating point values, a floating point fraction of the available height (.fraction()), or give a precise height in points with .height(). You can specify as many different stops as you like with the array you pass as a parameter to the .presentationDetents modifier. By default, SwiftUI will create a resize handle.

Be aware that the detent bound sheet will use all the available height if the device is rotated and this modifier is used on a rotated iPhone (compact-size screen device).

If you are developing a horizontal app, you should provide a button to dismiss the sheet. If you want to display a drag indicator, use the .presentationDragIndicator(.visible) modifier to show it. By default, this indicator is not shown.

Here is an example of presenting a detent bound sheet that is 250 points high when shown in a vertical format on an iPhone:

```swift
import SwiftUI

struct ContentView: View {
    @State private var showingDetentsBoundSheet = false

    var body: some View {
        Button("Show Detents") {
            showingDetentsBoundSheet.toggle()
        }
        .sheet(isPresented: $showingDetentsBoundSheet) {
            VStack{
                Text("presentationDetents allow the sheet to slide
covering the screen partially")
            }
                .presentationDetents([.height(250)])
                .presentationDragIndicator(.visible)
        }
    }
}
```

```
struct ContentView_Previews: PreviewProvider {
    static var previews: some View {
        ContentView()
    }
}
```

Detents specify the stopping points for a sheet when it's dragged up or down. In this code, a detent is set to make the sheet stop at a height of 250 units. This allows the sheet to partially cover the screen instead of taking up the full display.

The result is shown in the following figure:

Figure 6.9 – Presenting a sheet with detents

Summary

In this chapter, we looked at how we display tab bars in SwiftUI from the standard way of implementing tab bars called `TabView`. We have also explored modifying views to imitate a tab bar in situations where the standard system provided tab bar will not do, like when selection buttons have to be placed at the top of the screen.

We examined in depth how familiar modal views—sheets, alerts, and popovers—are shown in SwiftUI with focus on both iPhone and iPad, including using presentation detents, with attention on how to achieve this in different releases of iOS.

Moving forward, the next chapter will explore in depth the topic of navigation within SwiftUI.

7

All About Navigation

In this chapter, we will examine navigation in SwiftUI. We will begin with an introduction to the concept of navigation in iOS in general terms; then, we will examine navigation as a response to user interaction and programmatic navigation. We will cover the changes introduced in SwiftUI 4 (iOS 16), along with an explanation of navigation in previous versions. The most advanced techniques require iOS 16, and they make advanced navigation control easy – so easy and powerful that all the previous patterns for navigation become unnecessary.

We are going to cover these main topics:

- Navigation as a concept in iOS and other platforms

- Showing a tab bar title with `NavigationView`

- Presenting views with `NavigationLink` (pre-iOS 16)

- Adding buttons to `NavigationView` and activating navigation programmatically

- Using `navigationDestination` with `NavigationStack`

- `NavigationSplitView` – multicolumn navigation

- Direct navigation stack manipulation with `NavigationPath`

- Saving and loading the navigation stack

Technical requirements

You will find the code related to this chapter here: `https://github.com/PacktPublishing/ An-iOS-Developer-s-Guide-to-SwiftUI`, in the CH7 folder.

Navigation as a concept in iOS and other platforms

When we talk about navigation in an iOS context, we mean being able to "push" views on a stack and navigating "back" by popping them. You usually "pop" to the previous view by tapping a "back" button.

The main difference between a modal presentation and a stack-based "push" of a view is that with the modal presentation, the original view is kept active and "covered" by the presentation view. The modal presentation should be used to keep the user's attention focused within the same context and is typically a shorter-term interaction. Navigation push changes this context, that is, by switching away from, for example, a list selection to a detail view, that is, to a different interaction context.

Navigation is typically evidenced by a navigation bar containing a title and controls that can affect the screen content.

The navigation bar is shown at the top of the screen and enables navigating through a content hierarchy. The most common controls associated with a navigation bar are navigation buttons.

The back button is one of these. A typical navigation bar contains no more than two buttons, one to the left of the screen (typically the back button) and another on the right, which can change depending on context. Having more than one navigation button per side is possible. Still, it is not considered a best practice due to potential errors in selecting the wrong button, and it should be avoided.

> **Using non-recommended UI customizations**
>
> It is also not recommended to use the area provided for the title to place other controls. If a particular customization is mentioned in the Apple **Human Interface Guidelines** (**HIGs**) with terms such as "you should avoid…" you should regard it as a bad practice that you should avoid.
>
> You will find Apple's HIGs at this url: `https://developer.apple.com/design/ human-interface-guidelines`
>
> In that case, the customization is a bad idea that has already been tried and will likely cause technical problems and surprise or confuse the users. Besides, it is also likely to cause additional trouble for users relying on accessibility features. This is the case if a designer wants to add controls to the title space because they want to add another control to an already busy screen; please remind them to read the HIGs, and perhaps your company should invest more in training graphical designers. They can't just produce screens that look good on a hi-fi mock-up; designers need to have an understanding of how the UI is supposed to work on Apple platforms.
>
> Instead, place those control elements, if you need them, on a bar or a container view under the navigation bar.

The navigation bar does not exist as a UI element in **macOS** apps. In macOS, you usually use a sidebar or place a back button inside a toolbar. Also, a window's title is usually shown in the title bar in macOS.

Depending on the device and operating system platform, navigation will be translated differently by SwiftUI.

On an **iPad**, for instance, the navigation is usually shown by default as a split view, which implements the navigation concept by showing multiple columns simultaneously. This allows, for example, presenting a selection list on the left pane and a detail view on the right.

Normally, in iOS, the pushed view substitutes the existing one with an animated transition that makes the pushed view enter from the right while the current view is pushed out to the left.

When going back, the transition is reverted, called "popping" a view from the stack.

The title in a **navigation bar** should provide context to the users by describing the current screen and letting them understand where they are relative to the navigation hierarchy of the views on the stack.

Showing a tab bar title with NavigationView

`NavigationView` creates a navigation bar in SwiftUI, and it should be used as a container for whatever view you are trying to display. Here's a simple example:

```
import SwiftUI

struct ContentView: View {
    var body: some View {
        NavigationView {
            VStack{
                Text("This is a simple view")
                Text("inside a NavigationView")
                    .navigationTitle("Navigation Title")
            }
        }
    }
}

struct ContentView_Previews: PreviewProvider {
    static var previews: some View {
        ContentView()
    }
}
```

The result is shown in the following screenshot:

Figure 7.1 – A simple navigation view with a title

Observe that without the `.navigationTitle` modifier, the navigation bar won't have anything to display, and our view would look like any other container view and would be displayed without a navigation bar. Also, notice that `.navigationTitle` needs to be applied to the inner view, not the `NavigationView` itself.

`NavigationView` allows us to display new views by having them enter the main window from the right edge of the screen, and SwiftUI must display the title permanently attached to each view. The new title enters with the new view from the right, while the old one moves away off the left edge of the screen.

Notice that you can use the `.navigationTitle` modifier on any view inside `NavigationView`; it doesn't need to be the outermost view.

It is possible to customize the title by applying the `.navigationBarTitleDisplayMode()` modifier, which can have three options:

- `large`: This option will show large titles that are useful mainly for the top-level views in the navigation stack
- `inline`: This option will show small titles, which should be the preferred visualization for views belonging to secondary levels (and successive ones beyond the second level)
- `automatic`: This option is the default and will use whatever display mode the previous view used

In most cases, you should use the default display mode (`.automatic`) for your initial view, which can be obtained simply by not specifying the `.navigationBarTitleDisplayMode()` modifier. Then you can use the `.inline` option for all the other views following the initial one you want to push on the stack. `NavigationView` has been deprecated in iOS 16; you should use it only if you're working on a project that caters to previous versions of iOS.

Presenting views with NavigationLink (pre-iOS 16)

`NavigationView` is a container that wraps the contents of various views, preparing them for navigation. `NavigationLink` performs the task of designating which content to navigate to and providing the user with a UI component to initiate the navigation process.

`NavigationLink` in SwiftUI allows pushing a new destination view. You can use `NavigationLink` in a list or decide to push a view programmatically. The latter enables you to trigger a new screen from a different location in your view.

In this case, the user needs to tap on the link.

The next code example illustrates using `NavigationLink` to push a simple `Text` view on the stack:

```swift
import SwiftUI

struct ContentView: View {
    fileprivate func Destination() -> Text {
        return Text("This is the destination View")
    }

    var body: some View {
        NavigationView {
            NavigationLink(destination: Destination()) {
                Text("Navigation link!")
            }
            .navigationTitle("Navigation")
        }
        .padding()
    }
}

struct ContentView_Previews: PreviewProvider {
    static var previews: some View {
        ContentView()
    }
}
```

The destination view can be whatever you want, and the navigation link just needs to be embedded in a `NavigationView`. SwiftUI will present its content by default in blue, so the user recognizes that it will behave like a link.

Instead of `Text`, you could have used, for example, `Image`, for the content of the `NavigationLink`, or a stack containing both a `Text` and `Image`, like in the following example:

```swift
import SwiftUI

struct ContentView: View {
    fileprivate func Destination() -> some View {
        Text("This is a destination View")
            .navigationTitle("Destination")

    }
    fileprivate func Destination2() -> some View {
        Text("This is another destination View")
            .navigationTitle("Another Destination")

    }
    fileprivate func Destination3() -> some View {
        Text("This is yet another destination View")
            .navigationTitle("Yet Another Destination")

    }

    var body: some View {
        NavigationView {
            VStack{
                NavigationLink(destination: Destination()) {
                    Text("Navigation link1")
                }.padding()
                NavigationLink(destination: Destination2()) {
                    HStack{
                        Image(systemName: "globe")
                            Text("Navigation link2")
                    }
                    .padding()
                }
                NavigationLink(destination: Destination3()) {
                    Image(systemName: "cloud")
                }

            }
```

```
            .navigationTitle("Navigation")
        }
        .padding()
    }
}

struct ContentView_Previews: PreviewProvider {
    static var previews: some View {
        ContentView()
    }
}
```

The result is shown in the following screenshot, which shows embedding several instances of `NavigationLink` within the same `NavigationView`:

Figure 7.2 – Inserting multiple links in the same NavigationView

Adding buttons to NavigationView and activating navigation programmatically

As in UIKit, it is possible to add custom buttons to `NavigationView`. This is achieved by using the `.toolbar` modifier and placing a `ToolbarItem` inside it.

If you don't specify the placement, for left-to-right languages, the default placement of `.ToolbarItem` will be positioned on the right, and it will switch to the left for right-to-left languages.

Typically, you will add a `Button` to `ToolbarItem`. But if you are on iOS 16, `NavigationView` can be substituted with `NavigationStack`, without changing anything else.

The following code example illustrates how to add buttons to a `NavigationView`, specifying the placement explicitly in both cases:

```swift
import SwiftUI
struct ContentView: View {
    var body: some View {
        NavigationView {
            Text("Example of adding tabbaritems")
                .navigationTitle("Welcome")
                .toolbar {
                    ToolbarItem(placement: .navigationBarLeading) {
                        Button("Menu") {
                            print("Menu tapped!")
                        }
                    }
                    ToolbarItem(placement: .navigationBarTrailing) {
                        Button("Help") {
                            print("Help tapped!")
                        }
                    }
                }
        }
    }
}

struct ContentView_Previews: PreviewProvider {
    static var previews: some View {
        ContentView()
    }
}
```

The result is shown in the following screenshot:

Figure 7.3 – Navigation with a ToolbarItem with two buttons

You can also add multiple bar buttons in the same placement. If you do, it is recommended to wrap them inside a `ToolBarItemGroup`.

You can also use `.primaryAction` as a placement, which will default to trailing for left-to-right languages.

If you use `.secondaryAction` for a group, it will collapse multiple buttons into a single details button.

We can also use a `NavigationLink` to activate the navigation to a destination view programmatically. The `NavigationLink` is initialized with an `isActive` parameter bound to a `@State` variable that is set to `true` by the action of the **About** button. In the following example, the **About** button in the toolbar is initially hidden, as it is contained in the secondary action placement group:

```
import SwiftUI
struct AboutView: View{
    var body: some View {
        Text ("About view")
    }
}


struct ContentView: View {
    @State var linkActive = false
    var body: some View {
        NavigationView {
            Text("Activating a NavigationLink")
                .background(               NavigationLink(destination:
AboutView(), isActive: $linkActive) {})

                .navigationTitle("Home View")
                .toolbar {
                    ToolbarItemGroup(placement: .primaryAction) {
                        Button("Help") {
                            print("Help tapped!")
                        }
                    }

                    ToolbarItemGroup(placement: .secondaryAction) {
                        Button("Settings") {
                            print("Settings tapped")
                        }
                        Button("About") {
                            print("About tapped")
                            linkActive = true
                        }
                    }
                }
        }
    }
}
```

The result is shown in the following screenshots. The collapsed button shows three dots inside a circle:

Figure 7.4 – Tapping the collapsed button icon shows a menu

Figure 7.5 – Showing the destination view for About

For iOS 16, `NavigationLink`'s `isActive` and `NavigationView` parameters are deprecated, and should be replaced with `NavigationStack` and `navigationDestination(isPresented:)`.

The following code example shows how to correct the previous code, using the recommended approach for iOS 16, with NavigationStack and .navigationDestination(isPresented:). The results are the same as in the previous screenshots:

```swift
import SwiftUI
struct AboutView: View{
    var body: some View {
        Text ("About view")
    }
}

struct ContentView: View {
    @State var isPresentedAboutView = false
    var body: some View {
        NavigationStack {
            Text("Activating a NavigationLink")

                .navigationTitle("Home View")
                .toolbar {
                    ToolbarItemGroup(placement: .primaryAction) {
                        Button("Help") {
                            print("Help tapped!")
                        }
                    }

                    ToolbarItemGroup(placement: .secondaryAction) {
                        Button("Settings") {
                            print("Settings tapped")
                        }
                        Button("About") {
                            print("About tapped")
                            isPresentedAboutView = true
                        }
                    }
                }                        .navigationDestination(isPresented:
$isPresentedAboutView , destination: {AboutView()}
                )
        }
    }
}
```

```
struct ContentView_Previews: PreviewProvider {
    static var previews: some View {
        ContentView()
    }
}
```

NavigationStack is roughly equivalent to using the old NavigationView with .stack as a style. You can replace one with the other, and they will look and behave in the same way.

However, the new NavigationStack allows us to separate the navigation destination from NavigationLink.

We will show how to do that in the next section.

Using navigationDestination with NavigationStack

This is a feature introduced with SwiftUI 4 that is available with iOS 16. Another common use of .navigationDestination is passing an element from a list to a destination view, using a NavigationLink.

Let's begin with a simple array inside a List.

Here is our code example:

```
import SwiftUI

struct EmployeeView: View {
    let name: String

    var body: some View {
        Text("\(name)")
            .font(.largeTitle)
            .navigationTitle("Selected employee")
            .foregroundColor(.secondary)
    }
}

struct ContentView: View {
    let employee = [
        "Anne Loyd",
        "John Smith",
```

```
        "Sandra Brown",
        "Ken Richards",
        "Tommy Shepherd",
        "Amie Ross",
    ]

    var body: some View {
        NavigationStack {
            List(employee, id: \.self) { employee in
                NavigationLink(employee, value: employee)
            }
            .navigationDestination(for: String.self, destination:
EmployeeView.init)
            .navigationTitle("Select an Employee")
        }
    }
}

struct ContentView_Previews: PreviewProvider {
    static var previews: some View {
        ContentView()
    }
}
```

Our List displays an array of employee names. Each employee is shown within a clickable NavigationLink, which navigates to the EmployeeView detail view when clicked. EmployeeView is just a simple Text with a navigation title. NavigationLink takes two parameters: the text to display and the value to pass to the destination view.

In our case, the value passed is just the name of the employee, but it could be a user-defined type such as a struct, if you need to pass more information to the detail view.

ContentView also sets the navigation destination for NavigationLink. This tells SwiftUI where to navigate to when the link is clicked. The .navigationDestination modifier is used to set the destination for values of the String type; when the user clicks on a link, EmployeeView will be pushed on the stack, receiving the employee name as an argument.

The result is shown in the following screenshot:

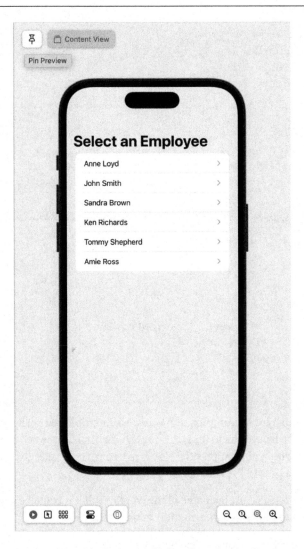

Figure 7.6 – List with NavigationLink and .navigationDestination

In the next section, we will examine how to use `NavigationPath` to control the navigation stack.

Using NavigationPath to control the navigation stack

Separating `NavigationLink` from the destination simplifies creating deep links and also jumping to arbitrary destinations or pushing or popping several views at once.

With `NavigationStack`, you can attach multiple navigation destinations to handle different types of data. In this case, your destination should be expressed with `NavigationPath`, rather than an array of data of a specific type.

The following example does exactly that, using two instances of `.navigationDestination`: one to handle a destination view to handle an `Int` parameter, and the other to handle a `String` one. Notice that `@State var presentedValues` is initialized to `NavigationPath()`, and that value is bound to the initializer's `NavigationStack(path:)` parameter.

Technically, `NavigationPath` is a type-erased list of data representing the content of a navigation stack, meaning that it can contain elements of different types.

> **NavigationPath as a type-erased collection**
>
> `NavigationPath` accepts elements of different types and behaves like a collection. It provides the usual collection features for adding, counting, and removing data elements. It allows for stack manipulation in sophisticated ways; for instance, you could remove all elements (popping directly to root).

Here's an example of using two different types of `.navigationDestination` within the same `NavigationStack`:

```
import SwiftUI
struct ContentView: View {
    @State private var presentedValues = NavigationPath()

    var body: some View {
        NavigationStack(path: $presentedValues) {
            NavigationLink(value: "String Example1") {
                Text("String Value")
            }
            Spacer()
            NavigationLink(value: "String Example2") {
                Text("Another String Value")
            }

            List(1..<30) { i in
                NavigationLink(value: i) {
                    Label("Int Number \(i)", systemImage: "\(i).
square")
                        .foregroundColor(.accentColor)
                }
            }
            .navigationDestination(for: Int.self) { i in
                Text("Int value \(i)")
                    .navigationTitle("Int DetailView")

            }
```

```
                .navigationDestination(for: String.self) { i in
                    Text("String Detail \(i)")
                        .navigationTitle("String DetailView")
                }
                .navigationTitle("Home")
            }
        }
    }


struct ContentView_Previews: PreviewProvider {
    static var previews: some View {
        ContentView()
    }
}
```

The result is shown in the following screenshot:

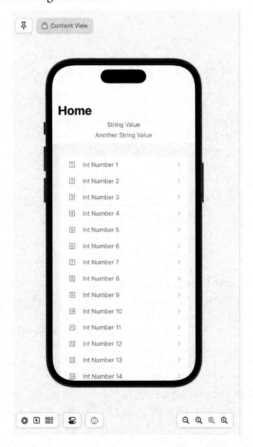

Figure 7.7 – Using NavigationPath to allow for different types of data on the stack

`NavigationPath` accepts an `init(codable:)` that has a `Codable` property. Therefore, if the values you place on the navigation stack conform to the `Codable` protocol, it is possible to use the `Codable` property of `NavigationPath` to obtain a serializable representation of the path that can be used to save and restore the state of the navigation stack.

NavigationSplitView – multicolumn navigation

`NavigationSplitView` is a view that presents views in two or three columns, where selections in leading columns control presentations in subsequent columns.

On large-screen devices, such as iPad and Mac, `NavigationSplitView` will represent detail-view navigation on multiple columns to better exploit large screens but will automatically default to a normal navigation stack when the screen width is compact (normal iPhone width in vertical format).

The simplest multicolumn view you can obtain in this way is simply a two-column static view, like in the following code fragment, which would work on an iPad:

```
struct ContentView: View {
    var body: some View {
        NavigationStack{
            NavigationSplitView {
                Text("Side View")
            } detail: {
                Text("Detail View")
            }
        }
    }
}
```

The result on the iPad would be the following (once you click on the **SplitView** button):

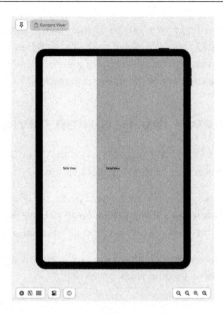

Figure 7.8 – A simple two-column NavigationSplitView

The result is not particularly interesting; however, it can be easily extended to three columns, by using the init(sidebar: content: detail) initializer instead of init(sidebar: detail:).

If presented on a narrow-width screen, NavigationSplitView will collapse its column in a stack and display the last column that shows useful information: the detail corresponding to the last selected item.

Typically, however, you would normally want to be able to select an item on the sidebar, and then load the detail view corresponding to that element. Take the following example:

```swift
import SwiftUI


struct ContentView: View {
    var body: some View {
        NavigationSplitView {
            List(1..<20) { i in
                NavigationLink("Row \(i)", value: i)
            }
            .navigationDestination(for: Int.self) {
                Text("You have selected row #\($0)")
                    .font(.title)
            }
            .navigationTitle("NavigationSplitView")
```

```
        } detail: {
            Text("Please select a row")
        }
        .padding()
    }
}

struct ContentView_Previews: PreviewProvider {
    static var previews: some View {
        ContentView()
    }
}
```

The result, for an iPhone **compact screen**, i.e. in vertical orientation, will be a normal navigation stack, with a list selection, as in the following screenshot:

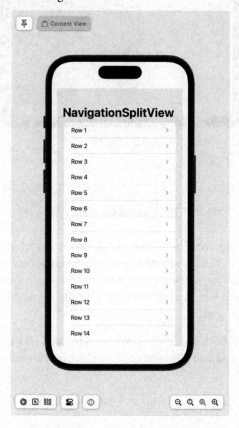

Figure 7.9 – NavigationSplitView on iPhone

On the iPad, it will instead look as in the following screenshot. You can switch the sidebar on or off by clicking on the sidebar button at the top of the screen:

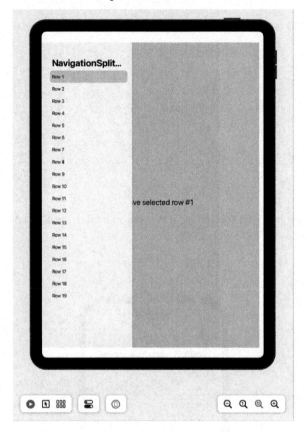

Figure 7.10 – NavigationSplitView on iPad

On an iPad or large screens (e.g., an iPhone with a large screen in the horizontal orientation), instead, this is shown as two columns, and the selected view will change according to the selected row. Once you have selected an element, you will want to remove the sidebar from the screen by tapping on the detail view; it will show a split view button on top of a detail view without the sidebar. Tapping that button will show the sidebar again.

On older versions of iPadOS (less than 16), you can instead show up to three views inside a `NavigationView`. The first one will behave like a sidebar, the second as content, and the third as detail.

In order to display a `List` on the first view as a sidebar, add the `.listStyle(.sidebar)` modifier to the `List`.

> **Lists in SwiftUI are lazy!**
>
> You may find some random articles on the Internet claiming that SwiftUI is not as memory efficient as UIKit in terms of displaying lists rather than UITableView on iOS, that's not correct. You don't have to worry about optimizing lists in terms of memory allocation. A list's contents are allocated as lazy by default, and SwiftUI will take care of dynamically allocating only the items displayed to the user.

In the next section, we will return to the topic of `navigationDestination`, giving more examples of how to perform programmatic navigation.

Direct navigation stack manipulation with NavigationPath

In the following example, we will demonstrate that `NavigationPath` is essentially a **type-erased collection**, by appending directly to the stack and directly removing items from the stack. With the buttons labeled **Jump to**, we will add a corresponding number of `Int` items to the stack, forcing navigation to the corresponding last view. We can navigate back, as usual, to the preceding item on the stack, until we reach the root, our home view. Or instead, we can click the button labeled **Go Back Directly to Home** to remove all the preceding items from the stack.

We also show a simpler navigation for items shown as a list. For those, we use `String` as a type, and we use `NavigationLink` with a value, thus pushing just one element on the stack. If we use `navpath.removeLast()`, that will have the same effect of navigating to the previous view with the back button. Here is our code example:

```
import SwiftUI
struct ContentView: View {
    @State private var navPath = NavigationPath()

    var body: some View {
        NavigationStack(path: $navPath) {
            Button("Jump to 1") {
                navPath.append(Int(1))
            }
            Spacer()
            Button("Jump to 2") {
                navPath.append(Int(1))
                navPath.append(Int(2))
            }
            Spacer()
            Button("Jump to 3") {
                navPath.append(Int(1))
                navPath.append(Int(2))
```

```
                navPath.append(Int(3))
            }
            Spacer()
            Button("Jump to 4") {
                navPath.append(Int(1))
                navPath.append(Int(2))
                navPath.append(Int(3))
                navPath.append(Int(4))
            }

            List(1..<5) { i in
                NavigationLink(value: "String \(i)") {
                    Label("Link String \(i)", systemImage: "\(i).
square")
                }
            }
            .navigationDestination(for: Int.self) { i in
                VStack{
                    Spacer()
                    Text("This is Detail View #\(i)")
                        .font(.title)
                    Spacer()
                    Button("Go Back Directly to Home") {
                        navPath.removeLast(i)
                    }
                    Spacer()
                    .navigationTitle("Numeric Detail")
                }

            }
            .navigationDestination(for: String.self) { i in
                VStack{
                    Spacer()
                    Text("This is Detail View '\(i)'")
                        .font(.title)
                    Spacer()
                    Button("Go Back Directly to Home") {
                        navPath.removeLast()
                    }
                    Spacer()
                }
            }
            .navigationTitle("Home")
    }
```

```
    }
}

struct ContentView_Previews: PreviewProvider {
    static var previews: some View {
        ContentView()
    }
}
```

The result is shown in the following screenshot:

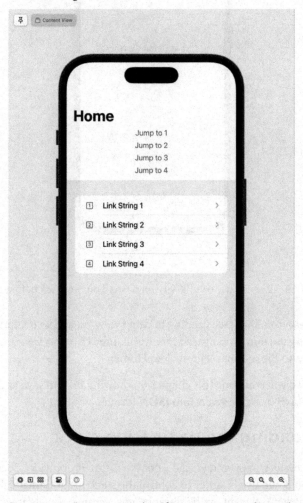

Figure 7.11 – "Jump to Number" forces n items on the stack

If, for instance, the user taps on **Jump to 3**, the following screen will be presented:

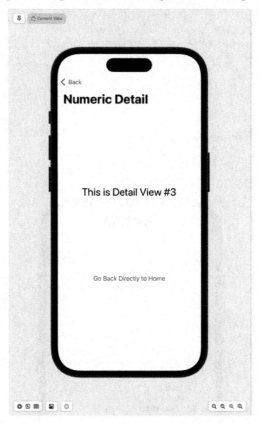

Figure 7.12 – Two other views have been pushed on the stack before this one

Back will pop this view from the stack, leading to detail view #2, and so on, until we reach the home view. **Go Back Directly to Home** will instead remove all three elements from the stack, including this one, thus returning us to the root navigation view, **Home**.

In the next section, we will conclude this chapter by showing how to save and load the navigation stack by converting `NavigationPath` into **JSON** format.

Saving and loading the navigation stack

`NavigationPath`, besides `.append()` and `.removeLast()`, provides `.count` and `.isEmpty` properties, which you could use in order to control the stack programmatically. Basically, you can delete and create whatever you want on the stack, in however many levels as you please, and you can do it all programmatically.

So, you could come up with your own solution to save the stack programmatically or manipulate it in any way you want. One possible suggestion could be using a state machine pattern if you have a really complex navigation structure in mind.

But in order to make things even easier, `NavigationPath` has a `.codable` property, which allows you to convert to and from JSON format. You could send the path to a server, deep link a view of your app from a web service, and so on.

One of the many applications is storing the path so that when the app is suspended or terminated, it is restored when the app is started, so that the app has a persistent navigation state.

To make things really simple, we will always store the navigation path when it is written to (set), and we will try to retrieve it at initialization if it had been stored during a previous app run, thus not even needing to take care of the app state.

To add an automatic save functionality of the navigation path to the previous example, we have to modify the `ContentView.swift` file slightly, declaring the `navPath` variable as follows:

```
@StateObject private var navPath = PathFileStorage()
```

We remove the old declaration:

```
@State private var navPath = NavigationPath()
```

We also change all other instances of the old `navPath` to `navPath.navpath` in the `ContentView.swift` file.

We finally have to add to the project the `PathFileStorage` class in a separate `PathFileStorage.swift` file, as follows:

```
import SwiftUI

class PathFileStorage: ObservableObject {
    @Published var navpath = NavigationPath() {
        didSet {
            store()
        }
    }

    private let fileURL = URL.documentsDirectory.appending(path:
"PathFileStorage")

    func store() {
        guard let json = navpath.codable else { return }

        do {
```

```
            let data = try JSONEncoder().encode(json)
            try data.write(to: fileURL)
        } catch {
            print("Could not store navigation stack representation")
        }
    }

    init() {
        if let data = try? Data(contentsOf: fileURL) {
            if let navigationStackRepresentation = try? JSONDecoder().
decode(NavigationPath.CodableRepresentation.self, from: data) {
                navpath =
NavigationPath(navigationStackRepresentation)
                return
            }
        }
    }
}
```

The `PathFileStorage` class conforms to `ObservableObject` and contains a `@Published` `navpath` property. That is to say, SwiftUI will automatically update all views that reference it, whenever it changes. The `didSet` belonging to `navpath` will call the `store()` method whenever `navpath` gets set.

The `store()` method first checks whether `navpath` can be converted into a JSON representation using its `.codable` property, and if so, it encodes it with `JSONEncoder`, then it writes it to a file in the document folder belonging to the app.

The `init` method of the `PathFileStorage` class is instead used to restore the navigation path from the saved file, provided this exists. First, it verifies whether there is data at the file URL, and if this is the case, it tries to decode it with `JSONDecoder`.

If the data is successfully decoded, it creates a new `NavigationPath` object with the data and sets the `navpath` property to this object.

If the decoding fails, or if there is no data at the file path specified by the file URL, the `navpath` property will be initialized to the default `NavigationPath()` value, which is an empty navigation stack, and this will happen at the first run of the app.

Summary

In this chapter, we have examined stack-based navigation in SwiftUI, illustrating the old approaches based on `NavigationView`, which are still useful on iOS versions prior to 16, and the new `StackView` and `.navigationDestination` approaches, which allow for a completely flexible approach to iOS navigation, to the point of rendering many of the navigation tricks and patterns used in UIKit totally unnecessary and obsolete.

We have also shown how to use `NavigationSplitView` on large screens to achieve the functionality of the old `UISplitView`, and we have shown that this can be used to automatically adapt the rendering of the navigation appropriately and automatically depending on the screen size of the device.

We have finally concluded by showing how the navigation stack can be manipulated programmatically in an arbitrary fashion using `NavigationPath`, and showing one of the simplest possible strategies for saving and restoring it programmatically using the JSON format.

In the next chapter, we will show how to create custom graphics in SwiftUI.

Part 4: Graphics and Animation

In this part, you'll be introduced to the art of styling apps with the least amount of effort, by creating custom modifiers and integrating Core Graphics within the Canvas view. You'll learn how it is possible to combine CALayers with SwiftUI and explore `CustomLayout` for tailored UI designs.

Additionally, you'll be introduced to the basics of SwiftUI view animations. You'll discover the built-in, state-driven, reactive approach to animating UI elements using SwiftUI's declarative syntax. You'll then delve into the use of built-in modifiers, such as animation, transition, and `scaleEffect`, to add dynamic, engaging elements to your UI app designs.

This part contains the following chapters:

- *Chapter 8, Creating Custom Graphics*
- *Chapter 9, An Introduction to Animations in SwiftUI*

8
Creating Custom Graphics

In this chapter, we will examine how to style your apps with custom graphics in SwiftUI. We will first examine how to create custom modifiers. We will explain how to use Core Graphics within the Canvas view. Then, we will explain how it is possible to use CALayers, and core animation layers in SwiftUI, and then, finally, we will introduce you to CustomLayout. The purpose of this chapter is to be able to style the graphical style of our views with more freedom than what is allowed by the default styling, allowing for more creative liberty, and, when possible, doing that in the most effortless way possible.

In this chapter, we'll be covering the following topics:

- Creating custom modifiers
- The Canvas
- CALayers in SwiftUI
- CustomLayout

Technical requirements

You will find the code related to this chapter at `https://github.com/PacktPublishing/An-iOS-Developer-s-Guide-to-SwiftUI`, under the CH8 folder.

Creating custom modifiers

Whenever we need to style multiple screens with a similar look, which we can obtain by applying several modifiers, we usually don't want to apply the modifiers to all the views we have to design.

We would want to just apply a single modifier, to a view or another modifier, producing all the changes we need simultaneously.

We could, of course, design a single view and repeat it through the entirety of our application, but let's imagine that the views are different, with different content, but we would still like to style all of them in a similar way, without repeating code.

In SwiftUI, we can create custom modifiers to encapsulate styling or behavior across an entire app. Remember that SwiftUI takes a functional approach – modifiers are composable and can be applied to a view or another modifier, producing a new version of the original input value.

In order to create a custom modifier, you just need to conform to the `ViewModifier` protocol, which has just one required method.

Let's create a modifier, `CardStyle`, that we can then use directly to process the views – in our case, simple `Text` views, as shown in the following code example:

```swift
import SwiftUI

struct CardStyle: ViewModifier {
    var backgroundColor: Color

    func body(content: Content) -> some View {
        content
            .padding()
            .overlay(
                RoundedRectangle(cornerRadius: 15)
                .stroke(lineWidth: 2)
            )
            .background(backgroundColor)
            .cornerRadius(15)
            .shadow(color: .black.opacity(0.25), radius: 4, x: 0, y: 4)
    }
}



struct ContentView: View {
    var body: some View {
        VStack {
            Text("Blue card")
                .modifier(CardStyle(backgroundColor: .blue))
            Text("White card")
                .modifier(CardStyle(backgroundColor: .white))
            Text("Green card")
                .modifier(CardStyle(backgroundColor: .green))
        }
        .padding()
    }
}
```

```
struct ContentView_Previews: PreviewProvider {
    static var previews: some View {
        ContentView()
    }
}
```

Rather than styling the three tabs individually, we have created a single `Cardstyle` struct that conforms to the `ViewModifier` protocol. `CardStyle` implements the body closure and has `var` for the background color. This way, it styles the common modifiers for the view that it filters and allows the background color to be individually specified.

We have avoided repeating common styling modifiers. The result is "cards" that are styled with a different background color but have a common border, shadow, and corner radius, as shown in the following screenshot:

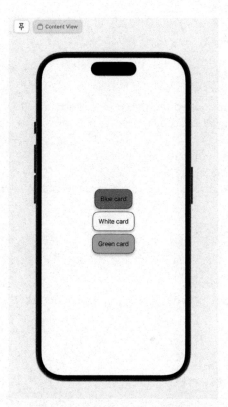

Figure 8.1 – Using custom modifiers

So far, we have applied our modifier to each of our views directly. As you can see, we have similar styling for all three Text views, but we only needed to write the styling only once. This style could be reused across a whole app, effortlessly and reducing the duplicated code.

It doesn't matter if the views we need to style have different content, as we are not addressing this problem by reusing views but rather by their style.

Moreover, should we need to restyle the whole app, we now have a single point where we can control this styling.

However, this is not yet the most efficient and convenient way of obtaining this result, as we could write an extension to the View itself and provide a custom method, cardStyling, that applies this modifier.

The following code example shows how to achieve that:

```swift
import SwiftUI

struct CardStyling: ViewModifier {
    var backgroundColor: Color

    func body(content: Content) -> some View {
        content
            .padding()
            .overlay(
                RoundedRectangle(cornerRadius: 15)
                    .stroke(lineWidth: 2)
            )
            .background(backgroundColor)
            .cornerRadius(15)
            .shadow(color: .black.opacity(0.25), radius: 4, x: 0, y: 4)
    }
}

extension View {
    func cardStyling(backgroundColor: Color) -> some View {
        self.modifier(CardStyling(backgroundColor: backgroundColor))
    }
}

struct ContentView: View {
    var body: some View {
        VStack {
            Text("Blue card")
                .cardStyling(backgroundColor: .blue)
            Text("White card")
                .cardStyling(backgroundColor: .white)
            Text("Green card")
```

```
                .cardStyling(backgroundColor: .green)
            }
            .padding()
        }
    }
}

struct ContentView_Previews: PreviewProvider {
    static var previews: some View {
        ContentView()
    }
}
```

Nothing changes in terms of the result, which is exactly like the previous example, but for a sufficiently large app, we will need to write even less code if we need to apply this more idiomatic way of styling our views.

We can now apply the `.cardStlying(backgroundColor:)` modifier to any view in our app.

In the next section, I will explain how to perform custom drawing, achieving the same level of freedom we have using Core Graphics in UIKit, thanks to SwiftUI's Canvas.

Drawing with the Canvas

According to Apple documentation, the Canvas is *a view type that supports immediate mode drawing*. In simpler and more familiar terms, if you have previous experience with UIKit, this is a view that allows you to implement custom bidimensional graphics that you are more accustomed to by using Core Graphics. It allows you to create custom and intricate graphics that you can use in your own user interface.

The programming is basically the same as in Core Graphics. The Canvas requires you to write a closure defining its contents. This closure receives two parameters, `GraphicsContext` and a size expressed in `CGSize` that can be used to customize the size of what you want to draw.

You can think about the context as a kind of "handle" of the drawing "pencil" inside the canvas, and you determine what you want to draw by calling the different methods supported by the canvas.

These are graphical primitives that allow you to draw different shapes (outlined and filled), images, text, and even complete SwiftUI views.

For instance, the following example will draw two circles within a square frame:

```
import SwiftUI
struct CircleView: View {
    var body: some View {
        Canvas { context, size in
            context.stroke(
```

```
                    Path { path in
                        path.addEllipse(in: CGRect(origin: .zero, size:
size))
                    },
                    with: .color(.green),
                    lineWidth: 2
                )
            context.stroke(
                Path { path in
                    path.addEllipse(in: CGRect(origin: .zero, size:
CGSize(width: size.width/2, height: size.height/2)))
                    },
                    with: .color(.green),
                    lineWidth: 2
                )
            }
        .frame(width: 300, height: 300)
        .border(Color.blue)
    }
}
struct ContentView: View {
    var body: some View {
        VStack {
            CircleView()
            Text("Canvas View")
        }
        .padding()
    }
}
struct ContentView_Previews: PreviewProvider {
    static var previews: some View {
        ContentView()
    }
}
```

In `CircleView`, a canvas is used for drawing shapes. The canvas contains two green ellipses. The first ellipse fills the entire canvas, while the second ellipse is half the size of the first and is drawn inside it. Both ellipses are drawn with a line width of 2 and are green.

The canvas itself has a fixed size of 300 by 300 units and has a blue border outline. `ContentView` arranges items vertically. At the top is the custom `CircleView` that displays the two green ellipses, followed by a text label with the title of the screen – "**Canvas View**". The result is shown in the following screenshot:

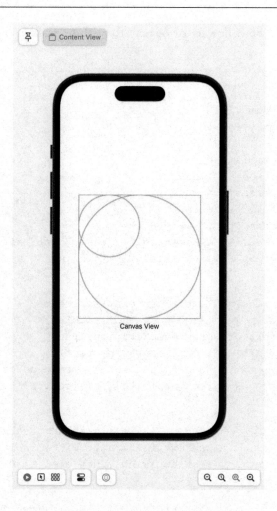

Figure 8.2 – Drawing shapes inside Canvas

Canvas allows you to add shapes, which do not offer any interactivity or any way to access the individual elements within the view. However, it may offer better performance for drawing complex shapes. It is also possible to add masks, filters, perform transforms, and control blending. You should not use the Canvas for drawing text primarily or for elements that require individual interactivity. If you need to address each view individually, it is usually better to use individual views inside ZStack or similar.

> **Important note – caveats on the units of measure**
>
> As with Core Graphics, you are expected to use CGFloat and CGSize to indicate typographical unit measures, and you won't be able to use colors directly if they are needed within a context method. Instead, you will need to convert them to their CG equivalents.

The following example shows how to use opacity, translation, scaling, and displaying text while drawing on `Canvas`:

```swift
import SwiftUI

struct ContentView: View {
    var body: some View {
        Canvas(
            opaque: false,
            colorMode: .linear,
            rendersAsynchronously: false
        ) { context, size in
            context.opacity = 0.6
            let rect = CGRect(origin: .zero, size: size)
            let text = Text(verbatim: "This is not a Text view!").font(.title)
                    .bold()
            var resolvedText = context.resolve(text)
            resolvedText.shading = .color(.blue)
            context.draw(resolvedText, in: rect)
            var path = Circle().path(in: rect)
                        context.fill(path, with: .color(.green))
            let rect2 = rect.applying(.init(scaleX: 0.7, y: 0.7).translatedBy(x: 150, y: 300)
            )
                            path = Circle().path(in: rect2)
                            context.fill(path, with: .color(.pink))
            let rect3 = rect.applying(.init(scaleX: 0.2, y: 0.2).translatedBy(x: 150, y: 300)
            )
                            path = Circle().path(in: rect3)
                            context.fill(path, with: .color(.cyan))
        }
    }
}
struct ContentView_Previews: PreviewProvider {
    static var previews: some View {
        ContentView()
    }
}
```

The result is shown in the following screenshot:

Figure 8.3 – A more complex example with Canvas

You can use the canvas to not only draw images or text but also draw any View.

Before we do that, we will need to register them using the `context.resolveSymbol(id :)` and declare them in the symbols closure.

You need to provide an **id** in the symbols closure, by means of a `.tag` modifier, and reference it with the `id` parameter in `context.resolveSymbol(id: )`.

The following example uses a TextView that is drawn on the Canvas, as shown in the following code example:

```swift
import SwiftUI

struct ContentView: View {
    var body: some View {
        Canvas(
            opaque: false,
            colorMode: .linear,
            rendersAsynchronously: false
        ) { context, size in

            let rect = CGRect(origin: .zero, size:
CGSize(width:400,height:400))

            if let mySymbol = context.resolveSymbol(id: 0x01) {
                context.draw(mySymbol, in: rect)
            }
        } symbols: {
            Text(verbatim: "Hello World")
                .foregroundColor(.blue)
                .bold()
                .tag(0x01)
                .padding()
                .background( .yellow)
        }
    }
}

struct ContentView_Previews: PreviewProvider {
    static var previews: some View {
        ContentView()
    }
}
```

The result is shown in the following screenshot:

Figure 8.4 – Rendering SwiftUI within Canvas

In the next section, I will explain how CALayers can be integrated into SwiftUI.

Using CALayers in SwiftUI

SwiftUI does not support **CALayers** directly, the equivalent functionality has been essentially combined within Views themselves.

There is also no compelling reason to use CALayers to obtain further acceleration, as that has also been implemented by other means in SwiftUI; in particular, there is no need to use CALayers to render really complex hierarchies of views because SwiftUI does not use **Auto Layout**. In UIKit, that would have had a rendering cost that increases with the number of views to be rendered. There is not a "layer" abstraction on top of `View` in SwiftUI.

That said, there are times when you need to implement code that was originally developed for UIKit. SwiftUI provides a protocol, `UIViewRepresentable`, that can be used for this purpose and allows to basically embed a **UIView** within a SwiftUI view.

If you need to use a custom UIView within SwiftUI, bear in mind that it is faster to use CALayers rather than Core Graphics.

You could use this technique for the few corner cases in which you want to embed a UIKit view in SwiftUI, as you need some of the increasingly sparse functionalities that are available in UIKit but have not been implemented yet in SwiftUI. As SwiftUI improves, this will increasingly become less frequent.

Also, there's often little need to use CALayers because some of its equivalent functionality is already exposed by SwiftUI views and their modifiers.

The following example illustrates how you can embed a **UIView** in SwiftUI and use CALayers on that UIView to render custom graphics:

```swift
struct ContentView: View {
    var body: some View {
        CircleView()
            .frame(width: 200, height: 200)
            .background(Color.cyan)
            .edgesIgnoringSafeArea(.all)
    }
}

struct CircleView: UIViewRepresentable {
    func makeUIView(context: Context) -> UIView {
        let containerView = UIView()

        // Create a CAShapeLayer to draw a circle
        let shapeLayer = CAShapeLayer()
        let path = UIBezierPath(ovalIn: CGRect(x: 50, y: 50, width:
200, height: 200))
        shapeLayer.path = path.cgPath
        shapeLayer.fillColor = UIColor.blue.cgColor
        shapeLayer.strokeColor = UIColor.white.cgColor
        shapeLayer.lineWidth = 4
        containerView.layer.addSublayer(shapeLayer)

        return containerView
    }

    func updateUIView(_ uiView: UIView, context: Context) {
        // No need to update anything for this simple example
```

```
        }
    }


struct ContentView_Previews: PreviewProvider {
    static var previews: some View {
        ContentView()
    }
}
```

Explaining CALayers in detail is out of the scope of this book; this is just an example that, if necessary, this integration can be achieved within SwiftUI.

The result is shown in the following screenshot:

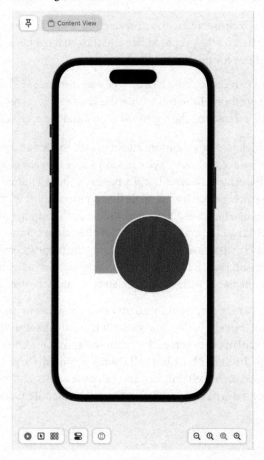

Figure 8.5 – Using CALayers with UIViewRepresentable

In the following section, we will explain how to implement a full custom layout for a grid.

Custom layout

Suppose that you have some special requirement for the design of the **layout** of a "grid" that cannot be achieved by placing items on an orthogonal geometrical grid. Instead, you would like them to be positioned according to some other arbitrary geometrical requirement that is not implemented natively in SwiftUI.

In SwiftUI, `Layout` is a protocol that allows you to precisely create your own custom layouts to arrange subviews within a container, according to your own geometrical choice.

By conforming to `Layout`, you can design layouts to fit your own design requirements. In order to create a custom layout, you need to implement two main functions:

- `sizeThatFits(proposal:subviews:cache:)`: This function calculates the ideal size for the layout based on the proposed size and the cell it contains. It returns a `CGSize` that represents the ideal size for the layout.

- `placeSubviews(in:proposal:subviews:cache:)`: This function is responsible for computing the position of the cell within the layout. It receives as parameters the layout bounds and the cell, calculating the appropriate position for each cell.

We will now use this approach to create a custom layout named `SpiralLayout` that conforms to the `Layout` protocol. The purpose of `SpiralLayout` is to arrange the cells in a spiral pattern rather than a grid. The distance from the center increases linearly based on the cell number, and the angle increases with the cell number, also placing the cell at an angle that is proportional to the division of `2*PI` by the total number of cells, with a maximum of 20. In order to change the number of cells, we will use a slider, with a range of 1 to 20. In `SpiralLayout`, our `sizeThatFits(proposal:subviews:cache:)` function takes `ProposedViewSize` as input, representing the proposed size for the layout. It invokes `replacingUnspecifiedDimensions()` on the value specified as a proposal, ensuring that any unspecified dimensions are replaced with sensible defaults. It finally returns a `CGSize` for the layout.

Our `placeSubviews(in:proposal:subviews:cache:)` function is responsible for computing the positions of the cells within the layout. It first calculates the radius of the bounds and defines the angle step in radians between each cell on the spiral. It also sets a `maxCellNumber` constant to determine the distance of the last cell from the center. Then, for each cell, it computes the radius for that cell, based on its cell number, and calculates the X and Y positions so that the cell lies on the spiral. Finally, it returns the position of the cell to the calculated position relative to the center of the layout.

The following code example shows how you can place the cells in a spiral, using the approach we have just described:

```swift
import SwiftUI
struct SpiralLayout: Layout {
    func sizeThatFits(proposal: ProposedViewSize, subviews: Subviews,
cache: inout Void) -> CGSize {
        proposal.replacingUnspecifiedDimensions()
    }

    func placeSubviews(in bounds: CGRect, proposal: ProposedViewSize,
subviews: Subviews, cache: inout Void) {
        let radius = min(bounds.size.width, bounds.size.height) / 2
        let maxCellNumber = 20.0
        let angleStep = 2 * .pi / maxCellNumber

        for (index, subview) in subviews.enumerated() {
            let cellNumber = Double(index)
            let cellRadius = radius * (cellNumber / maxCellNumber)
            let xPos = cos(angleStep * cellNumber - .pi / 2) *
cellRadius
            let yPos = sin(angleStep * cellNumber - .pi / 2) *
cellRadius
            let point = CGPoint(x: bounds.midX + xPos, y: bounds.midY
+ yPos)
            subview.place(at: point, anchor: .center, proposal:
.unspecified)
        }
    }
}

struct ContentView: View {
    @State private var count = 15.0
    private let colors: [Color] = [.red, .orange, .yellow, .green,
.blue, .purple]

    var body: some View {
        SpiralLayout {
            ForEach(0..<Int(count), id: \.self) { cellNumber in
                Text("\(cellNumber)")
                    .foregroundColor(colors[cellNumber % colors.
count])
            }
        }
        .safeAreaInset(edge: .bottom) {
            VStack {
```

```
                Text("Count: \(Int(count))")
                Slider(value: $count.animation(), in: 1...20)
            }
            .padding()
        }
    }
}


struct ContentView_Previews: PreviewProvider {
    static var previews: some View {
        ContentView()
    }
}
```

`foregroundColor` used in the cell also cycles through an array of six different colors within the ForEach cycle.

The result is shown in the following screenshot:

Figure 8.6 – Using an arbitrary Layout in SwiftUI

Summary

In this chapter, I showed how you can customize your SwiftUI user interface with custom graphics and custom layouts. We began with custom modifiers, allowing us to apply the same style and behavior to different views with little code.

In order to place arbitrary graphics inside a SwiftUI view, we used the Canvas, a view that allows you to draw arbitrary graphics and other views, and we have shown how to use `CALayers` with `UIViewRepresentable`.

Finally, IS showed how it is possible to create completely arbitrary layouts for container views.

In the next chapter, we will examine SwiftUI animation.

9

An Introduction to Animations in SwiftUI

There are quite a few ways to animate content in SwiftUI. SwiftUI animations have a declarative syntax, meaning you describe what results you want to achieve, and SwiftUI does the heavy lifting. Animations in SwiftUI tend to be state-driven (i.e., they depend on state changes, making them reactive and easy to reason about).

SwiftUI provides pre-made modifiers such as `animation`, `transition`, and `scaleEffect`, which allow the effective application of animation effects to views. It is generally more straightforward than UIKit, as you don't need to meddle with an imperative syntax or manage synchronization manually, nor do you need a deep understanding of layer properties.

SwiftUI offers a good balance of flexibility and control using **implicit** and **explicit animations**. In contrast, more complex custom animations can be achieved using animatable properties and modifiers, which will require additional effort.

On the other hand, to this date, UIKit still provides potentially more flexibility and fine-grained control, but it requires a deep understanding of Core Animation. Developers familiar with Core Animation might still want to use it if they need to orchestrate extremely complex animations. At the same time, SwiftUI's approach will meet most of the requirements for most app needs but with a much easier learning curve.

We will begin by briefly examining user **gestures** as these are typically combined with animation to create custom **user interfaces** (**UIs**).

In this chapter, we're going to cover the following main topics:

- Gestures
- Implicit animation
- Explicit animation

- Custom animations with animatable properties and modifiers
- Transitions

Technical requirements

You will find the code related to this chapter here: `https://github.com/PacktPublishing/An-iOS-Developer-s-Guide-to-SwiftUI`, under the `CH9` folder.

Gestures

Gestures are a way to recognize and respond to touch events. They are used to add interaction to SwiftUI views. Some examples of gestures that are used include zooming in on images by pinching, dismissing views by swiping down, and double tapping.

We can conceptually divide gestures into three categories: basic, advanced, and composite.

Basic gestures attach a single simple straightforward gesture to a view, such as tapping or swiping, and they are typically simple to implement because they can be implemented with a few lines of code. These actions mimic natural human actions and are intuitive for human users. Their behavior is what the user normally expects by having been exposed across multiple applications and as such they minimize the cognitive load required to interact with the app; users don't need to think hard to remember complex gestures.

Complex gestures, both advanced and composite, instead involve multiple touch points (multiple fingers) and multiple different movements or a combination of several simpler gestures. These are more difficult for users to use and discover and are more challenging to implement.

In the next section, we will introduce basic gestures.

Basic gestures

The most basic form of gesture is `TapGesture`, which can be attached to a view to provide an action that gets invoked when the view is tapped. It can have a `count` parameter that can specify the number of taps required to recognize the gesture. It is commonly used for navigation, button pressing, and selecting an item.

`LongPressGesture` instead recognizes when a user presses on a view and holds it on the screen. It allows two parameters: `minimumDuration`, which specifies the time in seconds the user needs to maintain the pressure before the gesture is recognized and `maximumDistance` indicates the maximum distance in points that the finger can move from the initial touch point before the gesture fails. `LongPressGesture` is commonly used for entering edit mode, activating context menus, and similar purposes.

DragGesture recognizes a user dragging a finger across the screen. Its optional parameters are minimumDistance, which indicates the minimum distance the user needs to drag the view before the gesture succeeds, and coordinateSpace, which specifies the geometrical frame of reference for measuring the points and distances during the drag gesture. The coordinate space is important because it specifies how offsets and locations are calculated. A coordinate space refers to the system or context in which sizes, positions, and other layout attributes are defined. SwiftUI uses different coordinate spaces to define and manage the layout and positioning of individual views. The coordinate space can be local, global, and named.

.local is the default coordinate space; it means that all the coordinates are relative to the center of the view that the gesture is being attached to, and the translation of the drag will be relative to the view's frame.

.global means that the coordinates are relative to the entire screen, meaning, for instance, that a drag event starting in the top-left corner of the screen will have a coordinate of (0,0) independently from the view the gesture is attached to. The translation of the drag will also be relative to the screen's frame.

.named(_:) signifies that the frame of reference is named, and it accepts a parameter of the AnyHashable type. This coordinate space allows us to define a coordinate space by giving it a name; this could be useful if the same coordinate space is to be used in multiple views to coordinate their behavior. For instance, you could have multiple views responding to a drag gesture in the same way.

Here is the code of a simple app showing the usage of simple gestures:

```swift
import SwiftUI

struct ContentView: View {
    // The state is used to keep track of the gesture states
    @State private var scale: CGFloat = 1.0
    @State private var dragOffset = CGSize.zero
    @State private var longPressToggle = false

    var body: some View {
        Image(systemName: "paperplane.circle.fill")
            .resizable()
            .frame(width: 150, height: 150)
            .scaleEffect(scale) // apply scaling effect
            .offset(dragOffset) // apply dragging offset
            .opacity(longPressToggle ? 0.4 : 1.0) // change opacity on
long press
            .foregroundColor(.cyan)
            .gesture(
```

```
                TapGesture(count: 2)
                    .onEnded { _ in
                        // Double tap resets all transformations
                        self.scale = 1.0
                        self.dragOffset = CGSize.zero
                    }
            )
            .gesture(
                LongPressGesture(minimumDuration: 1.0)
                    .onChanged { _ in
                        // Update longPress state
                        self.longPressToggle = true
                    }
                    .onEnded { _ in
                        // Revert longPress state
                        self.longPressToggle = false
                    }
            )
            .simultaneousGesture(
                DragGesture()
                    .onChanged { value in
                        // Update the dragOffset state
                        self.dragOffset = value.translation
                    }
                    .onEnded { _ in
                        // Scale up the image on drag end
                        self.scale += 0.2
                    }
            )
        }
    }
}

struct ContentView_Previews: PreviewProvider {
    static var previews: some View {
        ContentView()
    }
}
```

This example shows a paper plane inside a cyan circle; a long press of a minimum of 1 second will alternate between an opacity of 0.4 (semitransparent) and 1 (opaque) while allowing the user to drag the image across the screen. Each time the drag stops, the picture size is increased by 20% while the paper plane is rotated left by 15 degrees. Finally, a double-tap resets all transformations and returns the picture of the plane to the center of the screen.

The following screenshot shows the result of the preceding code example:

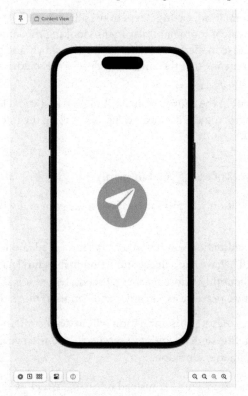

Figure 9.1 – Using gesture recognizers in SwiftUI

As we can see, the picture follows our fingers, but it is as if something is missing; the movement is too mechanic and appears somewhat less fluid than what we normally are accustomed to in iOS. What we feel is missing is animation, and we will begin exploring simple animations in the next section.

Creating implicit animations

Implicit animations are animations where the behavior of the animation is implied and not described in detail. They are the most straightforward way to add animations to your app views. The simplest requirement to implement them is to apply the `.animation` modifier to a view, and SwiftUI will automatically apply any changes to the properties of that view.

Implicit animations will automatically occur when a value changes in a view, without you needing to specify the animation effect to apply. SwiftUI will apply interpolation while transitioning between animation states automatically. This allows you to add animation effects with minimal code. The default animation is often what the user is accustomed to seeing in an iOS app, and therefore it is often the right choice in terms of usability.

> **Note**
>
> When talking about animation, **easing** refers to the adjustment of the speed and movement of the animation to create a more natural, organic-looking movement (than simple linear motion). For example, **ease in** means that animation starts slowly and gathers speed with time, non-linearly. **Ease out** means that the animation decelerates before stopping; `easeInOut` implies that it does both.
>
> These gradual transitions in the animation make it more realistic and less "rigidly mechanical." Easing is crucial in improving the user experience by making the interaction with the UI feel more natural and fluid.

There are four different types of easing you can specify:

- `linear`: The animation will proceed at a constant pace and will just stop when it reaches its conclusion.

- `easeInOut`: The animation will start at a very slow speed and will accelerate gradually and smoothly, and it will behave like a linear animation in its central part, only to start decelerating progressively and smoothly before reaching its completion. It is the animation that will more closely follow what we perceive as "organic" and "smooth" movement.

- `easeIn` and `.easeOut`: This animation will instead contain just the initial or the final "smoothed" acceleration or deceleration respectively, and will behave "linearly" during the rest other half of the animation duration.

It is also possible to specify `spring()`; instead of easing, which will constrain the speed of the animation effect as if it were a mechanical spring, that can be modified in terms of elasticity, stiffness, and dampening. Please see the Apple developer's documentation for more information: `https://developer.apple.com/documentation/swiftui/animation`.

There are two ways of inserting a simple animation in a view: the `.animation` modifier, which was deprecated in iOS 15 but could still be useful if you need to add simple animations to apps that need to run on old versions of iOS, and the `.withAnimation` closure.

The easiest, but now deprecated, way to add animation would be to add `.animation(.default)` whenever there is a change in either position or other visual properties, such as transparency, on a view. This is referred to as implicit animation because we do not need to specify what to animate, animation will just occur.

However, this use of `.animation` was deprecated in iOS15 and should be used only for compatibility with old devices.

The other way is by using `.withAnimation` with a closure. In this case, the animation will be explicit because we need to indicate how to animate each one of the parameters of the view we are interested in changing during the animation. We will begin with this approach, giving a simple example in order to get started.

Let's modify the previous gesture example by adding simple animation. We are modifying the image by adding `.withAnimation`, as shown in the following code block:

```
import SwiftUI

struct ContentView: View {

    @State private var scale: CGFloat = 1.0
    @State private var dragOffset = CGSize.zero
    @State private var longPressToggle = false

    var body: some View {
        Image(systemName: "paperplane.circle.fill")
            .resizable()
            .frame(width: 150, height: 150)
            .scaleEffect(scale) // apply scaling effect
            .offset(dragOffset) // apply dragging offset
            .opacity(longPressToggle ? 0.4 : 1.0) // change opacity on
long press
            .foregroundColor(.cyan)
            .gesture(
                TapGesture(count: 2)
                    .onEnded { _ in
                        withAnimation {
                            self.scale = 1.0
                            self.dragOffset = CGSize.zero
                        }
                    }
            )
            .gesture(
                LongPressGesture(minimumDuration: 1.0)
                    .onChanged { _ in
                        withAnimation {
                            self.longPressToggle = true
                        }
                    }
                    .onEnded { _ in
                        withAnimation {
                            self.longPressToggle = false
                        }
                    }
            )
            .simultaneousGesture(
                DragGesture()
```

```
                .onChanged { value in
                    withAnimation {
                        self.dragOffset = value.translation
                    }
                }
                .onEnded { _ in
                    withAnimation {
                        self.scale += 0.2
                    }
                }


            )
        }
    }


struct ContentView_Previews: PreviewProvider {
    static var previews: some View {
        ContentView()
        }
    }
```

In the preceding code block, we have wrapped the changes to `scale`, `dragOffset`, and `longPressToggle` within the `withAnimation` closures. This determines changes to these state variables to be automatically animated.

`withAnimation` runs the code of the closure and, if there are state changes, it animates the transitions of all the views that depend on this state. By default, it uses ease-in-out animation, with a duration of 0.33 seconds, but this can be customized further.

In the next section, we will examine the explicit animations that can be achieved using the `withAnimation(_: value)` closure.

Explicit SwiftUI animations

Explicit SwiftUI animations allow more control over the animation. They are used when we need more complex behavior, or we need to trigger the animation based on logic.

In order to create explicit animations, you use the `.animation(_: value:)` modifier rather than the simpler `.withAnimation` closure.

With `.animation(_: value:)`, you have more control compared to `.withAnimation`, as the animation is applied only when the specified value changes, and you can pass as a first parameter an `Animation` instance. The first parameter specifies the behavior, how the animation will behave, and the second what value it will affect.

There are quite a few functions that produce an `Animation` instance which can be used as a first parameter for the `.animation(_: value:)` modifier. These can be used with or without parameters, and the parameters of these functions allow to specify the duration and the delay.

You could also use `delay` and `repeatCount` as modifiers of `Animation`, and chain them. If you want you can also indicate a value parameter for the animation, allowing you to use animate specific state properties of the view. In order to get a complete list, please consult Apple's developer documentation: `https://developer.apple.com/documentation/swiftui/animation`

The following list will give you a sufficient number of examples to help you understand the patterns you can create the following:

- `animation` or `.animation(.default)` will produce a default animation

- `animation(.linear)` will produce a linear animation (without easing)

- `animation(.easeInOut(durationL 0.5)` will produce an animation with ease in and out and a duration of 0.5 seconds

- `animation(.easeInOut)` will produce an animation with the default duration, but with easing in and out

- `animation(.easeOut)` will produce an animation that starts linearly and has an ease out conclusion

- `animation (.spring(response: 0.5, dampingFraction 0.8, blendDuration: 0)` will produce a spring-like bouncy effect, and you can customize the stiffness, elasticity, and damping of the spring by passing parameters

- `animation(.easeIn(duration: 0.5, delay: 0.2))` will produce an animation that has ease in, a duration of 0.5 seconds, and starts after a delay of 0.2 seconds

You can also chain these animation functions by composition, to create complex animation effects. For example, `.animation(.spring().delay(0.2).repeatCount(4))` will repeat a spring animation with default parameters four times, after a delay of 0.2 seconds.

In the following example, you can see a simple spring animation using `.animation(: value:)`:

```swift
import SwiftUI

struct SpringAnimationView: View {
    @State private var boxOffset: CGSize = .zero

    var body: some View {
        VStack {
            Text("Drag the circle then let it go")
                .font(.title)
```

```
            Circle()
                .fill(.red)
                .opacity(0.5)
                .frame(width: 120, height: 120)
                .offset(boxOffset)
                .gesture(
                    DragGesture()
                        .onChanged { gestureValue in
                            self.boxOffset = gestureValue.translation
                        }
                        .onEnded { _ in
                            self.boxOffset = .zero
                        }
                )
                .animation(.spring(response: 0.6, dampingFraction:
0.6, blendDuration: 0.1), value: boxOffset)
        }
    }
}

struct ContentView: View {
    var body: some View {
        VStack {
            SpringAnimationView()

        }
        .padding()
    }
}

struct ContentView_Previews: PreviewProvider {
    static var previews: some View {
        ContentView()
    }
}
```

Let's examine the preceding code:

- `boxOffset` is a `@State` variable that keeps track of how far the circle has been dragged from its original position. It starts off as `.zero` (that is, no offset).

- The `body` property of `SpringAnimationView` contains a vertical stack and inside that the following two views.

- A `Text` view instructing the user to drag the circle.

- A red-filled `Circle`, with an opacity of `0.5` (transparent), 120 by 120 points in size.

- `offset(boxOffset)`: This draws the circle displaced geometrically by the `boxOffset` value.

- `gesture(...)`: This adds gesture recognizers to the circle.

- `DragGesture()`: This recognizes the drag gesture.

- `onChanged`: This is called when the drag changes and it updates `boxOffset` based on how far the circle has been dragged.

- `onEnded`: This is called when the drag ends. It resets `boxOffset` to `.zero`, causing the circle to be repositioned back to its original position (with animation).

- `animation(...)`: This adds a spring animation for moving the circle, driven by changes to the value of `boxOffset`.

The result is shown in the following screenshot:

Figure 9.2 – A spring animation example

The semitransparent red circle follows your movements when you drag it, and will return to its initial position with a spring-like animation effect. Feel free to experiment with changing the spring parameters to get a feel for how changing them affects the resulting animation.

To conclude this section, we will add another simple animation example; in this case, I will show you how to combine animation with a gesture recognizer for magnification, allowing the user to pinch the screen to zoom in on an image.

If you want to test the pinch gesture (magnification) on the simulator or a preview, rather than on a physical device, hold the *option* key while you keep the mouse button pressed.

In our case, the image is just a triangle inside a circle that, to make things more interesting, cycles endlessly between rotating left and right.

Here's our code example:

```
import SwiftUI

struct ZoomableRotatingView: View {
    @State private var rotateImage = false
    @GestureState private var scale: CGFloat = 1.0

    var body: some View {
        Image(systemName: "triangle.circle.fill")
            .font(.system(size: 200))
            .rotationEffect(.degrees(rotateImage ? 360 : 0))
            .scaleEffect(scale)
            .gesture(
                MagnificationGesture()
                    .updating($scale) { currentState, gestureState,
transaction in
                        gestureState = currentState
                    }
            )
```

```
                .onAppear() {
                    withAnimation(Animation.linear(duration: 15.0).
repeatForever(autoreverses: true)) {
                        self.rotateImage = true
                    }
                }
            }
        }

struct ContentView: View {
    var body: some View {
        VStack {
            ZoomableRotatingView()
                .foregroundColor(.accentColor)
            Text("Pinch me to zoom!")
        }
        .padding()
    }
}

struct ContentView_Previews: PreviewProvider {
    static var previews: some View {
        ContentView()
    }
}
```

ZoomableRotatingView handles both the animation and the gesture interaction:

- **Rotation**: The view uses a variable called rotateImage, which is a @State variable to decide whether to rotate the image or not. Initially, it is set to not rotate. When the view appears on the screen, an animation starts setting rotateImage to true, causing the image to rotate up to 360 degrees. This animation rotation is continuous, meaning it will keep rotating indefinitely. The animation is linear, taking 15 seconds to complete one full 360-degree rotation.

- **Zooming**: scale, another @State variable, is used to manage the zoom level of the image. Initially, scale is initialized to 1, scaling the image is at its original size. The pinch-to-zoom gesture, MagnificationGesture, is used to change the scale variable value tracking the user pinch gesture. This increases or decreases the image scale based on how the user moves their fingers.

The result is shown in the next screenshot:

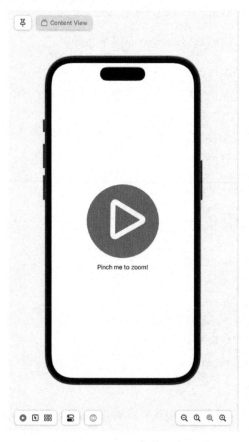

Figure 9.3 – A zoomable alternate rotating animation

In the next section, we will cover programming transition animations between two views.

Transitions

SwiftUI transitions allow you to animate the insertion and removal of views from the UI. To apply a transition to a view, we use the `.transition(_:)` modifier.

The basic transition types that SwiftUI provides include the following:

- `opacity`: This transition causes views to fade in or out when they're inserted or removed
- `scale`: This transition causes views to grow or shrink in size when they're inserted or removed
- `slide`: This transition causes a view to slide in or out from the edge of the screen when it is either added or removed

- `move(edge:)`: This transition moves a view in or out from the specified edge of the screen
- `offset(x:y:)`: This transition moves a view by the specified amount of typographical points when it is inserted or removed

By default, if you don't specify a transition, iOS will apply a default transition when presenting (adding) or removing views from the screen. There are several default transitions available in SwiftUI, and they use the basic transition types.

By default, SwiftUI determines the appropriate transition to apply based on the context in which the view is inserted or removed; for example, when a view is added to a list, SwiftUI applies the `.opacity` transition to fade in the new item.

When a sheet is presented or dismissed, SwiftUI applies a default slide or scale transition depending on the device and presentation style.

Bear in mind that as SwiftUI evolves, the default transitions may change, so please test on recent versions of the Apple operating system and consult the Apple developer documentation in order to stay current.

Besides the default behavior, you can customize the transitions to match your needs. SwiftUI offers modifiers such as `.transition()` and `.matchedGeometryEffect()` to apply custom transitions and animations to views. You can combine these modifiers with the animation techniques that we have seen previously.

These transition modifiers allow you to define the specific transition type, duration, and other parameters to achieve the desired visual effects.

In the next sections, we will learn how to use the `.transition()` and `.matchedGeometryEffect()` modifiers.

The .transition() modifier

Here's an example of how to specify a custom transition using `.transition`. The inserted screen is going to be just a red square with blue borders.

We begin by defining a new custom transition that combines two different basic transitions for insertion and removal of the view. The transition is asymmetric (with a different transition for insertion and deletion), and we decided to have a different duration in either case:

```
import SwiftUI


// Defining custom Transition
extension AnyTransition {
    static var myCustomTransition: AnyTransition {
        let insertion = AnyTransition.scale.combined(with: .opacity).
animation(.easeInOut(duration: 2))
```

```
        let removal = AnyTransition.scale.combined(with: .opacity).
animation(.easeInOut(duration: 1))
        return .asymmetric(insertion: insertion, removal: removal)
    }
}
```

Notice how we applied the `.combined` modifier on `.scale`, and then we applied a `.animation` modifier.

This is `ContentView` of our small example app:

```
import SwiftUI

struct ContentView: View {
    @State private var isShowingSquare = false

    var body: some View {
        VStack {
            Button(action: {
                withAnimation {
                    self.isShowingSquare.toggle()
                }
            }) {
                Text(self.isShowingSquare ? "disappear":"appear")
            }

            if isShowingSquare {
                Rectangle()
                    .fill(Color.red)
                    .frame(width: 250, height: 250)
                    .border(.blue, width: 5)
                    .transition(.myCustomTransition)
            }
        }
    }
}


struct ContentView_Previews: PreviewProvider {
    static var previews: some View {
```

```
        ContentView()
    }
}
```

In the preceding code block, ContentView is arranged vertically using a VStack, which contains a button and a red square. The button toggles the square's visibility on and off.

Here's a brief explanation of the previous code:

- isShowingSquare is a @State variable, keeping track of whether the square is to be displayed.

- Button(action: { ... }): When the button is clicked, its action toggles the value of isShowingSquare, making the square appear or disappear with an animation.

- if isShowingSquare { ... }: This block displays a red square with a blue border if isShowingSquare is true. It also specifies a custom transition for appearing and disappearing.

The result is in the following screenshot:

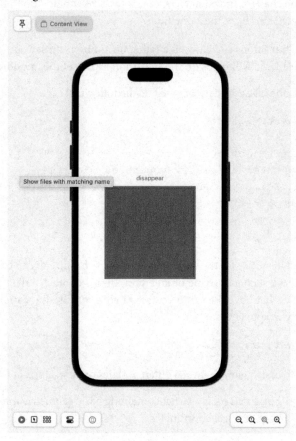

Figure 9.4 – A simple custom transition example

Pressing the "appear/disappear" button toggles between "appear" and "disappear." The red square being shown determines whether it is being animated on or off the screen.

In the next section, we will examine the other modifier `.matchedGeometryEffect`, to create another custom animated transition.

The matchedGeometryEffect modifier

The `matchedGeometryEffect` modifier is generally used when you want to create smooth transitions between views or animate the movement of a view from one position to another.

This SwiftUI modifier allows you to orchestrate simultaneously both the size and the position of a view between two different states or views. It has two different uses:

- Synchronize the size and position of two views, one that is being inserted and one that is being removed from the view hierarchy

- Synchronize the changes in geometries, that is the size and position of several views that are part of the view hierarchy at the same time

As we are dealing with transitions and case 2 is a rather uncommon corner case that can be understood in the same way as case 1, we will focus on the transition aspect of this modifier.

The definition of `matchedGeometryEffect` is the following:

```
func matchedGeometryEffect<ID>(
    id: ID,
    in namespace: Namespace.ID,
    properties: MatchedGeometryProperties = .frame,
    anchor: UnitPoint = .center,
    isSource: Bool = true
) -> some View where ID : Hashable
```

The `id` parameter is an identifier for the view you want to synchronize. It can be any value conforming to the Hashable protocol, such as a string or an enum. In this context, a namespace is a mechanism that prevents two views that have the same `id` from being confused; it can be declared with the @Namespace property wrapper:

```
@Namespace private var animation
```

This identifier is used to match views between different states or views, together with the `id` parameter.

`matchedGeometryProperties` is a struct containing basic geometric information about a view: the size, position, and frame, in local coordinates.

As an example, let's create a custom animation using `.matchedGeometryEffect`. We begin by having two views that are mutually exclusive: if one is presented on the screen, the other one disappears, and vice versa. In our case, we have either a selected view or none. In one case, we will display a list of items, and in the other, we will display the detail view.

Let's define `ViewModifier` based on `.matchedGeometryEffect`:

```
struct MyViewModifier: ViewModifier {
    var namespace: Namespace.ID
    @Binding var selectedRowId: String?
    let currentRowId: String

    func body(content: Content) -> some View {
        content
            .matchedGeometryEffect(id: currentRowId, in: namespace,
anchor: .leading, isSource: selectedRowId == nil)
            .onTapGesture {
                withAnimation {
                    selectedRowId = currentRowId
                }
            }
    }
}
```

Then we define `ContentView` as follows:

```
import SwiftUI

struct ContentView: View {
    @State var selectedItemId: String? = nil
    @Namespace private var animation

    var body: some View {
        ZStack {
            if let itemId = selectedItemId {
                VStack {
                    VStack{
                        Text("Detail view for item #\(itemId)")
                            .font(.largeTitle)
                            .padding()
                            .matchedGeometryEffect(id: itemId, in:
animation)

                        Text("Touch me to go back")
                    }
                    .onTapGesture {
```

```swift
                        withAnimation {
                            selectedItemId = nil
                        }
                    }

                    Spacer()
                }
                .frame(maxWidth: .infinity, maxHeight: .infinity)
                .background(Color.cyan.ignoresSafeArea())
            } else {
                ScrollView {
                    ForEach(1..<11) { i in
                        Text("Row #\(i)")
                            .font(.title)
                            .padding()
                            .frame(maxWidth: .infinity)
                            .background(Color.yellow)
                            .modifier(MyViewModifier(namespace:
animation, selectedRowId: $selectedItemId, currentRowId: "\(i)"))
                    }
                }
            }
        }
    }
}


struct ContentView_Previews: PreviewProvider {
    static var previews: some View {
        ContentView()
    }
}
```

The animation is triggered when a row cell is selected, and `matchedGeometryEffect` helps animate between the selected cell state (the view detail) and the unselected one (the list) smoothly. The result is the following screenshot:

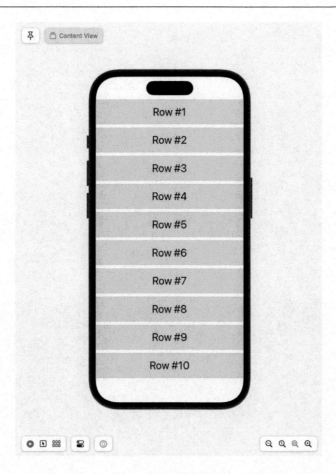

Figure 9.5 – Another custom transition example

The animation morphs the geometrical coordinates and sizes of the selected cell and the view representing the detail view, resulting in a diagonal elegant movement.

Summary

In this chapter about SwiftUI animation, we began by defining gesture recognizers, as these are often combined with animation. Then, we examined how to combine gesture recognizers with animation. We have covered simple implicit animation and more complex explicit animations. We completed the chapter by examining animated transitions, which are used to spruce up the presentation of views in the UI.

In the next chapter, we will begin discussing application architecture.

Part 5: App Architecture

In this part, we will focus on the transitional effect that SwiftUI brings in structuring applications within the Apple ecosystem. It kicks off with a pragmatic perspective on segmenting applications into more manageable units, emphasizing a tailored approach to architecture rather than following a cookie-cutter approach. This discussion highlights the importance of using architectural diagrams and following simple and minimalist design principles. This part explores the principle of dependency inversion, the basics of clean architecture, decoupling strategies for components, state management, and news about state bindings introduced in iOS 17.

Our journey then takes us deeper into the theoretical basis of modern application architecture, with particular emphasis on the iOS world. It will equip you with an understanding of software architecture and provide a framework to be able to evaluate the advantages of a good architecture. This part attempts to devise basic streamlined architectural principles, strategies for conflict resolution, and criteria for better architectural design. Other areas that we will focus on include the importance of software design patterns, consulting domain experts, and the effect that Conway's law has on software design and team dynamics.

This part contains the following chapters:

- *Chapter 10, App Architecture and SwiftUI
Part I – the Practical Tools*
- *Chapter 11, App Architecture and SwiftUI
Part II – the Theory*

10
App Architecture and SwiftUI
Part I: Practical Tools

This chapter will introduce the interesting topic of application structure and the impact SwiftUI has on modern mobile application architecture on Apple operating systems. This chapter will somewhat change the pace kept by this book this far.

We will begin the chapter by introducing the tools of the trade that help us partition apps into manageable software components, elegantly and practically.

I won't give you any premade "architectures" or architectural patterns. I will explain this point later. The reason is that I do not believe there is a perfect, premade architecture that you can just copy and paste. Your architecture will need to be unique and match the problem you are facing.

We will start with the practical angle, which you will need to be a better programmer.

You may already have encountered some of these topics – if this is the case, you are starting from a more advantageous place; if you haven't come across these concepts yet, don't worry because I will explain why these techniques are important and how to use them.

Be warned that learning about architecture is not the same as memorizing or practicing programming using a framework, not even a complex framework such as SwiftUI. In this field, you are practically required to do your own research, and think, acquire experience, study, and reflect mostly on your own. This chapter is going to be a shallow introduction to this important topic to begin your journey toward understanding architecture; you will need to read more books, a lot of them. This part of this book just tries to nudge you in the right direction.

SwiftUI by itself as a programming framework has an important impact on designing modern apps based on Apple operating systems. First, SwiftUI is inherently multiplatform, and second, it is designed to allow us to obtain the same functionality with far simpler designs than what was previously required using the UIKit or AppKit frameworks.

Due to the limits of this book, this will be just an introduction to the topic. Do not expect to become an architect by reading a book, much less just a few chapters. However, I will do my best to nudge you in the right direction and help you learn good habits, rather than propose some fixed easy-to-follow recipes. That would be swindling you, selling you snake oil. I will try to teach you how to fish, rather than give you pre-cooked fish ready to put in the microwave oven. In this chapter, we're going to cover the following main topics:

- Diagrams
- Dependency inversion
- Clean architecture
- Different ways to decouple
- A matter of state, binding state to views
- iOS 17 changes in state management

> **Legal disclaimer**
>
> The opinions expressed herein are solely those of the author and do not necessarily reflect the views or policies of his employers or other entities. Any reference to organizations, events, or individuals is purely fictional and intended for illustrative purposes only. Resemblance to any existing companies, events, or persons, living or deceased, is purely coincidental.

Diagrams

Architecture is better explained using diagrams, and as such, I suggest you familiarize yourself with at least one graphical editor. Being able to produce diagrams is a useful skill, and you need to start practicing. One diagramming tool that is open source and that I would recommend is Mermaid. It runs on the command line and produces diagrams using a simple textual interface.

The easiest way to use Mermaid on a Mac is by using the Mermaid Editor app from the App Store: `https://apps.apple.com/us/app/mermaideditor/id1581312955`. This is a cheap app that is well worth its modest price.

You will find documentation about Mermaid and its syntax at `https://mermaid.js.org/`.

While you will often need to express your architectural thoughts through a diagram, developers sometimes frown upon using diagrams, thinking that using diagrams is not agile, and some would just prefer to use code. However, being able to use a picture instead of the proverbial one thousand words is typically a reasonable choice, and architects who can't show their thinking on a whiteboard or with a diagramming editor are few and far between.

There are some architects and developers who prefer to use so-called C4 diagrams. I personally prefer a subset of **UML**, **Unified Modeling Language**, a traditional diagramming language that is sort of a "lingua franca" that most architects understand. UML is bigger and more complex, whereas C4 is easier but lacks some crucial diagrams that UML provides, such as timing diagrams and state diagrams, for instance. UML is large enough to require its own books, so beware: you are expected to read and do your own research, even about this side topic. Should you ever need to demonstrate the intricacies of expressing a protocol or a state machine, UML can convey your thoughts, while C4 won't.

You can use any other tool; **PlantUML** is another free command-line tool you may want to use in order to produce your diagrams (`https://plantuml.com/`). PlantUML supports both UML and C4 diagrams; which tool you choose is your decision.

Another online tool you could use is **draw.io**, which can be found at `https://app.diagrams.net`.

Some swear by Visio on Windows, and its closest match on macOS is OmniGraffle. Unfortunately, these are quite expensive programs. It is a matter of personal choice and preference.

In the next section, we will introduce the main tool we use to decouple software: dependency inversion.

Dependency inversion

Before we dive into this section, let me give you a brief overview of the first four of the five **SOLID** principles, which were created by Robert Martin:

- **S – Single Responsibility Principle (SRP)**:

    - **Concept**: A class should have only one reason to exist.

    - **Application**: Each class in your application should have only one specific job or responsibility. For instance, if you have a `UserHandler` class, its responsibility should be strictly limited to user-related operations, such as creating, updating, or deleting users, and not also include network functionality, for example.

- **O – Open/Closed Principle (OCP)**:

    - **Concept**: Software entities (classes, modules, functions, etc.) should be open for extension but closed for modification.

    - **Application**: Design your classes in a way that allows you to add new functionality through inheritance or extension rather than forcing fellow developers to modify existing code. For instance, using protocol-oriented programming can be a way to achieve this objective in Swift.

- **L – Liskov Substitution Principle (LSP):**

  - **Concept**: Objects of a superclass should be replaceable with objects belonging to a subclass without affecting the correctness of the program.

  - **Application**: In your iOS applications, ensure that subclasses maintain the behavior guarantees of their parent class. Avoid overriding methods in ways that change their expected behavior. This is not that important and, unless you do something really strange, would be the default behavior of any object-oriented language. Maybe an *L* was just convenient to produce a memorable acronym.

- **I – Interface Segregation Principle (ISP):**

  - **Concept**: No client should be forced to depend on interfaces it doesn't use.

  - **Application**: Instead of having one very large interface (or protocol in Swift) that contains too many methods, it's often preferable to break it into smaller, more specific ones. This ensures that classes that implement these interfaces only need to care about the methods relevant to them.

Dependency inversion is the *D* in SOLID and it is the most important letter in that acronym so we will concentrate on that principle in this section. It is pragmatically both a *technique* and a *principle* to be observed.

As a principle, it states the following:

> *High-level modules should not depend on low-level modules. Both will need to depend on abstractions.*

> *Abstractions should not depend on details. Details should depend on abstractions.*

Whenever you see the word *abstraction*, think about a **protocol**, or an interface/abstract class if you are used to other object-oriented languages.

To provide context and offer a more accessible example, if you encounter a situation where you are developing business application logic that relies on a low-level library, you can apply this principle to recognize a probable design flaw in your implementation.

Hey, but I need to use that library! Well, there's a solution to that problem, and here, this principle helps you pragmatically with a technique called **dependency injection**.

In Swift, we implement dependency injection using Swift protocols.

Let's imagine we need to send an email programmatically and let's examine the following code example:

```swift
import Foundation
struct EmailService {
    static func sendEmail(to: String, subject: String, body: String) {
        // Actually sending the email: Implementation detail...
    }
}

struct User {
    var email: String
    var name: String
    var surname: String
}

struct UserManager {
    let emailService = EmailService()

    func createUser(user: User) {
        // Create the user account...

        EmailService.sendEmail(to: user.email, subject: "Welcome new
user!", body: "Your email account has just been created.")
    }
}
```

We can observe that the `UserManager` struct is directly dependent on `EmailService`, and that is a violation of the **Dependency Inversion Principle** (**DIP**).

To correct this, we can define an `EmailSending` protocol that abstracts away the concept of sending an email; we just want to call a method, and we don't want to know how this is done, not at the `UserManager` level! Then, we modify `UserManager` to depend on this abstraction (the protocol!) instead of the concrete `EmailService`.

The resulting code is the following:

```swift
import Foundation

struct emailService {
    func sendEmail(to: String, subject: String, body: String) {
        // Implementation details...
    }
}

struct User {
```

```
        var email: String
        var name: String
        var surname: String
}

protocol EmailSending {
    func sendEmail(to: String, subject: String, body: String)
}
struct UserManager {
    let emailService: EmailSending

        init(emailService: EmailSending) {
            self.emailService = emailService
        }

    func createUser(user: User) {
        // Create the user...

        emailService.sendEmail(to: user.email, subject: "Welcome
user!", body: "Your account has just been created.")
    }
}
```

This has just been an appetizer. In the meantime, we also changed the class so that it is now necessary to instantiate it, rather than just call a `static` method in the process. This kind of change is minor and should not deter you from the main objective, which is decoupling your application software levels. This minor change is similar to what you will observe in practice when some detail needs to change for a design decision, may be taken by someone else.

You should read the book *Clean Architecture*, by Robert Martin, in which he talks about the application logic being the *core* and communication (e.g., your network code) and presentation (SwiftUI views) being *pluggable* via abstraction. Here, we talk about different layers, while he prefers to reason in terms of concentric circles and a core rather than outer layers. To be precise, the core is made of **entities** and **use cases**. The innermost part contains entities (or things) – concepts your application uses. Immediately above that, you have use cases – the implementation of user stories, and the interconnections, relationships, and methods that allow a user, in the most abstract way possible, to achieve their goals.

Do not be fooled: only the metaphor is slightly different. Robert Martin talks about "onion-like" concentric circles, whereas we (and the industry in general) tend to prefer thinking about horizontal layers when describing app architecture. The concept is the same.

Here is an example of the "onion layering" of a possible app using a **Clean Architecture** style:

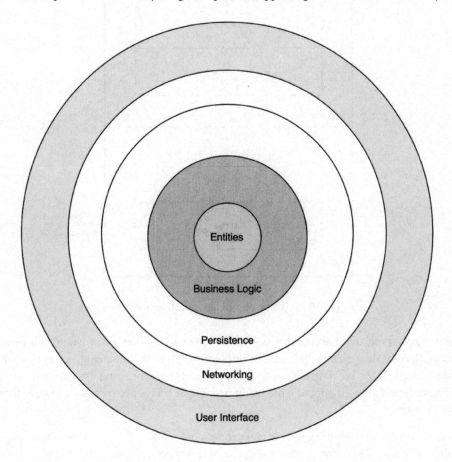

Figure 10.1 – An example of a possible Clean Architecture

The same concept can be expressed as horizontal layers, as shown in the next diagram:

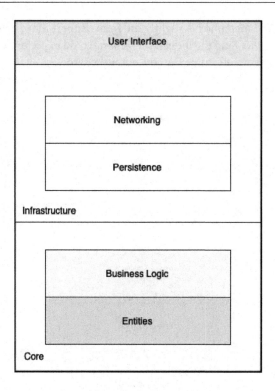

Figure 10.2 – The same architecture shown as layers

As we now have a protocol to decouple between one layer and another, and we don't rely directly on implementation detail, we can substitute our implementation without changing anything at all in the **business logic** layer. We have successfully decoupled them – *decoupled* means you can change the implementation without affecting the business logic. If this is not true, we consider these two modules *coupled*.

Of course, in real life, our *software layers* are going to be more complex than just a method to implement physically sending an email from a server. Our example was not even focused on mobile but was so generic, it could be used in any kind of application.

Ideally, we would like our entities to be the incarnation of the programming structures we need in user stories. And of course, use cases (the concrete programming methods that implement those stories) should depend on entities. Need to change a user story because you learned something new while you were implementing your system? The entities layer, the deepest one, does not need to change. Just implement your new story; no need to change anything. Also, the business logic does not need to know anything about how to display data, store it in a database, or interface with another system. Of course, if you need to change your entities, you will need to change the outer layers, but that's unavoidable. The main issue is intentionally reducing the need to propagate change when you need to modify a part of the code base as much as possible.

For now, let's start with the basics. In the next section, we will explore the concept of Clean Architecture.

Clean Architecture

We will focus on the Clean Architecture concept due to its didactic and practical value: it is one of the best architectural styles you can learn about. We will keep focused on using SwiftUI while avoiding some of the worst practices I have witnessed.

There are some practicalities in adapting Clean Architecture to a Swift-based context, as the relevant frameworks are in evolution. Due to recent changes to SwiftUI, which happened during WWDC2023, you may want to give some thought to whether to use SwiftData or whether to implement a data persistence layer yourself. Before WWDC2023, we would have suggested implementing a data persistency layer using Core Data. Now, this choice, which impacts your architectural choices, has become more varied. We will cover this in *Chapters 12* and *14* of this book.

Clean Architecture, a concept pioneered by the aforementioned Robert C. Martin (nicknamed "Uncle Bob"), prescribes the design of software systems with clear layering, where each layer has specific responsibilities and dependencies.

In the context of **Clean Architecture**, the DIP, Dependency inversion principle results in the outer layers (frameworks and UI) depending on the inner layers (business rules and entities), as shown in *Figure 10.1*.

This is often counter-intuitive as one might expect that business logic should depend on frameworks. However, inverting this dependency allows the core business logic to remain independent of external concerns such as databases, UIs, and frameworks, provided that the necessary data you depend on does not change.

By employing this architectural style, you can swap out databases or networking libraries, for instance, without the need to change the core business logic. This results in a system that is more resilient to change and easier to maintain and test.

And, of course, writing unit tests becomes easier, as you can mock implementation and declare conformity to the protocol you use for decoupling, without having to rely on a coupled implementation.

Testability and architecture

As a general criterion, if your architecture is difficult to test, you made an architectural mistake somewhere, and you need to refactor; you will have to decompose your software modules and reorganize the structure more logically. If your architecture is well decoupled, writing unit tests should be easy. If you lack unit tests, refactoring won't be easy as you won't know whether your refactoring activity introduced errors. So, start writing your tests while working on your code, from the very start. Learn to work using an approach called **test-driven development (TDD)**. Beware of architects not writing tests (https://en.wikipedia.org/wiki/Test-driven_development)!

What we write in this chapter does not mean that you should refer to authority, or that you can consider Robert Martin as a kind of prophet who you can rely on blindly. You should always question your sources, reflect, and find out whether they make sense. I personally disagree with a couple of things Martin says but find he is right in most of what he published, except in some special contexts where other concepts become prevalent. It is always a matter of balance.

There are a few instances where you would want your code cohesive and tightly coupled. This might be the case of extremely optimized code, which needs extreme execution speed, as sometimes needed in special cases. Architecture should adapt to context and to the problem at hand. There are no *absolute rules*: everything is a matter of engineering compromise. This is why principles are called *principles* and not *laws*.

But this does not mean that shoddy, badly written code should be accepted. In general, if you can't write tests, your architecture has problems, but choosing which tests to write is not easy and straightforward and is often a matter for debate:

> *Unit tests should form the vast majority of your tests. It is impossible to devise a strategy of tests that aims at complete coverage if you want to do integration tests prevalently, testing end to end, from the outer software layer to the next one, till you reach the higher application level.*
>
> *And that's even less safe if you want to actually test real external systems, such as servers, because your tests will become frail and unpredictable.*
>
> *– Anonymous*

Cohesion means leaving things close together. If you leave everything too close together, it will all become too entangled. A guideline may be **Demeter's Law** or the **principle of least knowledge**: an object should only communicate with its immediate neighbors and should not have direct knowledge of how other objects work internally.

For example, if you pass a parameter down 10 levels of nested calls and it changes something only on the 10th level, what you are doing is seriously wrong. Well, if you do it only once, it probably won't do any harm, but if you use this approach all around your code consistently, your application style can now be termed *callback hell*, or the *pyramid of doom*, as demonstrated in the following code example:

```swift
// This example is intentionally bad.
// You should avoid writing code like this.
import Foundation

func performTask1(completion: @escaping (Bool) -> Void) {
    // Simulate an asynchronous task
    DispatchQueue.main.asyncAfter(deadline: .now() + 1) {
        print("Task 1 finished")
```

```
            completion(true)
        }
    }
}

func performTask2(completion: @escaping (Bool) -> Void) {
    // Simulate another asynchronous task
    DispatchQueue.main.asyncAfter(deadline: .now() + 2) {
        print("Task 2 finished")
        completion(true)
    }
}

func performTask3(completion: @escaping (Bool) -> Void) {
    // Simulate yet another asynchronous task
    DispatchQueue.main.asyncAfter(deadline: .now() + 3) {
        print("Task 3 finished")
        completion(true)
    }
}

// Using the functions in a nested one after another, leading to
callback hell
performTask1 { success1 in
    if success1 {
        performTask2 { success2 in
            if success2 {
                performTask3 { success3 in
                    if success3 {
                        print("All tasks finiehed successfully")
                    }
                }
            }
        }
    }
}
```

The same applies if you "ping-pong" your parameters back and forth rather than just passing what is needed from a level to just one more level of distance from the calling function, and use the parameter immediately where it the parameter is needed.

Tools allowing the detection of this kind of behavior are known as **call diagrams** and are quite common in professional reverse engineering. They are uncommon in Swift, unfortunately.

Architecture is about **intentionality**; you should have a plan rather than refining your way step by step. This plan can be minimal, at the start. As such, beginning by defining some layers in the code with different responsibilities is a reasonable approach. This is called **horizontal layering**.

Why do we need to care about keeping things simple?

The main purpose of architecture, besides meeting requirements, is reducing risk and improving reliability. In practically all cases, this equates to reducing complexity, and this is one of the reasons why we choose Clean Architecture as an architectural style. A recommended book is *A Philosophy of Software Design*, by John Ousterhout. The whole book is about the pitfalls to avoid and is what you should read immediately after refreshing the SOLID principles.

You could also split your problem by the functional area you want to implement. For instance, in an insurance system, you could have a module that handles the user data, another that computes risk, and yet another one that describes the different possible states of an insurance policy.

This second approach is called **vertical layering**, which is like dividing a single horizontal layer into several slices. In complex applications, you might want to use both functional decomposition approaches.

It's worth noting that the dependencies point inward in Clean Architecture. For example, in a Swift iOS app, the UI might depend on a use case in the application layer, and that use case would depend on a protocol (which would be an interface or an abstract class in other OOP languages such as Java). The actual implementation of the UI would be in an outer layer and would depend on that interface. In this setup, the business rules (in the use case) are not affected by changes in the UI or the database.

Overall, using the DIP and Clean Architecture can lead to code that is more flexible, maintainable, and decoupled. Some other terms you might encounter relative to this architectural style elsewhere are *Ports and Adapters*, *Hexagonal Architecture*, and so on. These terms indicate architectural styles that are very close to the original Clean Architecture. We will stick to the original version. A good reason not to decouple is when extreme speed and computational efficiency are needed, for special purposes.

In the next section, we will dig deeper into the different ways you can use to decouple software using abstractions.

Different ways to decouple

In Swift, there are many ways to implement dependency injection. In this section, I will show you three methods by means of abstraction: get used to a humble protocol being described this way: calling it abstraction when we are speaking about decoupling via DIP. I won't show you the versions that are not decoupled via an abstraction, as that is not what I want to teach you.

The three approaches I will show you are as follows:

- Initializer injection
- Property injection
- Method injection

Let's look at these in more detail next.

Initializer injection

In a Mermaid diagram, due to the limitations of UML diagrams, which originated much earlier than Swift, we have to represent a Swift protocol with an abstract class. This is the closest concept to a Swift protocol, as UML was created with languages such as C++ and Java in mind, not Swift:

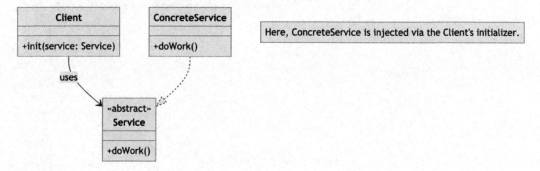

Figure 10.3 – Initializer injection

Initializer injection is usually the right choice in terms of dependency injection and tends to be the preferred way to perform dependency injection in Swift.

In Swift syntax, this would become the following code fragment:

```
import Foundation
protocol Service {
    func doWork()
}

class ConcreteService: Service {
    func doWork() {
        // Concrete implementation detail
    }
}

class Client {
```

```
    let service: Service

    init(service: Service) {
        self.service = service
    }
}
```

Method injection

Here, `Service` is again a protocol, and `ConcreteService` is a class that conforms to the protocol and does the dirty work of implementing our concrete implementation details; this is the class that does the actual work:

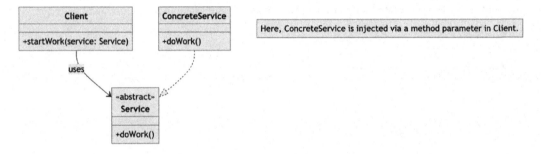

Figure 10.4 – Method injection

And the Swift code would be the following:

```
protocol Service {
    func doWork()
}

class ConcreteService: Service {
    func doWork() {
        // Concrete implementation details
    }
}

class Client {
    func startWork(service: Service) {
        service.doWork()
    }
}
```

The only difference is that `ConcreteService` gets injected by using a method parameter in the `Client` class.

Property injection

We can now complete our tour by using injection via a property of the `Client` class, as shown in the next diagram:

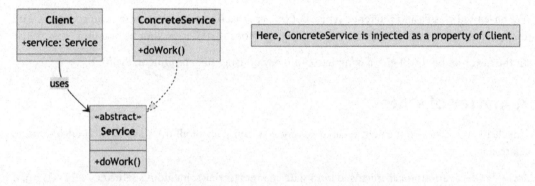

Figure 10.5 – Property injection

The corresponding Swift code would be the following:

```swift
import Foundation

protocol Service {
    func doWork()
}

class ConcreteService: Service {
    func doWork() {
        // Concrete implementation details
    }
}

class Client {
    var service: Service?

    func startWork() {
        service?.doWork()
    }
}
```

This approach is so simple that you might be tempted to think it is not important.

In all cases, it is the `Client` class that gets injected, and it can work totally oblivious to how the `doWork()` method is actually implemented by the `ConcreteService` class.

Suppose `ConcreteService` implements some HTTP methods to go and fetch some data from a server. You could go and swap it for some other mechanism, such as a Bluetooth stack or a socket-based library with custom encryption to do the same thing. `Client` would be totally unaware of the change.

We have used classes and reference types, but this approach is generic, meaning you can use it with other value types; the only requirement is using a protocol to describe your abstraction.

In the next section, I will give a complete summary of using state binding in SwiftUI.

A matter of state

This is intended as a convenient recap to give you a summary of all the ways SwiftUI allows you to share state.

SwiftUI offers various mechanisms to bind state changes to views, including `@State`, `@Binding`, `@ObservedObject`, `@StateObject`, and `@EnvironmentObject` (`@Environment` is used for system predefined values you want to observe). Let's go over these mechanisms in more detail:

- `@State`: This property wrapper stores mutable state for a specific view. SwiftUI manages the storage and ensures that whenever the state changes, the view is re-displayed. It's used for simple, private state management within a single view.

    Here's an example:

    ```
    struct ContentView: View {
        @State private var isOn = false

        var body: some View {
            Toggle("Toggle", isOn: $isOn)
        }
    }
    ```

The `@State` variable, `isON`, is bidirectionally bound to the value of the `isOn` parameter belonging to the `Toggle` view, so that its value changes in real time tracking the toggle position on the UI, and responding to the user.

- `@Binding`: This property wrapper allows you to create a two-way binding to a mutable state. If you need to modify a value from the `@State` property of a parent view inside a child view, you must use `@Binding`. Here's an example:

```
struct ParentView: View {
    @Binding var text: String

    var body: some View {
        TextField("Enter some text", text: $text)
    }
}
```

In this case, the parent's `text` variable gets updated when the user changes the content of `TextField`, a child view of `ParentView`.

- `@ObservedObject`: This wrapper is used for complex state management when the object can be shared across multiple views. The objects must conform to the `ObservableObject` protocol, and the properties that trigger view updates must be marked with `@Published`. Here's an example:

```
class User: ObservableObject {
    @Published var firstName = "Michele"
    @Published var lastName = "Fadda"
}

struct ContentView: View {
    @ObservedObject var user = User()

    var body: some View {
        Text("Good Morning, \(user.firstName) \(user.lastName)")
    }
}
```

- `@StateObject`: This is similar to `@ObservedObject`, but SwiftUI ensures it remains allocated and attached to the same view across view updates. It's used for observable objects owned by the view. SwiftUI ensures that only one instance of `@StateObject` is created per view. This allows you to solve problems of ownership of the reference object you want to observe. All other uses of this reference except the first one will need to be declared as `@ObservedObject`.

- `@EnvironmentObject`: This is used for sharing data across several views globally. Instead of passing data through each view hierarchy, we need to define a reference type as `@EnvironmentObject`, and SwiftUI will automatically ensure that it's available to all views. Beware that this might cause some unwanted refresh and will have some additional computational cost if you are not careful, so use it when needed and sparingly.

  (`@Environment` is similar but for objects owned and defined by the operating system, not the user. From iOS 17 onwards, only `@Environment` is the preferred form, with no distinction between `@Environment` and `EnvironmentObject`)

Here's a simple table to help you choose the right property wrapper:

Property wrapper	When to use	Advantages	Disadvantages
@State	Private mutable state within a single view	Simple, private	Only for basic data types or value types defined by the developer
@Binding	When a child view needs to mutate a value inside the parent view	Creates a two-way connection between views	Not for managing shared state across multiple views
@ObservedObject	Complex state management across multiple views	Shares state across views	Object's ownership (retention) is not managed by SwiftUI
@StateObject	When the view needs to own the data source	SwiftUI guarantees the persistence of the object	Misuse can lead to multiple sources of truth; you need only one
@EnvironmentObject	For global shared state among many views	Data is accessible to all views	Requires careful design; may lead to tight coupling

Other possible bindings in SwiftUI include leveraging `NotificationCenter` and the **Combine** framework. `NotificationCenter` allows objects to communicate without knowing about each other, which is useful when you want to share data across different parts of the app.

However, using `NotificationCenter` can make debugging more complex due to the loosely coupled nature of the notifications.

Combine is a reactive framework that allows you to process values over time. It was inspired by Rx, a third-party reactive framework made by Realm (`https://github.com/ReactiveX/RxSwift`).

We suggest you stick to Combine if you absolutely need a reactive framework, and to be precise, limit yourself to the parts that are integrated with the other frameworks such as the `@Published` properties.

You can use Combine publishers with SwiftUI's @Published property wrapper to monitor changes in the value to update the UI.

At the time of writing this book, Apple has just implemented a few changes, and Combine seems to be going to be phased out. Let's examine these new updates in the next section as these will have an impact on state management.

iOS 17 changes in state management

State management is related to architecture in SwiftUI applications as, in a SwiftUI application, you need to bind state changes to the UI, as SwiftUI is declarative and does not have "methods" that you can call to determine changes in the UI. These changes need to be achieved by declaration and state binding. SwiftUI will automatically redraw the views affected by the changes in the underlying data.

With iOS 17 and Xcode 15, presented during the WWDC2023 conference, Apple introduced some variations to all the binding mechanisms we have just examined: @Observable is used rather than ObservableObject, while we are expected to use @Bindable to mark individual properties we would want to be able to bind. @Bindable usage is limited to classes marked as @Observable. If you deliberately want to avoid observing a property, you can use ObservationIgnored to mark that specific property.

The @Observable property wrapper is the easiest way to create an object that conforms to the Observable protocol. The old @Binding, in comparison, just marks some part of the state information in your view as belonging to a child view, and that you have both read and write access to that data.

Besides that, there are many other changes throughout SwiftUI. The default animation is now a spring, and springs are created with a simpler programming interface; there are many improvements in scroll views, gestures, and so on.

You should always consult the developers' documentation to find out about the most recent documentation: https://developer.apple.com/documentation/swiftui/.

The Combine framework with this new update is going to be substituted with the **Observation** framework, which extends State and Environment to replace StateObject and EnvironmentObject. The net effect is a huge simplification.

You can introduce the new changes in your existing apps that use Combine incrementally, keeping the old approaches in place and substituting them as you progress; much of what you know already and is available in previous versions of SwiftUI will remain valid for quite a while. It normally takes a couple of years for the old approach to be completely replaced. But keep in mind that Combine is practically going to die eventually. And with Combine, the concept of Apple supporting reactive frameworks natively will also die.

So, relying on reactive frameworks is probably going to be a bad idea for your architectural choices on Apple systems, as the evolution of the Apple operating system seems to be moving away from that concept.

Another piece of big news just presented during WWDC2023 is the replacement of the **Core Data** framework with the new, simpler-to-use **SwiftData** framework for data persistence. SwiftData is compatible with Core Data to the point that it is possible to use both in the same app. Xcode is able to convert Core Data models into classes for use with SwiftData, so the conversion to the new framework is going to be rather simple. It still makes sense to use Core Data, as this transition will take about two years, and SwiftData is interoperable with Core Data.

There is, however, going to be less and less reason to depend on third-party frameworks such as Realm.

From a historical perspective, trying to innovate in front of Apple by introducing change means that you are going to spend quite a lot to keep your applications up to spec and maintain them. All technical engineering choices are economic choices, and trying to guess the future is part of the business.

Other ways to chop your code

There are many ways besides what I have shown you to structure your apps in Swift, all of which hold significance within SwiftUI. These are other mechanisms that Swift provides to partition a problem into components.

These alternatives haven't been overlooked, and while we'll touch upon them briefly, you likely have already come across them.

If any of these concepts are new to you, please revise them as you are likely to meet them. These concepts should be familiar to all Swift developers:

- **Extensions**: Instead of using inheritance, use Swift extensions to add functionality to existing classes, structures, enums, or protocol types. You can also extend types to conform to protocols. This is handy if you need to divide code related to a particular class into separate files or modules.

  Extensions can be used to group related functionality in separate files so that you avoid having, for example, too-long classes that are unreadable.

  In practice, what you define in an extension is still coupled to the entity it refers to but is less coupled in terms of code readability. It is also a better way to add functionality rather than using inheritance.

- **Namespaces**: Swift doesn't provide built-in namespaces like some other languages. However, enums can be used to create pseudo-namespaces. This can group related functionality together while maintaining separation between different parts of the code base. Beware that enums cannot support stored properties; if you need them, classes and structs are better choices.

  Again, this is about structuring code in a way that is easier to read for humans, rather than strictly decoupling.

- **Composition**: You should try to avoid inheriting as much as you can. Consider inheritance as something that only someone writing a framework or a library should use, and even so, sparingly. Rather than inheriting from a base class, consider building classes out of smaller components. Expressing this concept as relationships among objects, prefer containment ("has-a") rather than inheritance ("is-a").

  This will make your code easier to test and maintain, as each component can now be developed and tested independently. Besides, it will make your software easier to understand and people will probably already know the components you are using, rather than having to learn your "creations" from scratch. Try to be as gentle as possible toward your peers.

- **Generics**: Generic programming is a way to design functions and data types, letting the compiler do the "specialization" part for you while making minimal assumptions about the type of data being used.

  Generics normally allow for more flexible and reusable code, and they are easier to read than having to scan through a similar implementation of a function in 10 different variations, one for each different data type. Generics may occasionally be less efficient, but that's normally not a problem on modern hardware.

- **Higher-Order Functions (HOFs)**: Swift is also a functional language, and as such, it supports first-class functions and closures. This allows the developer to create HOFs. These can be used to create abstractions, and this can aid in creating clean, separated layers. Functional programming in depth would require volumes.

- **Separation of Concerns**: HOFs allow you to separate what is being done from how it's being done. For instance, the `map()` function doesn't concern itself with how each element is transformed. Instead, it focuses on applying a transformation to each element. The specific transformation is determined by the function passed to it.

- **Reusability and Composition**: Instead of writing monolithic functions that achieve a specific task, you can break them down into smaller, more generic functions. These can be reused and composed to achieve more complex behaviors.

- **Adaptable Code**: By decoupling specific behavior from generic operations, your code can easily adapt to changes. For instance, if you want to change the transformation logic, you can simply pass a different function without modifying the HOF itself.

- **Enhanced Testability**: HOFs can simplify unit testing. Instead of testing a large complex function, you can test smaller functions in isolation and then test their composition.

- **Delegates**: Are often used in Apple programming to respond to a specific action, or series of actions. In general, it is the "old way" of doing things. There are more modern and powerful approaches. You should use it where no other mechanisms are supported – for example, currently, in programming Core Bluetooth on iOS and macOS.

- **Observers (KVO/KVC and NotificationCenter)**: KVO stands for Key Value Observing and KVC for Key value coding. This approach was one of the many different Apple implementation of the observer pattern. The observer pattern is a software design pattern that was once called "publish and subscribe." This pattern is quite common as it is commonly used to allow decoupled systems to communicate.

  You can also implement your own simple queues when needed, but if you want something that is already supported by the OS, observers are a nice choice. This pattern allows one object to notify other objects about changes to its state. This can be another effective way to allow decoupled objects to interact.

  These mechanisms can be used if your project architect messes up so badly with the application architecture that you cannot use other means to integrate, for instance, a third-party library that needs to communicate with a part of your app that you cannot easily reach. Consider this like an emergency shortcut, such as joining two different circuits with a jumper cable.

  Use sparingly, otherwise, your application will begin to look like "spaghetti" and will become difficult to test. KVO/KVC and NotificationCenter can introduce arbitrary coupling between unconnected parts of your system.

Summary

In this chapter, I have tried to gently nudge you toward the most practical tools used to allow you to properly partition complex apps in a SwiftUI context, without using any of the terrible "architectural frameworks" that are unfortunately so common in the industry. Bear in mind that architecture needs to be adopted and understood by humans and, as such, is not about making optimal engineering choices; it needs to be balanced with the culture of the development team.

This treatment is not by any means complete, as we concentrated on the most practical approaches, avoiding "pre-cooked" approaches that might be useful in other contexts, such as Android and .NET, but are, in this author's view, less natural, less elegant, and less powerful in the context of Apple application programming using SwiftUI.

This is the end of our practical take on architecture. In the next chapter, we will take a more theoretical view: we will start by talking about the word itself, and its definition.

It will get less practical, but this part is as important as the first brush with some of the tools of the trade we have just introduced.

I tried to give you a glimpse of the main tools of the trade allowing an application architect to decouple and simplify program structure. In the next chapter, we will examine architecture from a more theoretical perspective.

11

App Architecture and SwiftUI Part II – the Theory

This chapter will proceed with an introduction to the interesting topic of modern application architecture in the context of SwiftUI. Bear in mind that what we discuss here in terms of preferred frameworks is specific to the iOS context. In other programming environments, other approaches such as **Model-View-ViewModel** (**MVVM**) may be perfectly valid. However, what we are really interested in is the rich field of "software architecture" itself, as a concept.

Due to the limited scope of this book, remember that this will be just an introduction to this interesting, vast, and complex topic.

We are going to introduce software architecture, with a focus on theory, and allow you to determine whether certain architecture is well designed.

In this chapter, we're going to cover the following main topics.

- Keeping it light enough
- Architecture – what is it?
- Conflict and the role of the architect
- What good architecture is and what it is not
- The importance of software patterns
- Don't be shy; ask an expert!
- Full-scale applications are different from examples
- The origin of software patterns
- Agency theory and bad architecture
- Clean Architecture

- The dark side of application architecture and Conway's law
- TCA, The composable architecture

Keeping it light enough

In this section, we will discuss the design part of software. We don't take the view that you should design everything from the start, with a "grand plan" that encompasses everything. That approach is often called *waterfall*, or *upfront architecture*. However, I don't subscribe that you should go completely free-range and start with no intentional initial design either.

Take, for example, starting a journey with just a map, a backpack with some spare light clothes, and enough money. It helps if you have a plan, research the country you want to visit first, and know at least a bit of the language. Also, you may have "rules" you want to follow in order to maximize some criteria, such as your gastronomic preferences, sunshine intake, and having abundant sunscreen oil in order to avoid sunburn.

When it comes to software architecture, the goal is not to begin with a completely blank slate. Instead, you aim to have the least amount of initial design necessary to address the specific problem at hand. This aligns with Stefan Tikov's and Douglas Fairbarn's minimalist perspective, which this author appreciates, emphasizing the concept of "just enough architecture" or "sufficient architecture" and the ultimate purpose of architecture being to minimize project risk.

In "real architecture" (i.e., the design of living spaces), famous minimalist architects include Massimiliano Fuksas and Renzo Piano. They tend to create buildings that are slender, elegant, beautiful, and simple fluid organic structures of steel and glass. As we will see in the next section, "real architecture" is often a source of cultural inspiration for software architecture.

Do not overcomplicate things; less is more.

When you embark on a project, it's essential to begin with at least a rudimentary design, much like sketching a preliminary line with a pencil on a map of the islands you intend to explore in a vast blue sea. I mention a pencil because it allows for flexibility; you may need to adjust your course as you gather more information during your journey.

Be prepared for your initial plan to evolve multiple times as you acquire more insights along the way.

In the next section, we will begin with the definition of the term *architecture*.

Architecture – what is it?

From *real* architecture, the one that deals with **buildings**, we borrowed a language and concepts that we use to describe our design activities and outputs when we build programs and systems.

This has happened multiple times during the history of the evolution of what we now call **application architecture**, or **software architecture**, in general.

Real architecture tends to predate its computer science-based sibling by a few decades, on average.

A very naïve definition of the term *architecture* in our field is "*an (ideally) appropriate structure of an application that (ideally) meets requirements.*"

This may also imply a "non-ideal" structure and organization of code that barely or does not at all meet requirements, in a descriptive rather than prescriptive way. It is exactly like a "family;" it could be a place full of love, or a dysfunctional environment, or a realm filled with horror.

A *requirement* is something that your system must do, a property that your system must have and often "guarantee" during its lifetime, always. Requirements may be *functional*, relative to the business problem to be solved, or *non-functional*.

The last category covers all the constraints that our application or software system needs to fulfill that are not simply derived from "user stories" and are relevant to the "business logic" description. A user story is a description of a software feature as seen from the perspective of a user of a system. User stories are normally written in the following format:

"As a user of the system, I want to <do something> to achieve <something else>".

There are more sophisticated and recent approaches to describe the functionality of a system from the perspective of a user; UX designers typically call these **user journey mapping** and **service design**.

Whatever we design typically has the sole purpose of serving the needs of a user. If your system is slow, your user will become annoyed. If your system works in a way that the user cannot predict and trust, your system is going to be essentially useless. Whatever you do, the sole purpose you have is serving the needs of the user. This is the main purpose of software architecture, like how "real" architecture has the purpose of providing living spaces for humans to use and live in.

A software system often consists of numerous components, with something such as the "iPhone app" representing only the most visible part that users encounter initially. Certain architects may argue that this description doesn't align with the proper definition of architecture. They might offer an alternative definition, one that reflects their self-identification and the tasks they engage in. For instance, an "enterprise architect" will often take the perspective that their job is to define **non-functional-requirements** (**NFRs**), almost exclusively, within the context of a business entity. They are interested in a strategic organizational perspective and do not want to get involved with the programming structure at all, delegating this activity as an "implementation detail" to programming leads and technical architects, or sometimes to the developers themselves.

Such architects will use enterprise *frameworks*; these organizational models and guidelines have practically nothing to do with programming and are more related to aspects such as business management consulting and user experience, service design, enterprise strategy, change management, digital strategy, and enterprise security.

This kind of "chief" architect will typically be a "non-programming architect" who focuses more on the organizational business aspects within a company, and they are not interested in technical details except in the more general, very high-level sense: We may say that their view of programming is based on a 10,000-mile business "aerial view.". This metaphor is so common in business to be referred as the helicopter view. These architects often look more like managers than engineers. Architects are supposed, in general, to be able to zoom in and out on technical and business issues, and see them at different "scales", from a very high level and abstract to very detailed and precise.

This is the kind of architect who would consider a personal achievement preventing an organization from trying out an uncommon programming language, requiring difficult-to-find expertise on the market. This architect won't personally make sure that the programming part is well structured, only being concerned that programming quality is a "process" that this kind of architect can control.

We will not challenge this view of the world, but this is not the kind of architecture we are going to describe here. If the non-programming-architect is interested just in dealing with non-technical stakeholders and is involved mostly in the pre-sale activities, some organizations would describe this role as a "pre-sales-engineer" or an "account manager/consultant" rather than call this role "architect." In some consulting companies, this is the role of the senior "partners" and high-ranking middle managers. These are the guys who bring big orders and ensure that a consulting company thrives.

Do not be surprised if different organizations and companies use the word *architect* in different ways. Selling and being able to build and maintain successful relationships with clients is a difficult key skill, and these more business-focused and less technical "architects" are of paramount importance for the success of a company. Sometimes, even within the same multinational company, you may meet different perspectives on this topic that vary by industry, and even regional or country, or change with time.

There is also often some tension between the more business-focused architects and "architects that program" who think that the role of the programming activities of the "architect" is "de-risking" a project, reducing its risk to a manageable level, and paving the road for other developers. These architects will often state that an architect should not deal with petty details such as program code and make sure that someone else does it, in some way, following a process they want to prescribe. Other architects would gladly invade the field of project managers, dealing with resource allocation and configuration problems. Practically speaking, no matter what the job description is, reducing risk is one of the main responsibilities of a software architect.

If anyone but the developers themselves decide about the prioritization of tasks, arguably the organization is not "agile," as this is typically one of the few areas where agile developers are supposed to self-organize. Do not expect to find a fit-for-all definition of *agile*, as organizations are supposed to adapt this process to their needs, and they can also use several different "project ceremonies," such as dailies and retrospectives.

If in your company an architect, in general, does not program, you should avoid doing so, and the same holds if you operate purely as a manager; stepping back into programming might indicate you are not at ease with your new managerial role and you are clinging nostalgically to your old times as a developer. Or you should step in to create the initial technical application structure. It all depends on the context, and the company organization and culture!

In some organizations and companies, this person giving structure to the code is often the role of the "lead" or the "principal" developer; in a start-up and some smaller or more traditional companies, this "hat" (role) belongs to the CTO, the chief technical officer, or the "technical director." This may sometimes be a "hands-on" project manager who understands both the business and the technical domain.

If you don't have appropriate technical leadership, you will often have developers jousting for power and for political reasons, rather than working together for the common good. The worst thing is a manager stepping in, losing impartiality, and contributing to a conflict.

Conflict is good, provided it can be expressed constructively, as this helps a team to be creative. Repressing conflict can make things way worse because the conflict will not actually disappear. It will become a matter of hidden "politics," things "that cannot be said" (an elephant in the room). It will often explode dramatically all of a sudden.

> **Note**
>
> Good communication requires transparency, honesty, mutual respect, and openness. It is the manager's function to ensure that this communication is possible. If you don't have an **open communication culture**, problems won't get reported and bad things will happen, as problems that don't get reported won't be solved.
>
> If you witness managers talking about openness but then punishing the bringers of bad news, you have just discovered what we commoners call "hypocrisy." In management speak, we can talk about the tension between the **theory in practice** (what people really do) and the **espoused theory** (what people want to be perceived as doing). For example, during a hackathon, a developer may ask to take the lead (after all, it is an exercise), and they are aiming at showing competence in order to be considered for promotion.
>
> The **highest-paid persons (hippos)** in the work group may get offended by their bad communication style and instead mark them as unfit for promotion. They may gladly proceed to leave the lead, during an exercise, in charge of people who "already know how it is done," such as existing managers.
>
> Modern well-structured organizations routinely allow their employees to "step out" of their roles, to learn on the job and grow. Some have explicit rules in their own quality manuals.
>
> Here's a question to consider: which organization type, in the long term, would favor better code production, create happier developers, and help a company make more money – the one with a closed, rigid system or a more open, flexible one?
>
> The interesting answer is that we don't actually know what will happen in the future, but we can make educated guesses and try to "cheat" at poker, using past experience as a predictor for future, preferably by using statistics in order to stay as objective as we can – until someone is kind enough to invent a working crystal ball, that is. Yes, software architecture involves heavy doses of "human engineering", understanding your colleagues as human beings, and having empathy, coupled with strong analytical skills.
>
> In another start-up, some of the developers during a similar competitive internal hackathon may have successfully twisted the collective arms of the CEO and the finance guys to write an app, using machine learning to distinguish a hot dog from a hamburger, with the developers operating as managers. I think they scored at least a third best, companywide.

In some companies, performing the activity of shaping a system so that it has a safe and reliable system design is a shared responsibility of the whole programming team. For this to happen, everyone needs to be able to contribute and is required to learn along the way.

This, for instance, is the perspective at Google and other modern companies where **site reliability engineering** (**SRE**) makes security and safety design a shared responsibility for all SRE engineers. Google has some good books on the topic of SRE that you should read in order to become a better developer: `https://sre.google/books/`.

This approach requires all developers to be good, dependable, and responsible adults, capable of having mature conversations and agreeing on common expectations. A SRE engineer is an architect who writes code and interacts with other peers in a democratic way.

In the next section, we will examine handling conflict within software projects.

Conflict and the role of the architect

If you have disagreements, most of the time it is a matter of unmatched expectations, and this can cause conflict. Alternatively, it could arise simply because of different roles and views. Conflict naturally occurs in teams, and if the conflict is respectful, this normally leads to increased performance and creativity. Like in a loving couple, you can quarrel about some choices but love and respect each other on a deeper level. If someone thinks we should always be forced to be friendly with everyone, and all decisions should be unanimously made, then really bad things will start to happen. You will not always be able to be friendly; sometimes, you are going to be sad or tired. There is no need to force everyone to smile all the time.

Go and research the term **Groupthink**. Groupthink is a phenomenon occurring in cohesive groups, identified by psychologist Irving Janis. Groupthink is a tendency within strong leadership that leads to ignoring signals from the surrounding environment and dangerously bad decision-making.

Conflict is a natural and anticipated aspect of any environment. However, if a leader's response to conflict is focused on cultivating a team of unquestioning individuals who are so homogenous that no opinions outside the leader's are allowed, the outcome can be bothersome. The team becomes so deeply committed to their own perspective that they dismiss any contradictory information from external sources. This unwavering adherence leads to creative stagnation within the team, frequently resulting in the generation of remarkably poor and perilous decisions. While the decision-making process may gain speed, it's akin to removing the brakes from a car that's rapidly descending a hill.

To be called a team, a work group must have a relationship of mutual professional trust and be preferably composed of diverse individuals, with different perspectives and skills. If someone says you must "conform," rather than accept you as an individual and just as you are as a person, prepare for a bumpy ride. The hard part of software is human relations; technology is the easiest part to work with.

There are no quick and fast rules. As a professional developer, expect lots of differences between one company and another, and you are a consultant between your current client and the next. If you are a solo developer, rejoice, as it is all on your shoulders, and you are often both the designer and the developer user of your own software designs.

In this book, we are interested in the perspective of a technical architect, who pretty much is capable of programming and should be ideally the most experienced and knowledgeable developer in the team, "leading" development – directing, mentoring, solving the hardest problems, and giving shape to a system.

A proficient architect plays a pivotal role in simplifying and taming complexity to mitigate project risks. By doing so, they enhance the likelihood of achieving a successful outcome, meeting project objectives, and ensuring overall satisfaction. This perspective on their purpose should be communicated with the project manager, particularly when these two roles are distinct entities.

An architect who increases complexity rather than reducing it, and who does not document and explain code and architectural choices, could be a bad apple and would probably be a better fit working for your competitors than in your own company. A likely reason for this bad behavior is "job security" – the architect wants to keep their usually very well-paid job by making a team's work harder.

Sometimes, this is not intentional, but the result is the same. Do you really want to become a true, effective, 10x developer? Don't write 10 times more code. Try instead to achieve the same result with a tenth of the effort. And some will take the pseudo-democratic view that "we are all equal, and we are all intelligent" to try to justify the bad, difficult-to-understand code they write by making you feel bad, and even stupid, if you object that it is more complex than it should be. Not caring about trying to reduce the complexity of the code you write betrays a lack of empathy and compassion. These types will often use exotic approaches – not because they are needed but to show off how good they are. This style is not considered "good" by this author.

A good concept to refer to in this context is the concept of **Intellectual Integrity** – a system that has this property is a system that is easy to understand by a single mind. A system lacking conceptual integrity will instead be so complex that it cannot be understood by a single mind.

Leaving a technical problem such as a bad application structure in place and not doing unit tests is called having "technical debt." *"I will fix this tomorrow,"* or *"I will fix this in production; now we are in development"* are the kind of lies we developers tend to say.

As in real monetary debt, **technical debt** tends to grow exponentially, and like "real debt," it can become crippling and out of hand quite rapidly.

If you see code cowboys who ignore best practices and just write complex hard-to-understand code that they only can grasp, your organization likely has a few problems. In nature, exponential phenomena tend to cause disasters – you have initially a small variation that we humans are not programmed to notice with alarm. Then, the speed of variation increases proportionally to it (time to revise some math?).

When the speed increases and the variation becomes noticeable, it is often too late. Whatever thing you were trying to control is now going out of bounds. All explosives in nature work this way.

There are engineering approaches that make this problem manageable – control theory and control (if you are interested in PID controls you may learn more about them here: `https://www.ni.com/en/shop/labview/pid-theory-explained.html`). Control theory is the approaches that allow planes to fly without pilots.

What grows faster than exponential, (O^n in Big-O-notation `https://web.mit.edu/16.070/www/lecture/big_o.pdf`), which computer science students sometimes may think is the fastest thing ever? They normally learn **Big O notation** and think that exponential growth, compared to polynomial growth, is the fastest thing in the mathematical universe. The answer might surprise you, and no, it is not the exponential function. A mathematical function that grows faster than the exponential one is the complexity of software systems.

This complexity grows with the **factorial function (O!)**, i.e. the number of ways you can reorder a number of items in a set, or the number of different paths a software system can take and that you have to test if you are not rigorous as an architect, doing your best to limit these possible interactions.

Now, add time (a delay) and feedback (some inputs) linked to the outputs of your system. If you are careful, apply everything you know, and research a lot, your system will still be stable, predictable, and dependable. If you are not, then what you will rediscover is **chaos**, the stuff nightmares are made of.

If you thought you could relax, the speed of light is constant, and you cannot physically guarantee a common time reference for all the parts of a complex system that are separated by distance – not in this universe. That is where the career of a mathematician, systems design theoretician, and Turing Award winner called Leslie Lamport began. Do a web search on the works of this author, and pray that this particular problem does not involve your next project because it would make your life interesting (meaning that you will be dealing with the design of a large distributed system, that has some peculiar difficulties).

If your system involves these things, **TLA+**, the formal language designed by Leslie Lamport, could help you understand better the problem you are facing.

As we live in the real world, and idealizations and reliable competence assessments are never what you observe in a real organizational context, not even in "meritocratic" multinationals adopting "competence-based systems" on paper, you may meet in your daily life people who have formal power and are classified as architects but don't have much to offer in terms of actual architectural expertise or knowledge.

Your mileage may vary depending on the "real politics" power structure within the organization you work for. You may also meet people lacking real-world experience being termed "lead developers," maybe since a very young age, and considered in a "leadership position" for no better reason than the trust relationship they may personally have had with the CEO; maybe they started as "employee number seven" when the company was small. They did contribute to the success of the company, and if you are lucky and want to think rationally, they learned a lot of wisdom during the process. In a non-meritocratic society, where social progression is not seen favorably, the risk minimization behavior of hiring managers will justify seeking only potential candidates who "held previous leadership positions" whenever hiring someone for a leadership position.

If you want a cynical perspective on this phenomenon, go and read up on a German historian named **Ernst Kantorowitz**: "*Power legitimizes itself, kings who had ancestors with humble origins create a narrative where their ancestors were knights in shiny armors rather than clad in sheep skin.*" And sometimes, controlling the narrative is all that power is about. Organizations, including the ones that create software systems, are composed of humans, and humans are never perfect. Welcome to the real world!

A good leader will be ideally empathic and would fight to defend their "resources" and will recognize merit and skill, fighting for their team members to be promoted. If a "leader" does not recognize merit in anyone but themselves, this is typically a rather big red flag, and it's even worse if no one ever saw the leader admit they ever made a mistake. As in many things in life, your mileage may vary, a lot, even at the best companies, which are never going to be "ideal,". Even multinational companies have different cultures depending on which of their country branches you consider.

If you want to understand leadership from a psychological perspective, you may want to read basically everything written by Manfred F.R. Kets de Vries, a psychiatrist and HR professor at the French business school INSEAD. He is not a light read but an interesting one. Basically, true leaders for him are leaders who are aware, as human beings, of their own weaknesses and overcome them. Then there are impostors, suffering from imposter syndrome in such an incapacitating way that it blocks their decision process. The last category is what he calls "fools" – leaders who have issues that they are not aware of and are not trying to correct (e.g., the kind of narcissistic leader who is always right because they are incapable of learning and admitting that mistakes are possible).

If you want to understand teamwork at a really deep level, you will often need to start reading about psychiatry because mere psychology won't explain some of the scenarios you will encounter in field work. Generally, though, just relax and be accepting and forgiving.

At some organizations, senior team members may lack formal power and role recognition but might have hard knowledge, and they may be recognized as the "go-to" authoritative people you know you can depend upon to ask tough questions when you have difficult problems to crack or need deep insights or advice about the design of a new system. These people, whether recognized or not formally, are architects, despite others claiming that "architecture is a club you need to be invited to by other members" or that they would only trust an architect having had that role for a long time. Even if you have been an architect your whole life, as with a software developer, there is no guarantee that those years of work equate to being dependable. In general, and this is the opinion of this author, and this author may be wrong, an architect who knows just one domain, for example, is just a mobile developer and tends to probably be a poor architect.

Nature favors a multidisciplinary approach when you have complexity. So, when you have finished this book, go and learn other languages, other programming paradigms, and some additional computer science theory. It is going to be a never-ending journey.

Good architects, in our limited and maybe questionable view, tend to be well-read; they often understand both the business and the technical domain, and often, they are well-versed in more than one technical domain. They tend to be old, with very few exceptions. They may have formal qualifications; some of them are PhDs and university professors, and some may lack formal qualifications, but then they typically have been studying all their lives. In general, we think that you require a lot in terms of autonomous thinking and rigorous thinking to become one.

This author's strictly personal view is that the field is open and learnable, and everybody could potentially become an architect. You are not "born" an architect, and some who think they are "born architects" may be bad at it, despite having been in the industry for decades, even if they are acclaimed as "thought leaders" by their companies. Some other employees may be better as architects, despite being less popular with management.

But don't get discouraged; you can learn. You may not be offered the role of an architect on a silver platter, or even at all, but you can and should learn to structure your applications better.

In the next section, I will try to give you some criteria to understand the difference between good and bad architectural designs.

What good software architecture is and what it is not

When we speak about software architecture, we don't have hard and fast "recipes" that you can regard as laws to be followed blindly and memorized to guide you in your journey. Instead, however, we have more guiding **principles** about architecture that allow us to judge the architecture (structure) of a system and help us determine whether this structure is appropriate or not. The first such principle is the prescriptive statement that that we can use to define as a sort of rule-zero of architecture –"*form must follow function*" or, even more simply, "*form follows function.*"

I borrowed this from **Bauhaus architecture school**. The Bauhaus school was founded in Germany in 1919 and literally means "building houses." It advocated for simplicity and practicality in form. When it comes to application structure, we discovered this philosophical view of the world in computer science between the end of the 1970s and early 1980s, when the first software "methodologies" such as "structured design and analysis" began to appear. As a principle, "form follows function" is still pretty much the very foundation of all software architecture today. Predating computer science by several decades culturally is a typical phenomenon we find when examining the cultural contributions from "architects of buildings." Sociologists call this *cultural contamination*, and it is a positive thing. This is one of the engines of innovation.

First, you could ask yourself, what kind of bad things could happen if "form does not follow function"? You could have some very typical unintentional architecture structures that, often, we would consider "inappropriate" and "unacceptable." For example, consider the following diagram:

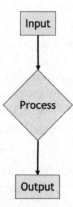

Figure 11.1 – An I/O-based batch process architecture

One such far too common and typical architectural structure would be the simple I/O batch computation model that accepts input, processes data, and outputs results. It may be appropriate (in moderation) for some specific tasks, but you cannot structure everything you do with a computer (and much less with a mobile phone) this way, always following this simplistic "recipe."

This I/O batch processing may well be the basis of all Cobol programs in existence. We won't even contend that it is "bad"; it is simply inadequate for most other purposes, such as writing modern event-driven mobile application software. If all you have is a hammer, the whole world looks like a nail.

This even applies in terms of describing what you do; if you describe things only with the words "process," "calculate," and "compute," they can apply to about 99.99% of everything we humans do with computers.

This is way too vague and generic to be useful. You should strive to find a better, more descriptive way of labeling what your system actually needs to do.

Now, instead imagine some bulbous, jelly-like, amoeba-like structure. Picture "the Thing" in John Carpenter's sci-fi horror movie. Are you scared already?

This unintentional (emergent) "architectural" style is what you get if you don't give any structure to your code, and simply lump all your processing in one place. This is what you get if you place a lot of super-complex logic and don't follow a structured approach, such as a **State Machine GoF** (**Gang of Four**) pattern, but just keep adding a conditional construct there, and a property there, incrementally – rinsing and repeating.

> **Note**
>
> The term GOF pattern is a go-ahead from "Gang of Four" patterns of the book: *Design Patterns: Elements of Reusable Object-Oriented Software* from *Erich Gamma, Richard Helm, Ralph Johnson, and John Vlissides*, collectively known as the "Gang of Four" or **GoF**. The book was first published in 1994, classifying and putting together a collection of design patterns aimed at solving common problems encountered during object-oriented design.
>
> Design patterns are essentially generic reusable solutions to frequently occurring problems.

Then, you proceed to modify your code, line by line, adding new things and changing other fragments of code, day after day, week after week, month after month as your requirements evolve.

You will end up with an entangled mess. No matter how intelligent you are, you soon won't understand your code anymore, and probably nobody else in the company will.

One day, your manager may ask you to add a new feature, and your honest answer becomes, "*Months*" or "*I don't have the faintest idea; probably less than a year.*"

Eventually, someone pulls the plug, and the old software system gets completely rewritten. But you don't have tests, and you can't know for sure whether the new software does exactly what the broken old system used to do. The worst thing that can happen is that you are so intelligent that you manage to prolong this agony by adding even more complex code for a while. Be smart; code in a way that does not require other people to be smart. Write smart code only if there is no other way to achieve your goal.

This is what could have happened with UIKit if you made the mistake of placing all your programming logic within Model View Controllers. And I won't be giving you any examples of this bad programming style because I want you to carefully avoid this "style."

This "architectural style" is often referred to as "**big blob of mud**," and this is not a compliment. We Italians tend to love food. When we ironically compare code to gastronomic terminology, such as "spaghetti," "minestrone," "risotto," "salad" to describe structure… well, we are not using these words to compliment clarity and readability. In English, we would say "clear as mud." In order to give clarity and structure to code, we use patterns, and we will introduce them in the next section.

The importance of software patterns

Now, let's talk about a much-maligned pattern, the **Model View Controller (MVC)**. A pattern is a "repeatable" solution to a problem that can be applied to known contexts and situations.

The first software pattern ever invented was the MVC, used originally by **Xerox** to create the first event-driven, object-oriented, windows-based software in the history of mankind. The language they used at the time was **SmallTalk**.

There is no such a problem as a "**fat MVC**" per se; the problem is just an inherent lack of structure. By fat MVC, we mean inserting all the application code in the MVCs rather than in distinct software layers.

MVC is the first programming pattern ever designed in object-oriented programming. It was conceived during the development of the Xerox Alto, which served as the precursor to all modern desktop computers in existence today. This framework is still used today in some web application contexts, notably with **UIKit** and **AppKit** on Apple systems.

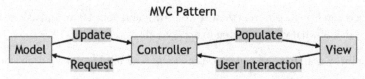

Figure 11.2 – The "infamous" MVC pattern

And this problem of "being fat" – that is, containing all application code in one place – does not arise just because you use the MVC pattern in an Apple context.

The problem root cause lays in doing all the processing within that pattern. We had structured programming, and before that we had gotos. Now, the `goto` statement is conspicuously absent from most modern language and is seldom found, even in modern code written in the C programming language. The ultimate purpose of a pattern is giving structure to what would otherwise be chaos.

In the old days of programming, we referred to bad programming style as "spaghetti programming." Again, the problem is lack of structure, making the life of a fellow developer who has to read the code and debug it really miserable. The purpose and intention of the original developer were hidden by the lack of structure and continually "jumping" back and forth. Again, there are no examples here; if you are interested in this bad programming style, grab some old BASIC program listings from the 1980s.

Envision the satisfaction you might derive from programming on an industrial microcontroller such as the Intel 8051, a highly favored option in the early 1990s. During that era, the primary flow control mechanism available in assembly language was essentially the "compare and jump if not equal" instruction.

A not-so-good developer (or a really bad architect) will produce fat View Controllers in UIKit, fat classes in object-oriented programming, fat **ViewModels** (in MVVM), long functions with thousands of lines of code (without the actual need for extreme processing speed), with nested gotos, and they will still try to place all the processing logic directly in Views if using SwiftUI.

In the next section, we will talk about the importance of asking for help when needed.

Don't be shy; ask an expert!

It is very difficult to say that a specific architecture design is "ideal" because, as with many things in engineering, everything here is a matter of compromise. You will never "get it absolutely right," and some of the questions you will meet will likely be so hard that sometimes even PhDs and university professors would end up on different sides of the discussion. Be humble and ask for help if needed;

don't rely solely on yourself and the few people you are working with. If there is a friendly data scientist with a penchant for stats and thorny statistics in your company, sometimes they will be the only soul who can help you. The same holds for cybersecurity, or some exotic expert domain subject that your system deals with.

An external expert can bring a different view to your own and your team, and asking for expert help will decrease the risk of what you are trying to achieve, always.

If you are not so lucky as to have an expert, do research, read books, and try to reason with math.

Prefer rigorous thinking, well grounded in reputable research and based on good academic science, and refuse opinion and hearsay, even when coming from "experts." If an expert has anything worth saying, the supporting argument must come from multiple verifiable sources, experiments, mathematical proofs, and "good science." Avoid experts who rely solely on their own experience without explaining their recommendations with rational arguments and sound, methodologically valid science. Experts tend to assume *they know*, and often, they can be too superficial to be trusted. Often, they will think that their expertise extends far outside their field, and in that case, their experience may not be relevant.

Don't trust a PhD in cybersecurity to understand anything about team dynamics, no matter how confident they look.

For instance, if you base all your work on false assumptions (e.g., just one unsubstantiated statement by a single "expert witness" telling you that something the expert says being false is actually true), this will open a really bad can of conceptual worms:

A friendly architect I know, Klaus Alfert, recently gently reminded me of this fundamental principle – *Ex falso quo libet*, which means "from a falsehood, anything can logically follow."

This is called the "explosion principle" in logic.

So, please don't base all your design on the concept that earth is flat, as you could use that wrong statement to logically prove anything you wanted (that time travel is possible, that the sun temperature is negative, or that this author likes pizza with ketchup if you are creative enough). Don't go there.

Unfortunately, some of the "science" in software engineering is not exactly sound, so if you compare the likelihood of making errors, statistically, between very different programming languages such as C and Swift, you end up making comparisons between apples and oranges, as these languages allow for very different constructs (as Klaus Alfert, a distinguished architect and PhD, I consider a friend of mine, would observe on this topic).

Swift in general is way safer than C, but declaring at point blank that Swift is safer in all circumstances, always, is kind of stating something without having actually bothered to find a good academically and scientific valid proof.

Some time ago, someone boldly declared that "managed languages" (and, at that time, that meant Java and C#) were *safer* than "unmanaged languages" such as C and assembly. Swift is technically unmanaged but has a fussy compiler, one that checks source code extremely rigorously. So, you can say that Swift kind of is a "managed language," if you broaden this academically unsound assumption just a tiny bit further.

I have a story to tell.

It is possible to write life-critical code in assembly, and this author participated to projects where aerospace **ESA (European Space Agency)** grade code for "ground-based" tests was written in assembly or HP BASIC. We were documenting our development process as "waterfall," but at that time we used "spiral" and scaffolding, incrementally writing code, and testing our assumptions every step of the way.

I did, write this kind of code personally, during the initial stages in my career. That code would be a lot safer than code written by safety unaware mobile developers today, even with a safe, strongly typed compiler such as Swift. The first generation of integrated automotive brakes and gear-shifting controls for trucks was built this way. Later on, the development process in similar contexts was regulated by means of standards, making it more rigorous. Still, no modern programmer today literally counts the microseconds needed to execute a particular programming branch or call a routine during an interrupt, and our code was designed to be simple and took care of some part of the system failing, handling failure in multiple worst-case scenarios, which was meticulously analyzed. Nobody got killed by our assembly, while many lost their lives due to accidental acceleration problems of more modern cars that use far more modern compilers (research the Toyota unintentional acceleration problem).

The skill of the developers rather than the language makes the difference.

I was sitting side by side with engineers who had a complete understanding of the physics, the electronics, and the mechanics of the system. *If you can, keep your domain experts at close range and talk to them, a lot.*

On academic approaches to architecture, prefer to have a rigorous stand.

Sometimes, you will need a boring, number-heavy approach, with the kind of mathematics that would scare small children.

This might involve statistics, or even economic theories based on a theorem that won a Nobel Prize for a bunch of university professors. The intellectually rigorous, hard approach is usually the better one that will reward you more if you follow it.

Pragmatic means just as complex as needed, but not any less; context is everything.

Between specifying a system "by example" using an "agile approach" and using the intellectually terrifying formal mathematical route of a language such as TLA+ (`https://lamport.azurewebsites.net/tla/tla.html`), the latter domain-specific language is the clear winner, even if its notational syntax looks more like scary math than a normal programming language. Leslie Lamport is just one expert, a mathematician who spent 25 years or so ruminating on the formal representation of software systems. What he says, and proves with formal mathematics, is worth thousands of run-of-the-mill agile methodologists.

Agile is important, but math, in a scientific context such as computer science, matters more.

Formal specifications make systems design safer. They are out of the scope of this book, but don't refuse to use a tool, as an architect, if only because the tool requires you to study. Some hard problems will require hard tools to be cracked.

Rigorous models developed in TLA+ helped the Xbox deliver as a project and are considered best practices at companies such as Microsoft and Amazon.

And now, in the next section, we will talk about real-life applications.

Full-scale applications are different from examplesIn previous chapters code examples, I indeed took this approach – I intentionally simplified matters, and I accept responsibility for that. My aim wasn't to create comprehensive applications, and I deliberately kept the examples quite compact. My primary goal was to showcase SwiftUI programming techniques within the limited space available for this purpose.

App architecture is what differentiates a programming example from real "industrial-grade," well-structured, rugged, and optimized applications.

Real "industrial-grade" apps normally have a quite different structure, so do not think you can get away with what we did in order to just show how to use a particular SwiftUI technique.

We chose not to write complete apps, as this would have given us less opportunities to cover SwiftUI programming techniques and would have been more difficult for you to understand, as we would not have been able to cover SwiftUI topics in isolation or with progressive difficulty in mind.

We have shown a few techniques that can be used in SwiftUI to decompose and refactor complex views. We won't repeat them here.

When it comes to structuring application code, many refer to "architectures" that would solve the problem of "fat view controllers" or allow better testability of software, as well as other claimed benefits. We can consider that this is probably snake oil and a "silver bullet" (a magic technique that would make the problem at hand magically disappear).

I will now invoke another consequence of the foundational "form follows function" principle that was mentioned by Robert "Uncle Bob" Martin in his book *Clean Architecture*.

Effective architecture is tailored to the unique challenges that your system seeks to address, akin to a custom, meticulously crafted garment rather than off-the-rack, mass-produced attire. While the human physique exhibits relatively consistent dimensions, the concept of "one-size-fits-all architectures" is typically less applicable and effective in the realm of software.

There are no good "architectures." These are usually patterns, presentation patterns, and these patterns are suspicious because they claim multiple benefits and list a universal applicability. So, they all claim to be "silver bullets," the ones you expect to fire in order to kill magical beasts. And magic is as real as Santa Claus.

In the next section, I will give you the origin story of software patterns.

The origin of software patterns

A pattern is another concept I borrowed from "real" architecture of the house building variety. The term was invented by **Cristopher Alexander** in his book *A Pattern Language* and was adopted by software architecture more than 20 years later by the "Gang of Four," the authors of the book *Software Patterns: Elements of Reusable Software* – Erich Gamma, Richard Helm, Ralph Johnson, and John Vlissides. The ominously named **Gang of Four** (GoF) was a team of two Siemens and two IBM engineers who discovered that most object-oriented computer systems tend to be composed by some "reusable solutions" that are specific to a context and can be reused, substantially independent from the programming language. Read the GoF book and keep it for reference.

Using software design patterns appropriately is normally considered a "best practice" when designing an object-oriented software system. Beware that a lot of learning has taken place since it was written. One of the major changes is the fact that multithreaded code is now commonplace, due to multi-core processors being the norm rather than the exception nowadays. So, some example implementations of the patterns you will find in the book are not anymore adequate, as they would lead to race conditions and different results, depending on the execution path, which will not be predictable. Some more modern languages also make some of these patterns meaningless, as the modern programming language might have support for better ways to solve the problem the old pattern tries to solve. For instance, the Singleton is now universally considered a bad practice – difficult to test, risks introducing global state, and probably linked to potential security leaks; that's not to mention the obvious race conditions that we all know and love if your implementation is naive. There is no angle where this specific pattern looks good, and in general, it is widely known as a bad practice that you should remove from your set of tools. You should examine the Singleton only for study purposes and consider it very carefully if you really don't have any other choice.

One of the measures of appropriateness when considering when to use a pattern, is its requirement to be used in a *specific, appropriate context*, a situation in which the pattern is considered a good solution for a specific problem.

No pattern should be ever used "always," in all circumstances. A pattern that someone claims you should *always use* becomes automatically a bad pattern, an **anti-pattern**, such as the **Singleton**.

So, these "architectures" that someone claims you should use to solve all the possible problems you may have in terms of architecture of your app are nothing more than presentation patterns (they normally deal mostly with the UI part) and are just third-party substitutes of the MVC pattern. You would normally end up with a better result, even with UIKit, by using just plain old MVC and using Clean Architecture and SOLID principles from the ground up.

Some of these software design patterns often were introduced to Apple, typically in an iOS context from other operating systems, as third-party frameworks. For example, the MVVM pattern was borrowed from Windows .NET programming, and in that OS, you have bindings that, at the time of the introduction of this framework to iOS, did not exist in Apple operating systems and were often simulated with some other clunky and complex "reactive frameworks" and bindings.

Other recent non-traditional presentation patterns made really wilder claims, offering a different file to customize to every different stakeholder in a big application design team, listing five or seven "roles," claiming to be "completely decoupled," and solving all possible imaginable architectural issues and, of course, "fat view controllers"

In general, if someone tells you that their "architecture" solves the fat view controllers problem, you can safely assume that to be an unsubstantiated claim, and you should consider whatever they are proposing with a big pinch of salt: "*I don't know what you are selling, but I am not buying it.*"

As such, we won't be covering **MVVM**, **VIPER**, **VPI**, and similar "architectures" because they are just presentation frameworks, are too old, and – surprise, surprise – you don't actually need them in SwiftUI.

To be completely precise, the Apple-suggested **VM pattern**, which uses just Views and Models, is actually MVVM, as the **ViewModel** functionality (state binding) in SwiftUI is supplied by the view and the binding mechanisms we have already explained.

If you say you want to have a **ViewModel** in a SwiftUI context, this generally proves you don't know what you are talking about.

A ViewModel in MVVM is supposed to be a class that, in addition to performing the bindings, translates from the Model data representation to whatever data format the view requires to display data to a user.

Some weird architectural patterns emerged a few years ago, including controllers, reactive frameworks and ViewModels, with Interactors and Presenters for good measure. All these were, in general, rather nightmarish to work with, and a constant source of "job security" for architects generally paid far too much, given their role in increasing rather than decreasing complexity.

The role of SwiftUI is decreasing this unnatural complexity, allowing better and simpler applications to be written. SwiftUI makes "doing the Devil's work" harder for bad architects. Thanks, Apple! In the next section, we will find out whether some architects have any economic rational incentive in producing systems more complex than useful.

Agency theory and bad architecture

The idea that a company employee (an "agent" in economic theory) might do something that does not benefit his employer (the "principal") if the employee can operate without being held accountable (e.g. because the employee knows that his actions are "hidden") is called "**Agency Theory**." This is a well-known, respected and well-researched sociological theory on the performance of decision-makers in organizations.

If your CEO does not subscribe to this theory, ask them to please give back their bonus, because them getting a generous managerial performance bonus is grounded in this theory being correct.

Agency theory, in practice, is difficult to prove, as proving beyond any doubt that someone is behaving less than honestly is really hard. In legal terms, what matters is not the actual truth (that is subjective most of the time) but what you can successfully prove in court.

However, according to this author, there is typically no good reason to make code less readable or more complex than it should that does not take into account either incompetence, malice, or being overwhelmed with work (because, otherwise, even after a bad day, we could have corrected that code the day after, or the day after that one, or maybe after one week). But let's not be judgmental; it is safer to assume everyone is always doing their best (even when you have a well-grounded suspect, this may not be actually true). So, bad design can sometimes be a rational decision in the best interest of the architect, individually, and not in the interest of the organization that the architect works for, the "Principal" in Agency Theory parlance.

We are all humans, and we all make mistakes, but if you see repeated, systematic bad behavior, you may still have no legal proof, but you might have a strong indication that something foul is afoot.

Agency theory is not "a conspiracy theory." It acknowledges that the system you are building is going to be the result of human interaction, and the human element part is often the prevalent, most risky part. Almost all technical problems are usually way easier than the interactions among the humans developing them. An expert on the management of software projects defined this kind of activity as "herding cats."

By increasing complexity, you will increase the probability of your project not reaching a successful outcome, and this is known as increasing project risk. It is also usually demotivating and exerts a heavy price in terms of the mental health of the development team in the process. Architects, and those of you who want to become architects, should use complexity only to achieve something for a well-defined purpose and not to look smart and be fancy. Failing to do so results in "crunches", "death marches", and overworking.

If you are a smart developer, you will want to be as lazy as possible and use your mind to better serve your client, do more with your system, and provide your user more value. Never use your intelligence to solve the complex-to-understand problems you caused all by yourself. If you do, there'll be no pats on the back for you.

Giving a promotion to an architect because they created a complex solution to a problem that was simple is like rewarding an arsonist who happens to be a firefighter for having done such a spectacular good job.

The fight may have been exhausting but was totally unneeded, and the consequences were harmful to begin with.

In the next section, I will take a closer look at what Clean architecture is and what it is not.

Clean Architecture

In terms of "pre-made" *ready meal-style* architecture, some might claim to have been inspired by "Clean Architecture" or that they offer an implementation of it. That is extremely strange, suspicious even. I doubt they actually read and, what's more, understood the book *Clean Architecture* by Robert Martin.

Sometimes, all these people do is implement at face value an architectural diagram that was given as an example in that book. You should stop asking for recipes and implementing them in a piecemeal fashion.

What Robert Martin really observes in his book, which we can consider a fundamental discovery, is that in "real architecture," the one related to houses and buildings, we have **blueprints** that are easily recognizable in terms of the purpose of the buildings they depict. *Architecture is about intent.*

You can tell the different intentional functions of a building by examining its blueprint.

A cathedral will not have the same blueprint (map) as a theater, a parking lot, a school, or a villa. Different buildings with different functionalities will have different blueprint maps, and they will have easily recognizable structures.

This is sadly often not the case in the architecture of computer applications, and mobile applications are just a sub-case of that more general case.

In software systems, you too often see that the resulting application system does not have its own unique recognizable structure, even in terms of folder structure, but often, the folder structure is instead just dictated by the framework.

Robert Martin augmented that he could just recognize that a particular web application had been written in Ruby on Rails, a popular framework for web application at the time his book was written, as he knew that framework well as a web application developer.

That was way different from having a different blueprint, like in "real architecture" (the one dealing with the design of living spaces), where a cathedral does not use the same blueprint as a parking lot.

So, the idea of just implementing "clean architecture" as a reusable pattern that you use by following boilerplate code, producing always the same structure, even in terms of file structures, their names, and having to rely on Xcode custom templates, due to the complexity of the boilerplate code, makes no sense. That is normally the case with VIPER, a pattern that was quite popular in the mobile community a few years ago.

VIPER stands for **View, Interactor, Presenter, Entitity, and Router**. It is not a pattern that I would recommend, as it entails writing a lot of boilerplate code that adds to the complexity of the code.

VIPER is not an implementation of a "clean architecture," and there are other popular (in UIKit) "architectures" that also claim to be "clean architectures."

So, one of the reasons why some "architectures" have **interactors** and **presenters** is just because these classes were needed in the Ruby on Rails-based example in the book *Clean Architecture*. We use Swift on Apple operating systems. Ruby on Rails is the wrong context.

Are these architectural patterns really needed in iOS, and in SwiftUI in particular?

In a word, no, and you don't need to implement MVVM by having a bridge class named ViewModel if you are in a SwiftUI context.

A very confused developer might call an observable object class "ViewModel" in SwiftUI without ever understanding what the function of a ViewModel should be, in a proper MVVM context.

Imagine that you have built some communication layer and had to declare that as an `ObservableObject` or a `StateObject`. Depending on who is responsible for its deallocation, you should probably refactor your app further, but what you have is not a **ViewModel**; it is your **Model**!

You may want to call it a ViewModel only for "cultural compatibility reasons" – that is, if this is the name that the team you are working with finds easier to conceptualize and understand because it is more commonly called this, despite this file not containing translation code from View to Model and vice versa.

In modern SwiftUI, the binding mechanisms offered by the ViewModel are already there and performed by the View. If you need to perform any form of data translation, you could use a simple wrapper or any other convenient technique offered by Swift.

In SwiftUI, the View is already your ViewModel.

So, if you write an additional bridging class between the Model and the View, in SwiftUI, you are doing things wrong; you are overcomplicating things. This will cost you at least twice the complexity, for no good reason.

In SwiftUI, you have native binding mechanisms, the ones we mentioned at the beginning of this chapter, that allow you to write models and views separately, with changing of the values in the Model state being automatically reflected in the View.

And if you say you use a ViewModel, at least please use a full-blown **MVVM** pattern; don't just go calling whatever pleases you arbitrary names that you don't really understand.

In the next section, we will discuss another sociological explanation of bad architecture, Conway's law.

The dark side of app architecture and Conway's lawConway's law states that organizations design systems that resemble their communication patterns and structure. Dysfunctional organizations end up designing dysfunctional software. The complexity of the seven ISO layers in network architecture is a kind of tongue-in-cheek joke about ISO's software standard being as complex as the organization that originated it. The ISO model in networking did not win; on the internet we all use, the networking protocol is TCP/IP. That protocol was produced by ARPA and was designed essentially as military research during the Cold War; it's simpler, with many levels of complexity less, easier to use and understand, and faster.

In organizations where technical decisions are more political than it is usual, it is common for lead developers and "architects" to be concerned with power and their role's position of privilege compared to other developers, to the point that they might be incentivized economically to keep their role by means of obscurity and, in general, by designing bad systems that are difficult to understand and maintain.

They might use some undocumented software design pattern of their own making, some proprietary framework or pattern that they never explain in great detail and is difficult to understand and maintain. I have seen some people, in old UIKit times, use proprietary frameworks of their own design that used as a single design element `UITableView`.

They needed `SplitView` and a custom tab bar on iPad. Instead of using the appropriate UI elements, and leveraging `ViewController` containment, they did everything using just `UITableViews`. When they needed a scrollable something horizontally they just used an affine transform and rotated the UI element by 90 degrees. I also saw people designing something weird, such as their own asynchronous multithreaded management of an iOS UI, within a really small team, by means of callbacks. That actually succeed, to an extent, due to bona-fide geniuses and extremely hard work, before eventually collapsing as an approach. That kind of creativity is seldom good for developers, the team, the client, or in general the company.

The managers in companies where these things tend to happen often delegate responsibility to lead developers exclusively, without any measure or accountability, and take a detached view, unconcerned with software quality. Sometimes, they don't want to be held accountable for personally having promoted bad "rockstar" developers, who may be experts at writing code that nobody else reads easily. This is not usually a merit; unless you have good reasons to write complex code that is hard to read, you should avoid doing so. If you need to write complex code, at the very least document it thoroughly and explain why you did what, very precisely and thoroughly.

If you want to learn why promoting a capable technician who lacks any managerial skills to a managerial role tends to be a bad choice, try researching *The Peter's Principle*. It is a book written by a humorist, but it is standard suggested reading for management consultants and project managers.

Managers empowering the worst developers to lead might even claim to be following an agile process, but without the developers having any form of autonomy or being respected or empowered. They too often see the developers as substitutable cogs that are just some kind of machinery they need to operate. Alternatively, they might idealize developers as not needing "creativity" or creativity in developers being bad, while it is good in designers.

They often refer to developers as "coders," implying that developers just must follow orders. They are not usually encouraged to perform any analysis or actually do any individual thinking. In some organizations, the developer is just asked to "implement" a design and *improve* the design to be "pixel-perfect."

In such organizations, which way too often claim to be "innovation-focused," innovation is allowed to happen only in the minds of selected individuals, and recognition is often denied or free thinking is frowned upon if this strange activity comes from "unsanctioned" free-range developers.

Then, this *strange thinking activity of thinking* about deep technical problems and structure, coming from lowly software engineers, is not considered socially acceptable and is too often sabotaged.

If an engineer gives too strong signals they are competent but risk overshadowing the highest-paid person in the room, then they might end up being attacked for talking too much and being too verbose, or poor communication may be used as an excuse not to promote the poor employee. After all, they were "just an engineer."

In such organizations, it is usually the "in-charge" architect, project manager, or lead who will try to quash too much free thinking, if the "thought leader" is so brittle in their leadership role to see themselves challenged, rather than helped by their more independently minded and capable contributors. Rather than trying to grow other leaders, these "leaders" will try to weed out the competition. And typically, the company rhetoric, symbols, and internal communication in these companies are focused on praising the leader's achievements, sometimes to the point of having personality cult status of the already selected few in power roles.

This is typically the situation in some start-ups and scale-ups, where the founding members are present in all company pictures, and when one of them, for any reason, leaves the company, history is rewritten. The former founding member, who was responsible for building the whole architectural stack and every form of advancement, is quickly airbrushed out of existence from the company brochures and the official portraits of the "founders." The founders of Apple were more than just two people in a garage; there were three different founders. As an exercise, please do some web research on the actual history of Apple and other very large companies; you will find surprises. The ancient Romans called this **damnatio memoriae** (breaking statues and erasing the name of the guilty from all written records).

In some architectural engineering approaches used in software development, such as SRE, some critical architectural functions are instead democratically delegated to everybody. Provided that the technical level of the developers is high, and all the developers are highly competent and cooperative, this is a quite an ideal approach.

If you want a secure and reliable system, it is everybody's job to understand and be trained to understand and decide appropriately about security, data integrity, protocols, and hard synchronization problems, and how to make sure that you can have a system running 24/7 and still be able to upgrade it, without stopping during the deployment of the upgrades!

Of course, this makes sense in some companies, but not necessarily in yours, and your mileage will vary, a lot.

TCA, The Composable Architecture

For completeness, I will mention one of the latest additions to the collection of third-party "architectures" for iOS and Apple development. **TCA, The Composable Architecture** is a framework implemented as a library developed by PointFree: `https://www.pointfree.co`.

Unfortunately, TCA is not fully open source nor fully explained by a textbook when it comes to its documentation, as the PointFree business model is based on a subscription model. Some information, however, is available publicly, in particular on GitHub: `https://github.com/pointfreeco/ swift-composable-architecture`

TCA is conceptually based on Redux, a software pattern used in Javascript frontend development, normally used with React.

Redux and TCA are two state management frameworks used in software development to manage and centralize the state of an application, making it predictable and easier to understand. Redux was originally designed for React applications in the JavaScript ecosystem, while TCA is specifically tailored for Swift and iOS development with SwiftUI. Despite their different target platforms, both frameworks share several core concepts and principles.

One of the core principles shared by both TCA and Redux is the idea of having a single source of truth for the application's state, which means storing the entire state of the application in a centralized store. This approach makes state management more predictable and debugging easier.

Another principle shared by both frameworks is the treatment of state as immutable. When the state needs to be updated, a new state is created instead of modifying the existing state directly. This helps prevent unwanted side effects and makes state changes easier to track, understand, and test. Redux and TCA both use reducers to handle state changes. Reducers are pure functions that take the current state and an action as arguments and return the new state. This approach ensures that the same state and action input will always produce the same new state output, enhancing predictability and testability.

Both frameworks use the concept of *actions* to describe state changes. Actions are dispatched to the store and indicate what kind of state change should occur. Reducers then interpret these actions and return a new state based on the type of action. Both frameworks also support the composition of reducers, which allows for breaking down the application state and logic into smaller, manageable parts that can be combined to form the overall application logic. This makes the code base more maintainable and scalable.

Finally, both frameworks have a mechanism for handling side effects that result from state changes or actions. Redux uses middleware, while TCA uses effects. Effects allow for operations such as API calls, logging, or asynchronous tasks to be executed in response to certain actions, without compromising the purity of reducers. Purity in the context of functional programming means that an FP language should in theory not have side effects, such as mutating the values of variables. However, side effects are always necessary whenever a program needs to interact with the external world, e.g., writing to a file or handling user I/O.

Conceptually, TCA is structured as shown in the following figure:

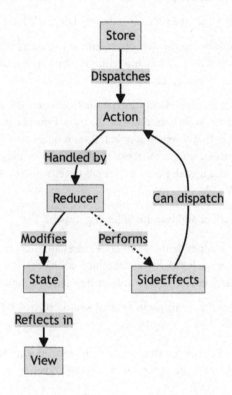

Figure 11.3 – TCA, The Composable Architecture

This diagram illustrates at a conceptual level the overall flow of data in TCA. This flow is very similar to Redux's:

- **Store**: The state of the application lives here. It is the core and single point of truth that must be easily accessible from any part of the application.

- **Dispatches**: These signal that something has happened within the app. These are action creators – simply JavaScript objects describing events – and they might have some data about some event that has taken place.

- **Action**: An object with the sole purpose of telling a reducer how the state should be changed. Normally, it has a property of type, describing the action to take, but it may also have other data.

- **Reduced by a Reducer**: A **reducer** is a function that determines how the state could change in response to an action and in so doing returns a new state. It takes in the previous state and an action as its parameters. This comes as an analogy with the **reduce** operation on collections, which executes an operation on a collection, for example, computing the sum of all elements in the collection, returning a result that has the same type of the elements of the collection.

  - **Modifies State**: The **reducer** produces a new state based on the received action.

  - **Reflects in View**: The updated state is used to update the UI to reflect the most current state.

  - **Side Effects**: The **actions** also involve operations with side effects, such as API calls. The side effects do not have a direct relationship with updating state and, therefore, state transitions are "pure" and easier to understand.

  - **Can Dispatch**: Once the **side effects** are handled, new **actions** can be dispatched as a result, and the cycle continues. Solid lines describe the usual flow of data, while dashed lines indicate an optional side effect that dispatches new actions if necessary. This pattern centralizes state, in the sense that it uses a single "source of truth" to help manage **state** in a more predictable way and tries to make it easier for developers to reason about state modifications inside the application.

TCA is not exempt from criticism and has the following drawbacks:

- Essentially, you become dependent on someone's else "architecture," which may or may not be adequate for the problem at hand. If you encounter problems, you may be worse off than with a completely custom architecture that you have developed yourself and you fully understand.

- TCA has a rather steep learning curve and seems to not be particularly efficient for large-scale applications.

In general, while being more articulated than most architectural frameworks commonly proposed for mobile applications, TCA has some aspects that I would consider red flags:

- TCA encourages a standardized approach to architecture, trying to transform the work of a software architect into a problem of memorizing a framework designed by someone else, with the developers being forced to make the problem at hand fit the pattern rather than the other way around. Architecture is all about intentional design; it should never be a mnemonic exercise.

- You can think of TCA as a "prefabricated" building plan in "real architecture," and it shares some of the drawbacks you can imagine with this approach: a pre-made standard design rarely compares with the quality of an ad hoc, precisely tailored design.

- You also need all your developers to learn TCA's approach, and the cognitive load (the mental effort necessary to understand this framework) will likely be higher than you would expect from reading the online description.

- Also, adopting TCA will introduce a dependency throughout your whole software architecture, at a fundamental level, making the maintenance of your application a lot more risky in the long term as you will have to depend on a third party at a very basic level and they may choose to maintain and evolve this framework in ways that do not necessarily match your own specific project needs.

Personally, I would suggest you study this architectural pattern, experiment with it, and learn from the techniques it uses, rather than espousing this approach in production on a piecemeal basis.

Unfortunately, not everything related to TCA is exactly spelled out and clearly documented, and if you encounter problems, you might need to pay its developers if you are not able to find a solution on your own.

I would consider trusting any such framework too much in a production environment a bad idea. You can easily achieve the same results on your own, provided you are familiar with software design patterns at a fundamental level. You will have more control over the end result by using your own DIY approach. And in using a DIY approach, you will learn more in the process.

Summary

In this chapter, we tried to give you a glimpse on the main concepts that underline software architecture and a brief description of what software architecture work entails. As this is not just a job involving programming concepts, we took the liberty to look at the topic from some other angles besides that of strictly computer science, as these different perspectives are related to working as an architect in a business context.

In the next chapter, we will start examining modern structured concurrency.

Part 6: Beyond Basics

This part tries to cover some parts that are indispensable for professional development, including the core aspects of data management within SwiftUI applications. We start with an examination of Core Data. You'll discover its capabilities for local data storage, seamless integration with SwiftUI, and practical applications. We will examine the evolution of concurrency in Swift, transitioning from old-school threading models to a contemporary structured concurrency approach, with a spotlight on the async-await pattern and task management to enhance application performance and responsiveness.

Then, we will introduce SwiftData, Apple's latest ORM framework, designed to refine data handling in SwiftUI, moving beyond the capabilities of Core Data.

We will then move on to integrating REST services within SwiftUI, a critical component for iOS applications requiring network communication. You'll acquire skills to make HTTP/HTTPS requests using `URLSession`, serialize and deserialize data with Codable, and ensure secure, efficient network communication.

Concluding this part, we will examine the innovative Apple Vision Pro mixed-reality headset. You'll discover its potential for spatial computing and the available development tools for visionOS, and you'll start developing immersive applications for this cutting-edge platform.

This part contains the following chapters:

- *Chapter 12, Persistence with Core Data*
- *Chapter 13, Modern Structured Concurrency*
- *Chapter 14, An Introduction to SwiftData*
- *Chapter 15, Consuming REST Services in SwiftUI*
- *Chapter 16, Exploring the Apple Vision Pro*

12
Persistence with Core Data

In this chapter, I will introduce Core Data in SwiftUI. Core Data is a persistency framework for Apple systems. We will also briefly talk about persistence from a more general perspective. As Core Data was introduced in 2003 and has constantly evolved since then, it is not possible to completely cover this topic; it would require a large book just by itself. This chapter will be just an introduction to this persistence framework.

In this chapter, we will define persistency, and then we will move on to explain what Core Data is and how it is structured. We will then explain how to use Core Data within SwiftUI and offer guidance on the practical use of Core Data in Xcode. Finally, we will discuss CloudKit, a framework that easily allows you to store persistent data on the cloud.

In this chapter, we're going to cover the following main topics:

- What is persistency?
- What is Core Data?
- Understanding Core Data framework classes
- Using Core Data with SwiftUI
- Creating a Core Data project
- Core Data migrations
- The SQLite data file
- CloudKit

What is persistency?

First, let's define the word *persistency*. Persistency is the ability of application data to survive between successive runs of an application. As is typical of the Apple ecosystem, there are many ways to achieve persistency of data, and each way has different use cases, advantages, and disadvantages.

If you just store application data in volatile memory – that is, RAM – then data won't survive across different launches of the same application; each launch would be "a new beginning," starting from scratch.

Although this approach might suit a handful of specific scenarios, such as projects where there's no requirement to retain information between launches (e.g., basic utility calculations such as unit conversions), you will need the capability to save data to non-volatile memory in most cases. Furthermore, apart from retrieving it, you'll often need to perform additional operations. The usual tasks you anticipate being able to carry out on data are so common that they warrant their own acronym, **CRUD**, which stands for **Create, Read, Update, Delete**.

As you might anticipate, the simplest method to achieve persistent data storage involves writing and subsequently reading files in the data folder associated with your application. However, considering that iOS emerged in 2007, and macOS (formerly known as Mac OS X) has a longer history, it's reasonable to suspect that you don't have to rely solely on a single tool to accomplish this task.

The following table gives you an overview of most of the many different mechanisms you can use that allow you to create data on non-volatile storage and retrieve it. You are expected to be familiar with a least a few of these:

Persistency framework	Use case	Advantages	Disadvantages and limitations
User defaults	User settings and lightweight data	Easy to use and does not need to be set up	Not suitable for sensitive or large data sets
Property List (Plist) files	Configuration files, and very simple data hierarchies	Human-readable, simple, and can be edited in Xcode	Not suitable for complex data, data that changes often, data that contains relations or needs complex queries efficiently
SQLite database	Local relational data storage	A lightweight, SQL interface. Really fast. You can implement a SQL relational database schema in SQLite with very few or no changes from a backend-specified one; just adapt the SQL tables and indexes' creation script. What you know about relational databases simply applies to SQLite. SQLite can be custom-compiled to support strong encryption.	The C API of SQLite can be a problem for strictly mobile developers. You will sometimes need to take care of some multithreading issues. To use SQLite efficiently in a modern object-oriented context, you normally need to create your own persistency/abstraction framework.

Persistency framework	Use case	Advantages	Disadvantages and limitations
Core Data	Complex object graphs, relational data	Object-oriented, feature-rich, fully configurable, acceptable performance, and can use different storage strategies – SQLite, files, RAM. Has support for versioning and automatic data migration across application version changes. Can be integrated easily with CloudKit.	Complex. Has a more difficult learning curve and could be not worth the cost for simple data. Not so easy to debug in complex scenarios. Cannot define tables and indexes using a SQL creation script. Some typical usage scenarios, such as updating data in the background from a backend while ensuring rapid responsiveness and correctness, are non-trivial. It is pretty much "Apple"-only and cannot be ported to non-Apple contexts. However, this approach is applied in the same way to multiple Apple devices, and in this context, it is multiplatform.
File system	User documents and binary data	Full control and flexibility	No built-in sync or backup. Not suitable for complex data, relations, complex queries, or data that keeps constantly changing.
iCloud Key-Value Store	Simple data sync across devices	Easy to use and iCloud integration	Limited to small datasets.

Persistency framework	Use case	Advantages	Disadvantages and limitations
iCloud document storage	Document synchronization across devices	Integrated with iCloud, user familiarity	Limited to user's own iCloud storage. Suitable for documents, but not for complex data, relations, and record-based information.
CloudKit	Structured cloud data and multi-user sync	Scalable, robust, and integrates seamlessly with Core Data. Data "follows" the user seamlessly across different devices belonging to the same user.	Limited to the Apple ecosystem. Data quotas impose limits on apps that are data-intensive.
Firebase Realtime Database/ Firestore	Real-time data sync and no-backend solutions	Real-time, scalable, and relatively simple	Dangerous vendor lock-in, not native to Apple, and similar products simply ceased to be supported/ exist in the past.
Custom backends	Custom server logic and RESTful APIs or other non-REST approaches, such as GraphQL, Apache Thrift, and Google protobufs.	Full control, a programming language, and a database of choice. Often, these tools generate code for both sides – the frontend and backend clients from a single interface description file. Binary communication protocols reduce the band-pass required compared to REST.	Requires server maintenance. Relies on an active internet connection and, therefore, is potentially slow, unavailable, and/or unreliable outside well-connected urban areas. May not support content delivery networks and caching on the server side.
Secure storage (keychain)	Small amounts of sensitive data such as authentication tokens	Encrypted and secure	Limited data types, complexity, and unsuitable for large/complex datasets.

Persistency framework	Use case	Advantages	Disadvantages and limitations
`NSCoding/Codable`	Object serialization is typically in conjunction with backend storage and/or a file system.	Native serialization of custom objects	Only for objects that conform to protocols.

Table 12.1 – The many persistency options in Apple systems

The interesting fact about *Table 12.1* is that this list of many different approaches to Data Persistency on Apple systems, despite being long, is quite probably incomplete and likely to be growing.

In this chapter, we will focus on Core Data as it is commonly used in a SwiftUI context. Core Data is the ideal choice when working with complex datasets that are typically found in professional-quality complex applications. Such applications require a powerful local relational database that can handle large datasets and efficient querying and updating in a systematic way. Additionally, Core Data allows you to select data based on complex criteria. Also, with Core Data, you can have the data integrity assurances that you normally expect from a relational database.

In the next section, I will briefly explain what Core Data is.

What is Core Data?

Core Data is an old Apple programming framework. It first appeared with Mac OS X 10.4 "Tiger" in 2004. It has undergone a lot of changes in the last 20 years. Core Data is an **Object Relational Mapping (ORM)** framework. An ORM is a "method" or framework employed to facilitate the conversion between two disparate type systems in object-oriented programming languages. In our situation, Core Data enables the mapping and conversion of object-oriented objects to and from an underlying relational database. Instead of relying on SQL queries and commands, developers can work in terms of objects, their attributes, and methods. Core Data normally abstracts upon **SQLite**, the default local relational database used by Apple applications. To be precise, besides an SQLite-based relational database, Core Data also allows other "stores" to be specified – for example, instead of a `.sqlite` file, you can use a RAM-based "store" that will not persist anything or even simpler data files, such as XML data files. A RAM-based store is an excellent choice if you need to perform queries rapidly, on data that you are never going to need to store, or if you just want to rapidly run tests and don't want to create any side effects.

To be more specific, Core Data consistently represents objects in RAM, and the process of "persistence" only occurs when you explicitly instruct Core Data to save these objects.

Without an ORM, relational database operations are handled using raw SQL statements embedded in application code. These statements, SQL queries, and commands don't interact with "objects" but rather with tables, rows, and columns.

An ORM allows to achieve a one-to-one predictable mapping of an object-oriented object with a row of a table, described by a corresponding class, and each object has properties that map to the columns of the database table.

Without an ORM, you would need "multiple language programming" within the same application. This becomes an organizational issue, as developers would need to know both the application language, Swift or Objective-C, plus two different languages, SQL and C, used for the database operations. This would introduce an additional level of organizational complexity.

Bear in mind that using an ORM with one-to-one mapping between database entities (tables) and object-oriented classes is not the only approach possible; it is just the approach normally followed by most of the industry.

Unfortunately, this one-to-one mapping approach (e.g., with typical Java ORMs) leads to unnecessarily considering every table and every result type (the result of a query) as separate objects. Traditional ORMs help little in reducing the complexity of large-scale applications, in general, and not necessarily mobile ones. To drastically reduce this complexity, you would need to write your own database persistence stack, return a single type for all possible tabular-based results, and do this efficiently. All these can be achieved in most object-oriented languages by using advanced techniques, but these are well outside the scope of this book.

This custom persistency approach would seldom be justifiable nowadays, as machines become constantly more powerful with every passing year. Also, as an additional disadvantage, if you went full-custom on top of SQLite when you needed to migrate data between application version updates, you would be completely on your own as this approach is not natively supported by any Apple framework. It is not all about maximizing "efficiency" and performance; it is also about minimizing application maintenance costs in the long run.

Most of the time, Core Data is the best possible choice, and writing custom code directly on top of SQLite is never worth it.

However, Apple, as usual, did an excellent job in incrementally refining and making Core Data easier to use with each iteration. The definition of a Core Data object can be implicit; normally, you can just define your data model, and Core Data will create your Entity classes and their properties automatically.

In the next section, I will briefly discuss the theory behind Core Data, explaining the classes that constitute the Core Data framework.

Understanding Core Data framework classes

The following diagram illustrates a simplified, conceptual schema of the relationship among the main objects that are part of the Core Data stack:

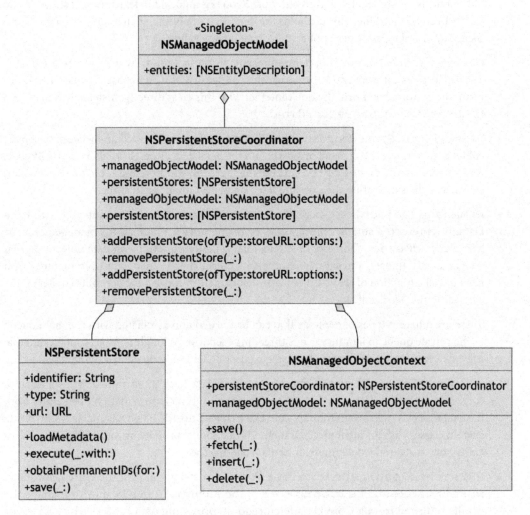

Figure 12.1 – A Core Data simplified conceptual stack

If you are unfamiliar with **UML** notation, the diamond means "contains" or "has-a." In a UML object diagram, the upper part of the rectangle represents the object type, the middle part its properties, and the lower part its methods. A minus sign represents instance properties and methods, while a plus sign represents static or class methods and properties.

Here is a description of the main classes that are the components of Core Data:

- NSManagedObjectModel: This class represents the data model of an application, essentially a database schema for all the entities, attributes, and relationships that a Core Data store contains. This model is usually created and edited using Xcode's graphical model editor and stored inside a .xcdatamodeld file. This file holds the definition of objects, such as property names and their names and types. It does not actually contain any values.

- NSPersistentStore: This class represents the actual physical store where the data is saved. The physical store can be, among other things, a SQLite database, a binary file, or an in-memory store. You normally don't interact with this class directly; instead, it is managed by NSPersistentStoreCoordinator.

- NSPersistentStoreCoordinator: This class acts as an intermediary between the object context, NSManagedObjectContext, and the persistent store, NSPersistentStore. NSPersistentStoreCoordinator manages the addition and removal of persistent stores, as well as mediating the save and fetch operations made against them.

- NSManagedObjectContext: This is the class most often used to interact with Core Data. It represents a single "object space" or in-memory scratchpad for managed objects, NSManagedObject. This is where data manipulation functions on data objects happen – fetch, create, update, and save. All these data object changes happen just in memory. You need to call a function of NSPersistentContainer, save, that commits (writes) these changes to the persistent store.

  There are different types of contexts that can be created and associated with the main queue or the private queue to handle various threading scenarios. A single app can contain multiple contexts – for example, one related to the main queue and one or more for background processing.

- NSManagedObject: This is the data object in Core Data. Each NSManagedObject instance corresponds to a row in the persistent store and is a runtime representation of an entity from the data model. When programming Core Data, NSManagedObject is subclassed to create custom classes with the attributes and methods that model the data in your application. Every entity you create in the data model inherits from this class.

- NSFetchedResultsController: While not strictly part of the Core Data stack, NSFetchedResultsController is commonly used in iOS apps to manage the results returned from a Core Data fetch request, providing data for UITableView or UICollectionView. It also has features to monitor changes in the dataset and automatically update the UI. This class is often considered a purely UIKit-related component. To use NSFetchedResultsController within SwiftUI, you will need to wrap it in an ObservableObject wrapper. Create a class that conforms to the ObservableObject protocol. This class will wrap NSFetchedResultsController and act as a bridge between Core Data and your SwiftUI views. Inside this class, you will need to initialize NSFetchedResultsController with the desired fetch request, context, and other configurations such as sectionNameKeyPath and cacheName if needed.

- Implement the fetching logic in this wrapper class, and use the `NSFetchedResultsControllerDelegate` methods to listen for changes in the data store. In response to changes in data, update the `@Published` properties to notify the SwiftUI views of the updates.

  To provide data to SwiftUI, use `@Published` properties to hold the fetched data (e.g., an array of entities or sections) in a format that SwiftUI can easily consume. You may need to translate from Core Data entities into more SwiftUI-friendly data types if necessary.

  To use the wrapper in SwiftUI views, instantiate your `ObservableObject` wrapper class within a SwiftUI view, either as `@ObservedObject` or via `@EnvironmentObject` if it's provided by a parent view. Use the data from the `@Published` properties to dynamically build your SwiftUI view hierarchy, making sure to respond to updates as the underlying data changes.

- `NSPersistentContainer`: This is a convenience class, first introduced in iOS 10 to simplify the setup of the Core Data stack. It encapsulates `NSManagedObjectModel`, `NSPersistentStoreCoordinator`, and `NSManagedObjectContext` into a single easy-to-manage object. It is the class you need to interact with in modern versions of Core Data. It reads your data model file, setting up `NSManagedObjectModel`. The persistent container controls where data is persisted on the device, loading data from the persistent device so that it can be used by the app. Once these functionalities were separated, developers needed a lot of setup work, but Apple simplified the use of Core Data with `NSPersistentContainer`.

- `NSFetchRequest`: This class defines a query on the data model, including aspects such as the entity to fetch, sorting, and filtering criteria.

If you have started programming on Swift recently, you might be wondering about the mysterious "NS" at the beginning of all these class names. **NS** stands for **NeXT**, which was the operating system for NeXT, the computer created by Steve Jobs after leaving Apple, which Apple used as a foundation of what would later become Mac OS X in 2000, when he came back to lead the company to success with product innovations, culminating with the iPhone. As no "namespaces" existed at that time, such as those nowadays provided by case-less enums in Swift, you would have obtained the same result by using the first two letters of all names inside your code as a substitute for a namespace. NS at the beginning of their names marked all the system provided, Apple's own classes.

In the next section, we will understand how to integrate Core Data with SwiftUI.

Using Core Data with SwiftUI

SwiftUI offers several basic mechanisms to interact with Core Data that are easier to use than UIKit.

The `@FetchRequest` property wrapper allows you to fetch entities from Core Data directly inside your SwiftUI views. It automatically observes the Core Data context, so it will update the view if the data changes.

You can use the @Environment property wrapper to inject NSManagedObjectContext into your SwiftUI view. This is useful for operations such as adding, deleting, or modifying entities.

For more complex scenarios where you want to encapsulate Core Data logic in separate layers, you can use either the @ObservableObject or @StateObject property wrapper, depending on your needs. This approach works well for views that require observing not just Core Data changes but also other types of state or data flow. This is how you can integrate, for instance, NSFetchedResultsController; this is a good choice if you are dealing with a large volume of data that you want to display in a table or a grid.

NSFetchedResultsController is a controller that you can use to manage the results of a Core Data fetch request and display those results to the user. Traditionally, it's used in conjunction with UIKit to populate UITableView or UICollectionView instances. It offers several features, such as caching, sectioning, and automatic updates when the underlying data changes.

NSFetchedResultsController was introduced long before SwiftUI, so it's often considered a UIKt-related component. However, you can use it with SwiftUI as well; it isn't limited to just UIKit applications. SwiftUI offers its own native ways to manage lists and other collections of data, but if you're dealing with large sets of Core Data entities, the efficiencies gained from NSFetchedResultsController can be beneficial.

To integrate NSFetchedResultsController with SwiftUI, you can use an observable object to wrap its functionality. This object can listen for updates from the controller and notify the SwiftUI view to redraw itself when changes occur.

In the next section, we will explain how to create a project that uses Core Data within Xcode.

Creating a Core Data project

The easiest way to create a project that includes Xcode is by choosing a template and checking the **Use Core Data** option box.

The following screenshot shows this:

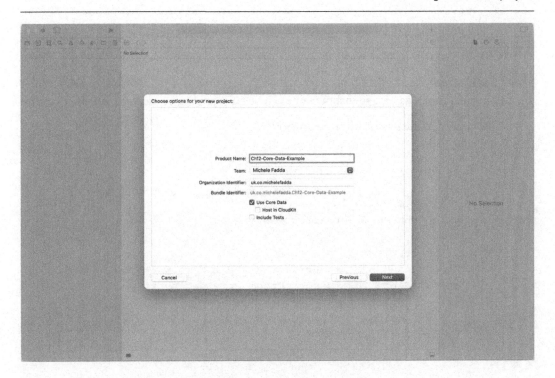

Figure 12.2 – Creating a project and enabling Core Data

By following this approach, the project template will create an `@main` App struct that instantiates `PersistenceController` as a singleton. The name you choose for the project in Xcode will be pre-pended to the app to determine the default name for that struct, and this will match the corresponding swift file generated by the template. The project creation template will create code inside that file that passes this `PersistenceController` and the public `managedObjectContext`, using `.environment` at the Composition Root so that they can be accessed globally by any view in the app. Note that `.environment` is used instead of `.environmentObject`, as these are system- rather than user-defined.

The "Composition Root" is a complex name for a simple concept – it is the single place where the instantiation of the application objects takes place. In SwiftUI, this is normally the instantiation of the app window, within the `@main` App struct.

In UIKit, this would have been inside `UIAppDelegate` or `UISceneDelegate`, depending on the version of iOS, typically the `application(_:didFinishLaunchingWithOptions:)` method.

The Composition Root is a common name used to discuss application structure that you should be aware of. It is also a good idea to place all the instantiation-related code in close proximity, in order to make the code base more readable and easier to understand.

The Core Data project template also creates the `Persistence.swift` and `ContentView. swift` files.

The `Persistence.swift` file defines a shared `PersistenceController` as a singleton, as well as `PersistentContainer` so that the same Core Data setup can be used across the application.

Here is the content of the `Persistence.swift` file:

```swift
import CoreData

struct PersistenceController {
    static let shared = PersistenceController()

    static var preview: PersistenceController = {
        let result = PersistenceController(inMemory: true)
        let viewContext = result.container.viewContext
        for _ in 0..<10 {
            let newItem = Item(context: viewContext)
            newItem.timestamp = Date()
        }
        do {
            try viewContext.save()
        } catch {
            // Replace this implementation with code to handle the
error appropriately.
            // fatalError() causes the application to generate a crash
log and terminate. You should not use this function in a shipping
application, although it may be useful during development.
            let nsError = error as NSError
            fatalError("Unresolved error \(nsError), \(nsError.
userInfo)")
        }
        return result
    }()


    let container: NSPersistentContainer

    init(inMemory: Bool = false) {
        container = NSPersistentContainer(name: "Ch12_
CoreDataExample")
        if inMemory {
            container.persistentStoreDescriptions.first!.url =
URL(fileURLWithPath: "/dev/null")
        }
        container.loadPersistentStores(completionHandler: {
```

```
(storeDescription, error) in
            if let error = error as NSError? {
                // Replace this implementation with code to handle the
error appropriately.
                // fatalError() causes the application to generate
a crash log and terminate. You should not use this function in a
shipping application, although it may be useful during development.


                /*
                Typical reasons for an error here include:
                * The parent directory does not exist, cannot be
created, or does not allow writing.
                * The persistent store is not accessible, due to
permissions or data protection while the device is locked.
                * The device is out of space.
                * The store could not be migrated to the current
model version.
                Check the error message to determine what the actual
problem was.
                */
                fatalError("Unresolved error \(error), \(error.
userInfo)")
            }
        })
        container.viewContext.automaticallyMergesChangesFromParent =
true
    }
}
```

Let's understand the code for this file:

- `PersistenceController` struct definition: The `PersistenceController` struct is defined to encapsulate Core Data stack management.

- **A static shared instance**: It defines a static property named `shared`, which follows the Singleton pattern to create and share a single instance of `PersistenceController`. This is the instance used in the application, and it can write data to the persistent store.

- **A static preview instance**: Another static property named `preview` is defined. It uses a closure to create and initialize an instance of `PersistenceController`. This instance is set up with an in-memory Core Data store and populated with 10 sample `Item` objects.

- **A container property**: A container property of type `NSPersistentContainer` is declared. This container is responsible for managing the Core Data stack. The persistent container is responsible for the management and retrieval of data.

- **Initializer (init)**: This defines the initializer for `PersistenceController`. This initializer takes an optional Boolean parameter, `inMemory`, which defaults to `false`. The initializer creates `NSPersistentContainer`, with the name corresponding to the project name.

- If the `inMemory` parameter of the initializer is `true`, it configures the container to use an in-memory store by setting the store's URL to a dummy URL (`/dev/null`). The in-memory instantiation is useful for tests and previews, and Xcode is smart enough to generate an in-memory version for this purpose automatically. For this specific use case, actual persistent storage is not needed for SwiftUI previews.

- The `loadPersistentStores` method is called on the container to set up the Core Data stack. This method loads the persistent store, normally the actual SQLite data file, according to the provided configuration. Any errors that occur during this process are handled in the closure.

There isn't typically much you can normally do, at application setup, if the Core Data data file load fails, as this failure would be normally catastrophic in production. You should test very thoroughly before submitting your app.

When the `save()` function is invoked on an instance of `NSManagedObjectContext`, if there are changes, this file will get physically updated and written to; this operation would be a "commit" in SQL parlance.

Core Data does not have automatic commit available as a feature; if you need to persist data, you have to invoke this write operation explicitly.

In the next editions of Xcode, Apple could decide to change this template, so it is best if you try to get the general gist of Core Data usage, rather than focusing on the exact details of the code generated by the project template, which might change in the future.

While, in general, using a Singleton is a bad practice, in this case, Core Data uses this pattern to share access to a single instance at the system level of a unique resource in the system. It is one of the few cases in which its use is acceptable. Bear in mind that Core Data is quite old, and some of the well-grounded "dislike" toward the Singleton pattern accumulated as time passed.

The `container.viewContext` view context is configured to automatically merge changes from parent contexts, which is a common setup to manage changes in Core Data. This is needed if the database is updated from different parts of an application UI or from a background thread.

Normally, you would want to have parent and child contexts if you want to be able to commit or discard changes performed – for example, while editing a form (a modal sheet could be used for that purpose in SwiftUI).

You would normally declare a parent context for the whole app and a child context for the input form view. If the parent form is updated, the child context will be updated automatically. However, if changes happen while editing the form, these can be discarded. For them to be committed, you would need to save both the child and the parent contexts. A change occurring just in the child context would "be lost" and ignored, unless it was also committed to the parent context.

The following code fragment illustrates the child context save code pattern:

```
let parentContext = NSManagedObjectContext(concurrencyType:
.mainQueueConcurrencyType)
parentContext.persistentStoreCoordinator = persistentStoreCoordinator

let childContext = NSManagedObjectContext(concurrencyType:
.privateQueueConcurrencyType)
childContext.parent = parentContext

// Perform changes in childContext
// ...
// Save child context. This pushes changes to parentContext but does
not save them to the disk
try? childContext.save()

// Save parent context to push changes to the persistent store (saves
them physically to disk)
try? parentContext.save()
```

The project template also creates a `ContentView.swift` file that creates an editable list of timestamps, which can be added and deleted. The `ContentView_preview` is initialized with a preview Core Data instance, also created in the Persistence file. That preview is initialized with 10 sample items and does not store data permanently, due to having been initialized as an "in-memory" database. While this template does a good job of demonstrating Core Data functionality, it places quite a lot of code in `ContentView`. Rather than showing you the swift file generated by the Core Data Xcode template as is, I will illustrate how we could refactor this code in a manner more suitable to a larger app, separating the view part from the Core Data operations related to the view. Here is the `CoreDataOperations.swift` file:

```
import CoreData
import SwiftUI

class CoreDataOperations {

    static func addItem(context: NSManagedObjectContext) {
        let newItem = Item(context: context)
        newItem.timestamp = Date()

        do {
            try context.save()
        } catch {
            let nsError = error as NSError
            fatalError("Unresolved error \(nsError), \(nsError.
```

```
userInfo)")
        }
    }


    static func deleteItems(context: NSManagedObjectContext, offsets:
IndexSet, items: FetchedResults<Item>) {
        offsets.map { items[$0] }.forEach(context.delete)

        do {
            try context.save()
        } catch {
            let nsError = error as NSError
            fatalError("Unresolved error \(nsError), \(nsError.
userInfo)")
        }
    }
}
```

Note that some would call this thing a "ViewModel." As we don't follow an MVVM pattern in SwiftUI, we don't need a ViewModel to handle both the data translation and the binding from a model to a view. Note that such a separate layer has a purpose, and we can call it with a more descriptive name, `CoreDataOperations`. If you needed to perform generic logic elaboration within the view, `ViewLogic` would probably be more appropriate than ViewModel, as we don't need any ViewModels properly called in a SwiftUI architecture. ViewModels are part of the MVVM architectural presentation pattern, which sometimes gets adopted in SwiftUI when developers try to mimic approaches that had a reason to exist on other platforms, such as Microsoft's .NET, but cannot be considered best practices in the SwiftUI Apple ecosystem.

In SwiftUI, you don't need MVVM at all; just use views, models, and the native bindings offered by SwiftUI.

Here is the refactored `ContentView.swift` file:

```
import SwiftUI
import CoreData

struct ContentView: View {
    @Environment(\.managedObjectContext) private var viewContext
    @FetchRequest(
        sortDescriptors: [NSSortDescriptor(keyPath: \Item.timestamp,
ascending: true)],
        animation: .default)
    private var items: FetchedResults<Item>

    var body: some View {
```

```
        NavigationView {
            List {
                ForEach(items) { item in
                    NavigationLink {
                        Text("Item at \(item.timestamp!, formatter:
itemFormatter)")
                    } label: {
                        Text(item.timestamp!, formatter:
itemFormatter)
                    }
                }
                .onDelete(perform: deleteItems)
            }
            .toolbar {
#if os(iOS)
                ToolbarItem(placement: .navigationBarTrailing) {
                    EditButton()
                }
#endif
                ToolbarItem {
                    Button(action: addItem) {
                        Label("Add Item", systemImage: "plus")
                    }
                }
            }
            Text("Select an item")
        }
    }
    private func addItem() {
        withAnimation {
            CoreDataOperations.addItem(context: viewContext)
        }
    }

    private func deleteItems(offsets: IndexSet) {
        withAnimation {
            CoreDataOperations.deleteItems(context: viewContext,
offsets: offsets, items: items)
        }
    }
}
private let itemFormatter: DateFormatter = {
    let formatter = DateFormatter()
    formatter.dateStyle = .short
```

```
    formatter.timeStyle = .medium
    return formatter
}()
struct ContentView_Previews: PreviewProvider {
    static var previews: some View {
        ContentView().environment(\.managedObjectContext,
PersistenceController.preview.container.viewContext)
    }
}
```

Let's understand the preceding code:

- `@Environment(\.managedObjectContext) private var viewContext`: This line sets up an environment variable, `viewContext`, that contains `managedObjectContext` used by Core Data.

- `@FetchRequest`: This is a property wrapper that fetches `Item` objects from Core Data. It sorts these items based on their `timestamp` property in ascending order.

- `NavigationView`: This contains a stack for navigating hierarchical content.

- `List`: Displays rows of data.

- `ForEach(items)`: Iterates over each `Item` fetched from Core Data.

- `NavigationLink`: Provides a navigation link to details of the selected item.

- `.toolbar`: This modifier defines the two toolbar items – a `ToolbarItem` "edit" button available only for iOS, and an "Add item" button to add new items is also present.

- `Text("Select an item")`: This is the default text shown on the detail side of `NavigationView`.

- `addItem()`: Calls `CoreDataOperations.addItem()` to add an item to Core Data.

- `deleteItems(offsets: IndexSet)`: Calls `CoreDataOperations.deleteItems()` to delete the selected items.

In the next section, we will understand how to create a Core Data data-model file.

Working with the data model file

When you enable Core Data, in the `App` struct file you will find a data-model file that you can edit with the Xcode editor, as shown in the following figure:

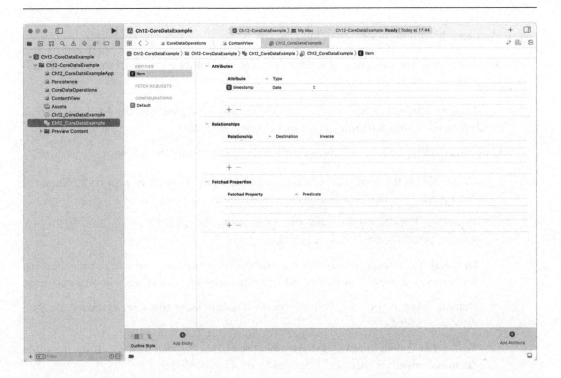

Figure 12.3 – Editing the data model

The editor is divided into two panes, a left pane and right pane.

Let's understand the options under the left pane:

- **ENTITIES**: These are the core building blocks of your Core Data model. You can think of an entity as a table in a database:

  - **Adding an entity**: Click the **Add Entity** button (the + button at the bottom) to add a new entity

  - **Renaming an entity**: Double-click on the entity to rename it

- **FETCH REQUESTS**: Predefined queries that can be executed to fetch entities that match certain criteria.

- **CONFIGURATIONS**: Configurations allow you to group different entities together under one name so that they can be used together more easily.

Let's understand the options under the right pane:

- **Attributes**: Attributes are the properties or fields of your entities; they correspond to columns in a database table:

  - **Adding an attribute**: Select an entity, and in the right-hand pane, find the Attributes section. Click on the + **Add attribute** option to add a new attribute.

  - **Setting data types**: After adding an attribute, you can specify the following:

    - **Name**: This is the name that you'll use to access this attribute in your code. Choose a descriptive name that clearly indicates the attribute's purpose.

    - **Type**: Core Data supports various data types, such as `String`, `Int16`, `Int32`, `Int64`, `Float`, `Double`, `Boolean`, and `Date`.

    - **Optional**: You can specify whether the attribute is optional or required. If it's required and you try to save an entity without a value for this attribute, Core Data will throw an error.

    - **Default Value**: If you wish, you can specify a default value that Core Data will use if no value is provided.

    - **Transient**: Transient attributes are not stored in the persistent store. These are often calculated attributes that can be derived from other attributes.

    - **Indexed**: For faster searches, you can index an attribute. However, keep in mind that indexing takes up additional disk space and can slow down insert and delete operations. However, it will be much faster in search, transforming an $O(n)$ seek operation on the database into an $O(1)$ one in terms of complexity, that is will execute in constant time independently from the number of elements rather than in time linearly dependent on the number of items involved in the operation.

    - **Validation**: You can also specify various validation rules here:

      - **Minimum and Maximum**: For numerical types, you can specify minimum and maximum values

      - **Regular Expression**: For string types, you can specify a regex pattern that the string should match

      - **Max Length**: For string and data types, you can specify a maximum length

- **Relationships**: Relationships define how entities relate to each other.

  - **Adding a Relationship**: Select an entity and then find the **Relationships** section in the right-hand pane. Add a new relationship and specify the destination entity and other details. The destination is another attribute belonging to another entity. A relationship can be configured as follows:

    - **Name**: It should be given a name that makes the purpose of the relationship clear.

    - **Destination**: Set the destination entity for the relationship. This determines what type of object the relationship will point to.

    - **Inverse**: Optionally, you can specify an inverse relationship. If you have a relationship from entity A to entity B, the inverse relationship would be from entity B back to entity A.

    - **Type**: Choose the type of relationship:

    - **To-One**: Indicates a one-to-one relationship.

    - **To-Many**: Indicates a one-to-many or many-to-many relationship.

    - **Delete rule**: Specifies what should happen when the object at the "source" of the relationship is deleted. You can choose among four delete rules:

      - **Nullify**: Deletes the relationship but doesn't remove the destination object.

      - **Cascade**: Deletes the destination objects of the relationship when the object is deleted

      - **Deny**: Prevents deletion of the source object if there's a relationship

      - **No Action**: Does nothing (allows relationships to be handled manually)

    - **Optional**: Specifies whether the relationship is optional or required.

    - **Transient**: Marks the relationship as not stored in the persistent store. Useful for temporary calculations and derived values.

    - **Ordered**: If this is checked, the relationship is treated as an ordered set; otherwise, it is treated as an unordered set.

- **Fetched Properties**:

  - **Adding a fetched property**: Select an entity and then find the **Fetched Properties** section in the right-hand pane. Add a new relationship by clicking on + and specify the fetched properties. These are queries that allow an entity to fetch objects based on a set of conditions. A fetched property has a name and a predicate; a predicate corresponds to the `Where` clause in SQL (e.g., `age > 35` to select all rows containing the `age` attribute with a value bigger than 35). Once you've added a new fetch request, you can configure it in different ways:

    - **Name**: Give your fetch request a meaningful name so that it's easier to reference in code.

    - **Predicate**: This is an optional field where you can specify the conditions that the fetched entities need to meet. You write predicates in a string format, like how you would write them in code for a WHERE clause – for example, age > 25.

    - **Sort Descriptors**: You can specify how the fetched results should be sorted. You'll need to provide the attribute name (key) and indicate whether the sort should be ascending or descending (`ascending` being a `Boolean`).

    - **Batch Size**: To improve performance, especially with large datasets, you can set the number of objects that the fetch request should return in each batch.

    - **Fetch Limit**: If you only need a certain number of results, you can specify a fetch limit to restrict the number of objects returned. This is equivalent to the `LIMIT` statement in SQL (e.g., a fetch limit of one would return the first fetched row).

    - **Result Type**: By default, this will be set to **Managed Object**, but you can also choose other types such as **Dictionary**, **Count**, or **Managed Object IDs**.

    - **Properties to Fetch**: If you're using a result type such as **Dictionary**, you might want to specify which attributes to include in the fetched results. You can do that here.

    - **Affected Stores**: Here, you can specify which persistent stores the fetch request should interact with, if you have multiple stores.

Once you have set up your entities, attributes, relationships, and so on, you can normally behave as if any entity you created inside the data-model editor had been created in code, as a class inheriting from `NSManagedObject`.

In the next section, we will talk about Core Data migrations.

Core Data migrations

Migrations are how Core Data helps developers adapt their data models to changing requirements. As applications evolve, it is often needed to change the data model; however, existing users will have their data stored in an old format. A Core Data migration helps move this old data into a new updated data model without losing vital information.

Core Data allows three types of migration:

- **Lightweight migration**: The simplest migration, which is almost automatic. It is achievable only if the database changes are minor, such as adding or removing one attribute, or changing an attribute status between mandatory and optional.

- **Staged migration**: This migration is more complex and required for more complex changes, such as renaming an attribute or changing data types or relationships.

- **Manual migration**: This is used when you need to perform complex transformations on data that cannot be covered by staged and lightweight migrations.

To prepare to migrate your data-model file, you need to follow these steps:

1. **Open your .xcdatamodeld file**: This file contains your Core Data model.

2. **Add a new version**: In Xcode, you can add a new version by selecting the data model and then choosing **Editor | Add Model Version...**.

3. **Give a name to the new version**: You'll need to give the new version a name and base it on the existing version.

4. **Make changes**: In the new version, perform the necessary changes such as adding new attributes, entities, or relationships.

5. **Set the current version**: In the Xcode Inspector, set the new version as the current version.

To enable lightweight migrations, you need to add a few options in the code when initializing `NSPersistentContainer`, as shown in the following code fragment:

```
let container = NSPersistentContainer(name: "YourModelName")
// Sets the container to automatically attempt lightweight migration
let persistentStoreDescription = NSPersistentStoreDescription(url:
storeURL)
persistentStoreDescription.shouldMigrateStoreAutomatically = true
persistentStoreDescription.shouldInferMappingModelAutomatically = true

container.persistentStoreDescriptions = [persistentStoreDescription]
```

For more complex migrations, consult the Core Data documentation: `https://developer.apple.com/documentation/coredata/migrating_your_data_model_automatically`.

The SQLite data file

When you compile an iOS app and execute it in the simulator, the SQLite file containing the storage for Core Data gets copied to the sandbox folder belonging to the application. This file physically contains the database objects and gets written to persist data. On some occasions, SQLite will also use additional temp files and, if write ahead is enabled, a WAL file for data not already persisted to the main `.sqlite` file.

You need to know the path of the sandbox directory, in order to access the `.sqlite` database file.

There are a many few ways to achieve this; the simplest is halting the execution of the app on a breakpoint and executing the following command on the debug console:

```
po NSHomeDirectory()
```

po stands for **print object**, and `NSHomeDirectory()` is an Objective-C function that returns the path to the sandbox folder of the app. You can open this folder with the finder, using its menu's `Go/ Go to` folder.

Your `.sqlite` file will be found inside the `Library/Application Support` folder. This file is where the SQLite database gets physically stored.

You can open this database file and edit it with a third-party database editor, such as Valentina Studio (`https://www.valentina-db.com/en/valentina-studio-overview`) or any other similar utility capable of browsing database data in this format. Another such tool is JetBrains' DataGrip: `https://www.jetbrains.com/help/datagrip/sqlite.html#connect- to-sqlite-database`.

Interestingly, with a database editor capable of handling SQLite, such as the ones suggested, you can also edit existing saved data.

Accessing the SQLLite data file is a quick way to gain a quick understanding of complex applications from a database perspective, and it is useful whenever you are tasked with understanding a Core Data based app and you don't have documentation.

This technique is often useful to be able to "see" what data looks like on a "table" while an application is running, to see what was changed on a table, and to better understand how an application actually works.

In the following code fragment, we provide a complete, very simple example of using Core Data without any data model file, by instantiating everything from the code:

```
import CoreData
import Foundation

// MARK: - Setup Core Data Stack

// Create Entity Description
```

```swift
let entityDescription = NSEntityDescription()
entityDescription.name = "Student"
entityDescription.managedObjectClassName = "Student"

// Create Attributes
let nameAttribute = NSAttributeDescription()
nameAttribute.name = "name"
nameAttribute.attributeType = .stringAttributeType

let ageAttribute = NSAttributeDescription()
ageAttribute.name = "age"
ageAttribute.attributeType = .integer64AttributeType

entityDescription.properties = [nameAttribute, ageAttribute]

// Create Managed Object Model
let managedObjectModel = NSManagedObjectModel()
managedObjectModel.entities = [entityDescription]

// Create Persistent Store Coordinator
let persistentStoreCoordinator =
NSPersistentStoreCoordinator(managedObjectModel: managedObjectModel)

do {
    try persistentStoreCoordinator.addPersistentStore(ofType:
NSInMemoryStoreType, configurationName: nil, at: nil, options: nil)
} catch {
    fatalError("Failed to setup persistent store: \(error)")
}

let mainContext = NSManagedObjectContext(concurrencyType:
.mainQueueConcurrencyType)
mainContext.persistentStoreCoordinator = persistentStoreCoordinator

// MARK: - Create and Save Data

let newPerson = NSEntityDescription.insertNewObject(forEntityName:
"Student", into: mainContext)
newPerson.setValue("Johanna", forKey: "name")
newPerson.setValue(24, forKey: "age")

do {
    try mainContext.save()
    print("Saved successfully!")
```

```
} catch {
    print("Failed to save: \(error)")
}

// MARK: - Fetch Data

let fetchRequest = NSFetchRequest<NSFetchRequestResult>(entityName:
"Student")
var fetchedPersons: [NSManagedObject] = []

do {
    if let results = try mainContext.fetch(fetchRequest) as?
[NSManagedObject] {
        fetchedPersons = results
    }
} catch {
    print("Failed to fetch: \(error)")
}

// MARK: - Update Data

if let firstPerson = fetchedPersons.first {
    firstPerson.setValue(27, forKey: "age")

    do {
        try mainContext.save()
        print("Updated successfully!")
    } catch {
        print("Failed to update: \(error)")
    }
}

// MARK: - Retrieve and Print Updated Data

do {
    if let results = try mainContext.fetch(fetchRequest) as?
[NSManagedObject] {
        for person in results {
            if let name = person.value(forKey: "name") as? String,
                let age = person.value(forKey: "age") as? Int {
                print("Name: \(name), Age: \(age)")
            }
        }
    }
```

```
} catch {
    print("Failed to fetch updated data: \(error)")
}
```

This code is just an example for educational purposes and does not actually use a database file; it allocates everything "in memory."

In the next section, we will briefly explain how CloudKit relates to Core Data.

CloudKit

This section offers a few words on CloudKit.

If while creating a new App, besides enabling Core Data, you also tick the **Host in CloudKit** option, Xcode will integrate Core Data with **CloudKit**, allowing your app to be cloud-enabled and automatically synchronized across a user's devices by means of iCloud.

We will now just briefly discuss the differences in project creation if CloudKit is enabled, and these differences are minor. An extra configuration option will appear in your .xcdatamodeld file, allowing you to specify which entities should be synced with CloudKit.

This is normally a checkbox in the entity's attribute panel in the data model editor. Instead of NSPersistentContainer, NSPersistentCloudKitContainer will be added to the generated code, which is a subclass of NSPersistentContainer, designed to work with CloudKit.

Xcode will generate code to initialize the CloudKit schema from your Core Data model. This will include creating CloudKit record types based on your Core Data entities.

You won't need to manually implement the synchronization logic between Core Data and CloudKit; NSPersistentCloudKitContainer will handle this functionality for you automatically, including conflict resolution and offline behavior.

If you have old applications based on Core Data, you can migrate them from NSPersistentContainer to NSPersistentCloudKitContainer.

Unfortunately, it is not all advantageous – you should consider whether the data privacy implications of storing data in the cloud are appropriate for your use case and are compliant with applicable laws. Also, iCloud has quotas based on storage and the number of requests, so high-volume apps will encounter limitations.

It might also be more difficult to debug apps supporting CloudKit, as errors might originate from both Core Data and CloudKit.

Summary

In this chapter, we introduced you to Core Data as used in SwiftUI.

We explained the main components of the Core Data stack, and you learned the basic practical skills needed to work with Core Data, such as creating a project that supports Core Data, what Core Data migrations are, and how to inspect data physically stored by Core Data in a SQLite data store. Finally, we briefly explained how Core Data can be persisted on the cloud using CloudKit.

In the next chapter, we will discuss modern concurrency.

13
Modern Structured Concurrency

Concurrency does not directly impact SwiftUI, but it is unavoidable as a concept in writing any application that is non-trivial, and as such, I think it is important enough a subject to deserve at least a chapter in this book. Concurrency is a concept that, over time, has become increasingly important in the development of mobile applications. Concurrency is the ability of a system to manage multiple tasks or operations at the same time. With the escalation in task complexity and the need for faster, more efficient processing to provide users with the best experience, the capacity to execute multiple operations concurrently has become progressively more crucial. Historically, programming languages have provided various mechanisms to manage concurrent execution, such as threads, callbacks, and event loops. These approaches, while functional, often lead to writing complicated and error-prone code. Apple has attempted several times to simplify concurrent programming, and modern structured concurrency is the latest take on this topic.

This chapter aims to provide a quick dive into structured concurrency in Swift, focusing on modern paradigms such as tasks and actors. We will first examine traditional concurrency mechanisms to understand their limitations, and then explore how structured concurrency provides a more intuitive, simpler-to-use and safer framework for concurrent programming. Most of the examples here can be run inside Swift Playgrounds.

In this chapter, we're going to cover the following main topics:

- A brief introduction to concurrency
- Understanding traditional concurrency mechanisms
- Callbacks and event loops
- **Grand Central Dispatch (GCD)**
- What is structured concurrency?
- Using `async`/`await`

- Async let

- Explaining tasks

- Task groups

- Asynchronous sequences

- Asynchronous streams

- Actors

- Bridging old GCD and structured concurrency

A brief introduction to concurrency

Concurrency in the context of iOS development with Swift is about managing multiple tasks that an application might need to perform simultaneously, such as fetching data from the internet, while keeping the user interface responsive by avoiding blocking the main thread, which is responsible for UI updates.

In this chapter, we will focus on the most recent approaches.

Parallelism, while related to concurrency, is specifically about executing multiple tasks at exactly the same time, particularly on devices with multi-core processors, and this includes all modern mobile devices and computers in general. iOS devices leverage parallelism to perform complex computations or handle multiple operations at once, enhancing performance. Swift and iOS provide several mechanisms to facilitate the parallel execution of tasks.

Race conditions in Swift development become a concern when multiple tasks try to access or modify the same piece of data concurrently.

This can lead to unpredictable outcomes because the final state of the data depends on the sequence in which the tasks are The essence of concurrency in this context lies in the CPU's ability to rapidly switch between tasks, creating the illusion of simultaneous execution from the user's point of view, even on single-core devices.

A race condition is a flaw that occurs in a system where the output is dependent on the sequence and timing of uncontrollable events. In the context of software, it manifests when the order of operations leads to unintended consequences, making the final state of the data unpredictable. This unpredictability is due to the non-deterministic ordering of task execution, which can vary with each program run, resulting in bugs that are notoriously difficult to identify and correct.

Synchronization is crucial in preventing race conditions and ensuring data integrity in Swift applications. In the context of modern structured concurrency, the main mechanism allowing the synchronization of multiple tasks are actors and `async/await`, which we will explain later in this chapter.

Concurrency is especially important in multi-core iOS devices, where efficiently utilizing the available cores can significantly improve application performance and responsiveness.

Swift's modern concurrency model, including `async`/`await`, actors, and structured concurrency, allows developers to write safer and more efficient concurrent code.

Understanding traditional concurrency mechanisms

My recommendation is that, although old concurrency paradigms can be still used, you should not mix concurrency paradigms together, and you should use the newer approaches in new projects. However, let's have a quick recap of older concurrency mechanisms.

Threads

A thread in concurrent programming is the smallest unit of a CPU execution that can run independently. Threads within the same process share the same memory space but execute independently. Each thread owns its own copy of registers, stack and program counter, but shares heap memory and file handles. Threads are one of the oldest and most traditional ways to achieve concurrency. A modern CPU can both switch the execution sequentially among several threads (concurrency) and can also process several threads in parallel on different CPU cores (parallelism).

It is nowadays uncommon to find a modern mobile device with less than four CPU cores. In a threaded model, each concurrent operation runs in its own thread, sharing the same memory space with all other threads in the process. This allows threads to read from and write to the same variables, making data sharing simple and computationally cheap, but also prone to race conditions and deadlocks. A **race condition** means that if two threads write to the same shared memory resource, the end result will be different based on the order of execution. A **deadlock** happens when two concurrent threads can remain waiting for each other to free resources needed by the other one, essentially stalling program execution. **Thread starvation** is another concurrency issue that occurs when a thread is unable to access the shared resources it needs for a long period of time, usually because these are hogged for too long by another thread. These difficulties are really hard to avoid in complex applications using threads, and they are also spectacularly difficult to debug; normal tests usually do not reveal concurrency problems. These issues are better avoided with careful design, and that is hard. *Naked* threads – that is, threads as they are available on Unix system programming – can be used on Apple systems, mostly for compatibility with Unix-based code, but they should be carefully avoided in an Apple context.

The following are the limitations of threads:

- **Threads are complex**: Programming threads is not intuitive and requires manual synchronization.

- **Threads are resource-Intensive**: Each thread consumes system resources, eventually degrading performance if too many threads are spawned. Some languages provide "coroutines" and light threads, but these are not present yet on Swift.

- **Threads are error-prone**: It is difficult to avoid the concurrency issues we have just discussed with thread-based programming.

Callbacks and event loops

To mitigate the difficulties of threaded programming, the event-driven programming model uses callbacks and event loops. In Objective-C, these were often implemented with blocks and, more recently, in Swift with closures. Apple does use closures quite often in its programming APIs, and they are commonplace in SwiftUI. While closures are useful, they should not be used too extensively in concurrent code written by the user. The reasons for not overusing this approach are the following limitations:

- **Callback hell**: Asynchronous code containing deep nested callbacks can become hard to read, a phenomenon known as "callback hell"

- **Error handling**: Handling errors across multiple asynchronous operations is difficult

- **Debugging**: Debugging is also challenging because the code's execution flow is not linear; this makes understanding the logic of the code flow complex, and placing a breakpoint and even console printing will modify the timing of the code

GCD

GCD, introduced with OSX 10.6 ("Snow Leopard") in 2009 was till recently Apple's solution to some of the limitations of threads and callbacks listed previously. GCD uses a queue-based approach to execute tasks concurrently; developers enqueue tasks into either serial or concurrent queues, and GCD manages their execution across multiple cores. You don't need to know the thread, just the queue in which a particular thread is executed.

As such, in Apple systems, you normally don't talk about "the main thread," but, rather, refer to the "main queue."

In Apple operating systems, UI rendering occurs on the main queue. Trying to use other queues "concurrently" to perform UI rendering normally results in crashes and malfunctions. If this error occurs, you should often see a warning on the debugging console, provided your application does not crash before allowing you to see it.

While simpler than threads, GCD-based programming is still rather difficult due to these limitations:

- **Abstraction level**: While simpler to program compared to raw threads, GCD still requires manual management of queues.

- **Synchronization**: Although easier than synchronizing threads, state management and synchronization remain challenging.

- **Thread explosion**: Creating too many concurrent threads requires constant switching; if thread switching occurs too often, it slows down the application execution

- **Priority inversion**: Tasks in GCD can suffer from priority inversion, meaning that a higher priority thread can be hindered by a low priority thread, which before releasing a process to the highest priority thread is, in turn, evicted by a "medium priority" one, affecting the overall system performance

- **No execution hierarchy**: Asynchronous GCD code lacked the concept of an execution hierarchy, making it difficult to cancel existing tasks or return a result to the caller

Each of these approaches that I have mentioned has its merits and downsides, but none are free from pitfalls. You should familiarize yourself at least with GCD if you need to work on old code. In the remainder of this chapter, we will explore how structured concurrency aims to offer a more robust and intuitive model for writing concurrent code. If you program iOS versions prior to 13 and macOS 12, you have no choice; you need to program concurrency using GCD and queues. If you are allowed to support more modern operating system versions with your applications, you can use the modern approach. In the next section, we will begin defining structured concurrency.

What is structured concurrency?

Structured concurrency is a programming paradigm that aims to make concurrent programming as straightforward, safe, and simple to understand as writing sequential code. It takes its name as an analogy stemming from structured programming.

The basic assumption of structured concurrency is that it should bring the same simplification to concurrency that structured programming brought to program sequencing, by removing goto-based branching.

Every asynchronous task is now part of a hierarchy and has a priority. The hierarchy allows the runtime to cancel all the child tasks of a parent task when the parent is canceled. It also simplifies waiting for all children to finish before the parent is allowed to complete. Also, the compiler checks whether code can or should be run asynchronously. Although not perfect, the compile-time check catches the most common programming errors. It will, for instance, detect some race conditions and potentially unsafe code, and Xcode will mark these errors in violet.

In structured concurrency, the life cycle of concurrent tasks is tightly scoped and managed by the program's structure, using language constructs such as `async` and `await`. This scoping ensures that tasks are started and completed within well-defined boundaries and are easy to reason about, making it easier to understand task execution and avoiding pitfalls such as resource leaks and "dangling" tasks (that never complete).

Here are the main advantages of structured concurrency:

- **Task lifespan**: Tasks are bound to the context or scope they are created in, assuring that they start and complete within defined boundaries.
- **Nesting**: Structured concurrency allows for concurrent tasks to be nested: A parent task can spawn "child" tasks. The parent task will complete its execution as soon as its code block ends, irrespective of whether all its child tasks have completed their execution or not. However, you often want to await child tasks to allow that they have completed before proceeding with the parent task execution. If the parent is killed before the child completes, the child will continue its execution in the background.

- **Error propagation**: Structured concurrency simplifies error handling.

- **Cancellation**: Tasks can be canceled programmatically based on conditions. This cancellation propagates to nested tasks; canceling a parent task automatically cancels its children also. This simplifies task management.

- **Resource clean-up**: As tasks have a well-defined scope, it is easier to manage resources such as memory and file handles, reducing the likelihood of resource leaks.

- **Readability**: Code is easier to read and understand because the control flow is more linear and less complex compared to older alternatives.

- **Debuggability**: It is easier to debug structured concurrency code because of its structured nature.

- **Safety**: It is less likely to have concurrency issues such as race conditions, deadlocks, and resource leaks.

- **Developer productivity**: It is easier to write concurrent code more quickly, creating fewer errors. This reduces the time to market for software projects.

In Swift, structured concurrency uses a limited set of constructs – **async/await**, **tasks**, **task groups**, **async let**, and **actors**.

In the next section, we will begin examining the first of these constructs, `async/await`.

Using the async/await syntax

The `async/await` syntax is the backbone of this structured concurrency. Let's begin by understanding the `async` keyword.

`async` in Swift means that a function will perform some asynchronous operation, suspending the thread till the operation completes, and returning only when that operation is complete. Unlike a standard function, a function marked with the `async` keyword doesn't block the caller but, rather, allows it to continue executing other tasks.

This is useful to perform IO-bound tasks, computationally intensive calculations, networking calls, and file operations, as it won't stop the CPU while waiting – for instance, while waiting for data from a network operation.

An example of a Swift `async` function, illustrating the `async` syntax, is the following example code fragment:

```
// an example async function
import Foundation
func fetchData() async -> Data {
    // perform a network call
    sleep(1) // simulate a call by waiting (doing nothing)
```

```
        return Data()
}
```

An `async` function is an asynchronous one that can perform some long-running operation, without blocking the calling thread.

A function or method designated as asynchronous can pause its execution at certain points. In contrast, standard synchronous functions and methods can run either to completion, generate an error, or never conclude. While an asynchronous function or method can also end in one of these three ways, it has the added flexibility of halting temporarily, typically when it's waiting for a particular event or operation to finish.

Within the code block of such an asynchronous function or method, you indicate each potential pause point with specific markers, denoted with the `await` keyword.

An `async` function cannot be invoked like a normal function. If you try invoking it, the compiler will give you the following error – **error: 'async' call in a function that does not support concurrency**. You need to wait for the `async` function to complete via the `await` keyword, such as the following:

```
let data = await fetchData()
```

`await` is used in conjunction with `async` functions, and it pauses the execution of the caller scope until the `async` function that is called completes. Importantly, `await` doesn't block the thread; it merely suspends the current asynchronous context, freeing the CPU to execute other tasks. You can use `await` multiple times, sequentially, within the same asynchronous function. From your programming perspective, you treat code containing `async`/`await` as if you were writing normal sequential code. The only difference is that `async` code is code that can be suspended and `await` waits for `async` code to return from suspension. The Swift scheduler will take care of execution on your behalf, and most of the time, you can ignore the exact details of how the Swift scheduler operates.

Regarding error management, `async` integrates with the `try`, `catch`, `finally`, and `throw` clauses to handle errors. Everything you learned in terms of exception handling works naturally with `async`, without any changes.

As a quick reminder, an `async` function can process an error locally with exception handling, as shown in the following example:

```
func fetchData(from url: URL) async throws -> Data {
    let (data, _) = try await URLSession.shared.data(from: url)
    return data
}func processData() async {
    do {
        let data = try await fetchData()
```

```
        // Continue processing
    } catch FetchError.invalidData {
        print("Invalid data received.")
    } catch {
        print("An unexpected error occurred: \(error)")
    } finally {
        print("This executes whether an error happened or not")
    }
}
```

Typically, the `finally` clause is used to clean up resources (e.g., to close files and deallocate resources).

Otherwise, an `async` function can throw an error, allowing it to be processed by the caller – for example, if our `fetchData()` network function fails, it can be declared as a throwing function, as shown in the following example:

```
func fetchData() async throws -> Data {
    // throwing an error from an async function
    throw FetchError.invalidData
}
```

> **Important note – waiting time without blocking the thread**
>
> In order to simulate the passing of time due to network operations and while learning concurrency, instead of `sleep()`, which would block a thread, you can use the `Task.sleep()` method. This method *does nothing*, but it waits for the given number of nanoseconds before returning and does not block execution. It is a way to measure time.

Apple introduced support for `async/await` in multiple frameworks that rely on completion handlers and delegates. Among these, `async/await` was adopted by `URLSession`, Core Data's `fetchRequest` and `FileManager`.

I will provide a couple of examples of using `URLSession`, and similar approaches can be used with other frameworks that support `async/await`.

With `URLSession`, it is now possible to use a much simpler syntax to fetch data, as shown in the following simple example:

```
import Foundation
import PlaygroundSupport

// Enable indefinite execution to allow the asynchronous code to
complete
```

```
PlaygroundPage.current.needsIndefiniteExecution = true

func fetchData(from url: URL) async throws -> Data {
    let (data, _) = try await URLSession.shared.data(from: url)
    return data
}

Task {
    do {
        let url = URL(string: "https://google.com")!
        let data = try await fetchData(from: url)
        print(data)
    } catch {
        print("Error fetching data: \(error)")
    }
}
```

The `await` keyword is used to wait for the result of the asynchronous `data(from:)` method without blocking the thread. The `try` keyword is used because this method can throw an error (for example, if there is no network connection).

`let (data, _) = try await URLSession.shared.data(from: url)` returns a tuple, but only the `data` part is used (indicated by `_` for the unused response part).

Do not worry about `Task` right now; I will explain it soon. Also, we can, of course, we can use URLSession to fetch data using `Result`, encapsulating error management in a structured way, as shown in the following example:

```
import Foundation
import PlaygroundSupport

PlaygroundSupport.PlaygroundPage.current.needsIndefiniteExecution =
true

enum NetworkError: Error {
    case badStatus, koStatus
    case badURL, failedRequest
}
func fetchData(from urlString: String) async -> Result<Data,
NetworkError> {
    guard let url = URL(string: urlString) else {
        return .failure(.badURL)
    }
    let request = URLRequest(url: url)
```

```
    do {
        let (data, response) = try await URLSession.shared.data(for:
request)

        guard let httpResponse = response as? HTTPURLResponse,
200..<300 ~= httpResponse.statusCode else {
            return .failure(.koStatus)
        }
        return .success(data)
    } catch {
        return .failure(.failedRequest)
    }
}


// Invoke fetchData()
Task {
    let result = await fetchData(from: "https://jsonplaceholder.
typicode.com/todos/10")
    switch result {
    case .success(let data):
        if let json = try? JSONSerialization.jsonObject(with: data,
options: []) {
            print(json)
        }
    case .failure(let error):
        print("Error: \(error) ")
    }
}
```

The `NetworkError` enum defines potential errors such as an invalid URL (`badURL`) and failed request (`requestFailed`).

The `fetchData()` function fetches data from a given URL string; it checks whether a valid URL object can be created from the provided string. The function then makes an HTTP request using the URL. It proceeds to fetch data from the URL using `async/await`. If the fetch is successful, it checks that the response's status code is successful (i.e., the status code is within the range 200-299). Finally, if the call is successful, the function returns the fetched data; otherwise, it returns an error from the `NetworkError` enum.

In the next section, we will examine **async let**.

Async let syntax

`async let` is an asynchronous assignment. It is conceptually like `Promise` in some reactive frameworks and JavaScript. The basic syntax is as follows:

```
async let myVariable = someAsyncFunction()
```

This assignment is launched as a task, concurrently with the rest of the enclosing asynchronous caller scope. The variable declared with `async let` becomes a placeholder for a value that will be assigned later. In order to actually access this value, you need to use `await`.

If you declare several `async let` assignments at the same time, these will be executed concurrently. The enclosing caller context, typically a function containing the `async let` assignments, won't complete unless explicitly awaited or canceled.

You can decide to use `await` to wait for the results with multiple `await` statements or follow `await` with a tuple containing all the placeholder variables declared with `async let`. This is treated as a case of multiple assignments in idiomatic Swift, as shown in the following code fragment:

```
func performTask() async {
    async let result1 = someAsyncFunction1()
    async let result2 = someAsyncFunction2()

    // Do other work ...

    let finalResult1 = await result1
    let finalResult2 = await result2
    // Use finalResult1 and finalResult2
}


func performTask2() async {
    async let result1 = someAsyncFunction1()
    async let result2 = someAsyncFunction2()

    // Do some other work ...

    let (finalResult1, finalResult2) = await (result1,
    result2)
    // Use finalResult1 and finalResult2
}
```

In order to handle errors, `async let` must be enclosed in `do/catch`, as in the following code example, where we use `let async` to fetch data from the main page of `google.com` within a Swift playground:

```
import Foundation
import PlaygroundSupport

// Enable indefinite execution to allow the asynchronous code to
complete
PlaygroundPage.current.needsIndefiniteExecution = true

// Async function to fetch data from a given URL
func fetchData(from url: URL) async throws -> Data {
    let (data, _) = try await URLSession.shared.data(from: url)
    return data
}

// Async function to demonstrate the use of async let and do-catch
error handling
func performTask() async {
    let googleURL = URL(string: "https://www.google.com")!

    async let googleData: Data = fetchData(from: googleURL)

    do {
        let data = try await googleData
        print("Fetched data from Google with length: \(data.count)
bytes")
    } catch {
        print("An error occurred: \(error)")
    }

    // Finish indefinite execution when the task is complete
    PlaygroundPage.current.finishExecution()
}

// Start the asynchronous task
Task {
    await performTask()
}
```

There are a few caveats you should be aware of regarding `async let`:

- Variables declared with `async let` are read-only. They cannot be re-assigned.

- You must use `await` on an `async let` variable before being able to either use its value or handle any errors it might throw. The variable cannot be ignored, and doing so will result in a compiler error.

- `async let` can only be used within an `async` context; it cannot be used within normal, non-asynchronous functions and methods.

In the next section, I will explain another foundational construct of the structured concurrency framework in Apple systems – tasks.

Understanding tasks

Tasks are "units of work" that can run concurrently, and they are a higher-level abstraction over threads, queues, and similar concurrency primitives. Essentially, in Swift, a task is simply a piece of work that can run in parallel with other tasks. In contrast to threads and queues, tasks are managed by the Swift runtime and not by the operating system. This makes them more lightweight and efficient. Moreover, this allows structured concurrency to be backported by Apple to iOS 13 just by updating Xcode, as iOS 13 did not offer this feature when it was first introduced.

Beware that in the first iterations of structured concurrency, you were supposed to be able to declare a task just by using the `async` keyword, followed by `do/catch`. The `async` keyword followed by `do/catch` syntax method has been replaced with task initialization. You won't find that in this book; if you happen to find it in old code, just replace `async` with an appropriate task creation.

You can create a task in several ways. The simplest way is just using the `Task` initializer with a block of code, as shown in the following code example:

```
func someAsyncFunction() async -> Int
    return 5
}

// A simple task that computes a value asynchronously
Task {
    let value = await someAsyncFunction()
    print("Computed value: \(value)")
}
```

To run tasks concurrently, you can create child tasks within a parent task. These child tasks run in parallel, but their lifetimes are tied to the parent task – for example, in the following example, the `parentTask` async function creates a child task that runs concurrently, and then it uses `await` to wait for it to complete. Without `await`, `parentTask` would complete without waiting for the completion of the child task:

```
func anotherAsyncFunction() async {
    sleep(3)
}

func someAsyncFunction() async {
    sleep(2)
}

func parentTask() async {
    // Spawn a new child task
    let child = Task {
        return await someAsyncFunction()
    }

    // Do something else concurrently
    await anotherAsyncFunction()

    // Wait for the child task to complete and get the result
    let result = await child.value
}
```

`Task` offers several different initializers that create tasks with different configurations. Let's look at them:

- `Task(operation: )`: This operation is the closure that contains the work to be performed by the task. If your operation is asynchronous, you should mark it with `await`. If your operation can throw errors, mark it with `throws`. This is the default `Task` initializer, the one you will get by instantiating `Task` followed by a code block.

- `Task(priority: )`: The optional parameter `priority` allows you to specify a task's priority, which is an enum value of the `TaskPriority` type. The priority, from highest to lowest, can have one of the following values:

  - `.high`: The task should be executed immediately and ahead of others.

  - `.default`: This is the normal priority of tasks.

  - `.low`: The task can be deferred and does not need to be run immediately.

  - `.background`: This is the lowest priority for a task, and it should be reserved for tasks that can take place in the background and won't delay the UI response.

- `priority`: This can also be used with `TaskGroup`, which we will examine in the next section. The system does not guarantee the respect of priorities. Priorities are, more than anything, "hints" for the Swift scheduler, and actual behavior can vary, depending on system load and memory available. You can also change the priority dynamically, during the task execution, by assigning a value to `Task.currentPriority`, but it is preferable to assign priorities of tasks when they are created, in order to allow the scheduler to have information about priorities as soon as possible, allowing for better optimization of the program flow.

  Tasks with higher priority are scheduled to run before tasks with lower priority, and it is useful to remember that higher priority tasks could potentially "hog" the CPU and starve lower priority tasks. Higher priorities should be reserved for important, infrequent, and short-lived tasks.

  You can also set the priority to `.unspecified`, allowing the the scheduler to decide on your behalf.

- `Task(detachedOperation:)`: The `detachedOperation` parameter accepts an alternate closure that creates a **detached task**. A detached task does not belong to any hierarchy, meaning that it is not tied to the lifetime of its parent task. So, if you need a task to outlive the context that creates it, it should be created as detached. This can be written in Swift as follows:

```
Task.detached {
    //detached task operation
}
```

- `inheritPriority`: This is an optional Boolean parameter, available when creating detached tasks. If its value is `true`, it indicates that the new detached task should inherit the priority of the context where the new task is created. If its value is `false` or is omitted, the task will have the default priority.

In the following section, we will examine task groups, a way to execute a number of concurrent tasks:

Task groups

A task group is a way to manage multiple task children that run concurrently within the same given scope. This ensures that the tasks belonging to the same group are executed at the same time. The group ensures that all spawned tasks complete before the scope terminates, allowing for multiple tasks to be run concurrently, and for their results to be collected.

`TaskGroup` is a struct, defined as follows:

```
@frozen
struct TaskGroup<ChildTaskResult> where ChildTaskResult : Sendable
```

You don't however instantiate `TaskGroup` by using its constructor; rather, you use the `withTaskGroup(of:returning:body:)` method to create a new `TaskGroup`.

The optional of: parameter indicates the type of TaskGroup, which is the same type returned by the child processes.

The optional returning: parameter indicates the type returned by GroupResult, and body: is the code closure associated that the task group executes.

> **Important note – the Sendable protocol**
>
> Sendable is a protocol that was introduced to help define types that can be safely transferred across different threads and tasks. All fundamental Swift types such as Int, Boolean, String, Float, Double, and Character are Sendable.
>
> Composite types such as struct and enum based on Sendable properties are also Sendable, provided that the conformance with the Sendable protocol is declared.
>
> Closures that capture Sendable types are automatically considered Sendable and should be marked with @Sendable, such as the following:
>
> ```
> let myClosure: @Sendable () -> Void = {
>     print("This closure is Sendable!")
> }
> ```
>
> Exchanging data between threads using classes is more tricky; classes can be Sendable, provided that they are declared as conforming to the Sendable protocol, they are either internally immutable, or if their synchronization is handled manually.
>
> **Boxing**, in the context of concurrency, generally refers to wrapping non-Sendable types in a Sendable container to safely pass them across task boundaries. This is because not all types can be safely sent across threads or task boundaries, leading to potential race conditions and other threading issues, such as the following:
>
> ```
> struct Box: Sendable {
>     var nonSendable: NonSendableClass
> }
> async let x = Box(nonSendable: NonSendableClass(value: 5))
> ```
>
> This would not, however, prevent race conditions.
>
> Boxing can, however, also mean, more traditionally, wrapping a value inside a reference type so that it can be addressed in heap memory. While this allows you to share state across multiple concurrency contexts, it also has the potential to determine race conditions and can have an impact also on performance, due to contention and the increased complexity of allocation/deallocation.
>
> In both uses of "boxing," you end up sharing a reference type, which tends to be problematic in terms of potential race conditions, unless the underlying type is immutable. This use of boxing, in general, should be avoided if at all possible and would require additional synchronization to not cause issues. This synchronization can involve locks, which are best avoided in all types of concurrency, and actors.

TaskGroup makes it easier to collect results from all the child tasks of the same TaskGroup, simplifying the writing of concurrent code.

TaskGroup is designed to work seamlessly with Swift's structured concurrency model, ensuring that all child tasks complete before the parent task moves on.

In order to collect results, you have to use await in conjunction with withTaskGroup, as in the following example that simulates throwing six dice:

```
import Foundation
var results: [Int] = []
func rollDice() async throws -> Int {
    // wait from 1 to 2 seconds
    try await Task.sleep(nanoseconds: UInt64(Int.random(in: 1_000_000_
000...2_000_000_000)))
    return Int.random(in: 1...6) // simulate casting a die
}
// Create an async function to run the task group
func rollMultipleDice() async {
    await withTaskGroup(of: Result<Int, Error>.self) { group in
        // Add 6 tasks to the group
        for _ in 1...6 {
            group.addTask {
                do {
                    let value = try await rollDice()
                    return .success(value)
                } catch {
                    return .failure(error)
                }
            }
        }

    // wait for children completion, collecting the results
        for await result in group {
            switch result {
            case .success(let value):
                results.append(value)
            case .failure(let error):
                print("An error occurred: \(error)")
            }
        }
    }
}
```

```
// Execute the async function that instantiates the Group
Task {
    await rollMultipleDice()
    print("Results: \(results)")
}
```

Error handling: If any task within `TaskGroup` throws an error, the error will propagate out of the `withTaskGroup` scope. The parent task can catch this error using `do/catch`.

In the previous example, as `Task.sleep()` is a throwing function that can potentially fail, we used a task group of type `Result<Int, Error>`, allowing the error to be processed easily.

Unless you get an error from the compiler, you won't typically notice that all types returned from child tasks and `TaskGroup` conform automatically to `Sendable`.

Error propagation: If the parent task of a task group is cancelled, all child tasks are also cancelled. Instead, if a child task is cancelled, its cancellation will not affect the remaining tasks in the group, nor the parent task. Cancellation of `TaskGroup` is propagated automatically through all its child tasks, recursively to all their children and children of children, and so on.

The `cancelAll()` method cancels all the remaining child tasks belonging to the same `TaskGroup`.

If a task has been cancelled and then new tasks are added to it, they are automatically cancelled.

However, to avoid instantiating them, they can be added with the `addTaskUnlessCancelled(priority:body)` method rather than the `addTask(priority:body)` method.

Task can be executed within a SwiftUI view as well; from iOS 15 onwards, if you need to call an asynchronous method when the View appears, you can use the `.task(priority:)` view modifier.

This is different from the `.onAppear` modifier, which is performed synchronously when the view appears and should not be used for tasks that take long to complete.

`.task`, in contrast, being asynchronous, can be used to perform tasks that may require time to complete, such as fetching data from a database. For example, in the following code fragment we use the `.task` modifier to invoke the simulated fetch of items to fill a list:

```
import SwiftUI

// simulate fetching items from an API.
func fetchItems() async throws -> [String] {
    // Simulating a network delay of one second
    try await Task.sleep(nanoseconds: 1_000_000_000)  // this function
is throwing and can potentially fail
    return ["row 1", "row 2", "row 3", "row 4", "row 5"]
}
```

```
struct ContentView: View {
    @State private var items: [String] = []

    var body: some View {
        List(items, id: \.self) { item in
            Text(item)
                .foregroundColor(.green)
                .bold()
        }
        // Using the .task modifier to fetch items when the view
appears.
        .task(priority: .userInitiated) {
            do {
                items = try await fetchItems()
            } catch {
                print("an error occurred")
            }
        }
        // shows a progress view while the items are being fetched.
        .overlay(items.isEmpty ? ProgressView().scaleEffect(3.0) :
nil)
    }
}
struct ContentView_Previews: PreviewProvider {
    static var previews: some View {
        ContentView()
    }
}
```

The result is shown in the following screenshot:

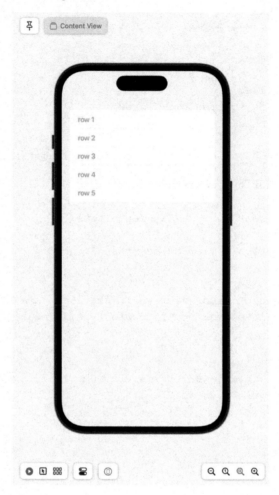

Figure 13.1 – An example of a .task view modifier

In the next section, we will examine asynchronous sequences.

Asynchronous sequences

An asynchronous sequence is a sequence that produces values over time, rather than all at once. This is useful to represent a series of values that are computed asynchronously – for example, reading lines from a file or waiting for a number of network requests to complete.

An asynchronous sequence conforms to the `AsyncSequence` protocol, and it can be iterated using `for await` within an asynchronous context. In order to implement a sequence conforming to `AsyncSequence`, you need to do the following:

1. Declare conformance to the `AsyncSequence` protocol.

2. Define the associated `Element` type that represents the elements produced by the sequence.

3. Implement the `makeAsyncIterator()` method that returns a type conforming to `AsyncIteratorProtocol`.

Here's an example of defining an asynchronous sequence that emits integers at one-second intervals, counting from 1 to 4, with a second wait between each number:

```
import Foundation
import PlaygroundSupport

// Enable indefinite execution to allow the asynchronous code to
complete
PlaygroundPage.current.needsIndefiniteExecution = true

// Define a struct that conforms to AsyncSequence
struct AsyncCounter: AsyncSequence {
    typealias Element = Int
    let maxCount: Int

    // AsyncIterator defines how to generate elements
    struct AsyncCounterIterator: AsyncIteratorProtocol {
        let maxCount: Int
        var currentCount = 0

        mutating func next() async -> Int? {
            // Produce nil when reaching the max count to terminate
the sequence
            if currentCount >= maxCount {
                return nil
            }

            let nextValue = currentCount
            currentCount += 1

            // Simulate an asynchronous operation
            do {
                await try Task.sleep(nanoseconds:
UInt64(1_000_000_000))
            } catch {
```

```
                    print ("An error occurred")
            }// 1 second
            return nextValue
        }
    }

    // Make an instance of the iterator when starting to loop
    func makeAsyncIterator() -> AsyncCounterIterator {
        return AsyncCounterIterator(maxCount: maxCount)
    }

}


// Use the asynchronous sequence
Task {
    for await number in AsyncCounter(maxCount: 5) {
        print("Received number: \(number)")
    }
    print("Sequence complete.")
}
```

The `AsyncCounter` struct is defined to conform to `AsyncSequence`. It specifies an `AsyncCounterIterator` struct that adheres to `AsyncIteratorProtocol`. The `next()` method of the iterator returns the next element in the sequence asynchronously. In this example, it simulates a delay using the `Task.sleep(nanoseconds:)` method.

Finally, the usage of the `AsyncCounter` asynchronous sequence is demonstrated within an asynchronous task.

The `for await` loop iterates through the asynchronous sequence, awaiting each value as it's produced, printing it.

Swift's runtime offers several utility methods that deal with asynchronous sequences, similar to those available for regular, synchronous sequences. These asynchronous functional methods, such as `map`, `filter`, and `reduce`, behave like their normal counterparts, facilitating various operations on asynchronous sequences.

Asynchronous sequences have some limitations; they cannot be randomly accessed or split like regular arrays or other collections. Asynchronous sequences are only designed to produce elements over time, which you consume one after another.

Asynchronous sequences use cases are similar to those belonging to the Combine framework but are at a lower level, allowing potentially for more control. Under the hood, `TaskGroup` child tasks are managed by means of asynchronous sequences and can themselves be considered asynchronous sequences, and at the time of writing, the Swift task scheduler uses asynchronous sequences.

In SwiftUI, the use of asynchronous sequences is only limited by a developer's imagination, and they can be used to lazy-load image galleries, tweets, stock prices, and similar.

In the next section, we will explain asynchronous streams.

Asynchronous streams

Asynchronous streams are similar to asynchronous sequences. `AsyncStream` is the Swift protocol that defines asynchronous streams. It is less flexible, simpler to use, and requires less code than `AsyncSequence`.

The `AsyncStream` protocol conforms to `AsyncSequence`, but it offers a more streamlined method for generating asynchronous sequences and does not require you to define manually an asynchronous iterator.

`AsyncStream`'s initializer is defined as follows:

```
init(Element.Type, bufferingPolicy: AsyncStream<Element>.Continuation.
BufferingPolicy, (AsyncStream<Element>.Continuation) -> Void)
```

The initializer builds an asynchronous stream for an element type, with the specified buffering policy and the element-producing closure "continuation."

Continuations in computer science are abstract representations of the control state of a computer program. A continuation captures the computation that remains to be executed at a certain point in a program – that is, the "rest of the computation" to be performed. This is a concept used in programming languages and paradigms that allows a developer to have complete control of the program flow and execution state by means of function calls. Basically, a continuation is a function that, besides data parameters typical of a function, also receives as a parameter the execution context.

Within a language that has first-class support for continuations (in a similar way to high-order functions in functional languages) – for instance, in the programming language Scheme – you can return from a function by calling a continuation method, and similarly, you have complete control over the flow of execution of code. In such a language, continuations can be stored, passed as parameters, and returned as a type. Swift does not offer such support, and continuations can be partially simulated with closures.

This style of programming is called "continuation-based programming" and has applications, for instance, in writing compilers for functional languages and simplifying some programming patterns (e.g., writing backtracking algorithms).

In our case, `Continuation` is not a full-fledged continuation but, simply, a closure that supports mechanisms for both yielding a result and terminating the stream flow. It is a continuation only in the narrow sense that it allows you to control "what to do next" (i.e., adding an element or terminating the stream), and does not "automatically terminate" by itself. Its stream can be left open till you want to close it, allowing you to capture a potentially indefinite number of elements (e.g. from a chat, a stock price tracker, or readings from a sensor).

Note that these use cases are quite similar to Combine's. In general, `AsyncStream` is adequate for simpler use cases, and it also has much lower memory requirements than Combine.

`AsyncStream` is documented here: `https://developer.apple.com/documentation/swift/asyncstream`.

There's also a throwing version of `AsyncStream`, `AsyncThrowingStream`:

```
struct AsyncThrowingStream<Element, Failure> where Failure : Error
```

`AsyncThrowingStream` is documented here:

`https://developer.apple.com/documentation/swift/asyncthrowingstream`.

An asynchronous stream is ideally suited for seamless integration with `async/await` of old callback-based code and to process asynchronous fetching of data.

To instantiate `AsyncStream`, you need pass it a closure that takes `AsyncStream.Continuation` as its parameter. Within this closure, elements are added to the stream via the invocation of the continuation's `yield(_:)` method.

The element production is halted by invoking the continuation's `finish()` method, leading the sequence iterator to yield a nil, ending the sequence.

As it conforms to `Sendable`, the continuation can be accessed from external concurrent contexts outside the `AsyncStream` iteration.

As an example, we can use `AsyncStream` to fetch the conversion rate from dollars to euros from the Frankfurt Stock Exchange, updating it every 10 seconds, as shown in the following simple example. As it is just an example, we haven't structured it in layers but kept it all within `ContentView.swift`.

Let's begin with our `ContentView`:

```
import SwiftUI

struct ContentView: View {
```

```
@State private var exchangeRate: Double = 0.0
@State private var isFinished: Bool = false

var body: some View {
    if isFinished {
        Text("Finished")
            .font(.largeTitle)
            .padding()
    } else {
        NavigationView {
            VStack {
                HStack {
                    Image(systemName: "dollarsign.circle.fill")
                        .resizable()
                        .foregroundColor(.blue)
                        .frame(width: 50, height: 50)
                        .padding()
                    Image(systemName: "arrow.right")
                        .resizable()
                        .frame(width: 40, height: 40)
                        .padding()
                    Image(systemName: "eurosign.circle.fill")
                        .resizable()
                        .foregroundColor(.blue)
                        .frame(width: 50, height: 50)
                        .padding()
                }
                Text("1 USD is \(exchangeRate, specifier: "%.4f")
EUR")
                    .font(.largeTitle)
                    .padding()
                Button(action: {
                    isFinished = true
                }) {
                    Text("Stop")
                        .padding()
                        .background(Color.orange)
                        .foregroundColor(.white)
                        .cornerRadius(8)
                }
            }
            .navigationTitle("USD to EUR Rate")
            .toolbar {
                ToolbarItem(placement: .navigationBarTrailing) {
```

```
                              Button(action: {
                                  Task {
                                      do {
                                          exchangeRate = try await
refreshExchangeRate()
                                      } catch {
                                          print(error)
                                      }
                                  }
                              }) {
                                  Text("Refresh")
                                  Image(systemName: "arrow.clockwise")
                              }
                          }
                      }
                      .task {
                          for await rate in exchangeRateStream() {
                              exchangeRate = rate
                          }
                      }
                  }
              }
          }
```

The `AsyncStream` definition, which is the interesting part and where the magic happens, is the following:

```
func exchangeRateStream() -> AsyncStream<Double> {
    AsyncStream(Double.self) { continuation in
        Task {
            while true {
                if isFinished {
                    continuation.finish()
                    break
                }
                do {
                    let rate = try await refreshExchangeRate()
                    continuation.yield(rate)
                } catch {
                    print("Error fetching exchange rate: \
(error)")
```

```
                        continuation.finish()
                        break
                    }
                    try await Task.sleep(nanoseconds: 10 * NSEC_PER_
SEC) // sleep 10 seconds
                }
            }
        }
    }
```

To conclude our code, we need to add the following final part of the file, which contains a simple function that fetches the current rate of exchange from the public API of the Frankfurt Stock Exchange and decodes it:

```
func refreshExchangeRate() async throws -> Double {
        let url = URL(string: "https://api.frankfurter.app/
latest?from=USD&to=EUR")!
        let (data, _) = try await URLSession.shared.data(from: url)
        if let rate = parse(data) {
            return rate
        } else {
            throw NSError(domain: "Unable to parse exchange rate",
code: 0, userInfo: nil)
        }
    }

    func parse(_ data: Data) -> Double? {
        do {
            let result = try JSONDecoder().
decode(ExchangeRateResponse.self, from: data)
            return result.rates["EUR"]
        } catch {
            print("Error parsing JSON: \(error)")
            return nil
        }
    }
}

struct ExchangeRateResponse: Codable {
    let rates: [String: Double]
}

struct ContentView_Previews: PreviewProvider {
```

```
    static var previews: some View {
        ContentView()
    }
}
```

As we have shown, the `AsyncStream` part is really simple.

`AsyncStream` can be used whenever you need to adapt old code that was initially written using callbacks, such as calls based on the old version of concurrency, to modern structured concurrency.

The recipe is quite simple and is exactly like the example we have shown here. You declare `AsyncStream` with its continuation initializer, and inside it, you call `continuation.yield` to add data to the stream, and `continuation.finish()` when you want to close the stream.

If your asynchronous operation throws errors, you should use `AsyncThrowingStream` and call `continuation.finish(throwing:)` to propagate the error.

Actors

Actors are a reference type, similar to a class. However, actors protect their internal state by enforcing a single thread that is able to access them at any given time. This is achieved by making sure that each one of the actors' methods and properties can only be accessed in a strictly sequential serial order. This determines data isolation, making it very hard to write code that could determine common concurrency problems, such as data races.

In **structured concurrency**, Actors should be used to perform synchronization. You should avoid locks, mutexes, and semaphores, as these are much more likely to introduce race conditions, and reasoning about their behavior is more difficult.

In Swift, actor isolation is enforced at the compile level, meaning that the compiler does not allow you to access the mutable state of the actor from outside the actor.

Swift actors are **reentrant**, meaning that while an actor awaits the result of an asynchronous operation, it can process other tasks. The properties of actors are isolated; they can be accessed only within the actor itself, and its methods need to be awaited when called externally.

This allows for more flexibility, but it comes with some additional risks, such as potentially out-of-order execution, meaning that there is no guarantee that methods of an actor are executed in the same order as they are called. This depends on multiple factors, such as the scheduling of tasks and system load. To enforce the order of execution, you would need higher-level synchronization or other design patterns, such as state machines, that ensure that tasks are executed in the order you would expect. An actor serializes access to its properties, but that doesn't mean that actor methods run without interruption. If an `async` function is called within an actor, the task might suspend and wait for the result, thus allowing some other tasks to access the actor's methods. The reentrancy of actors is not a bug; it is a deliberate design choice that allowed the Swift language designers to prevent deadlocks, which would have been commonplace had they not allowed reentrant behavior.

The following example shows an example actor and also illustrates the reentrancy problem with actors:

```
import Foundation
import PlaygroundSupport

// Enable indefinite execution to allow the asynchronous code to
complete
PlaygroundPage.current.needsIndefiniteExecution = true

func log(_ i: Int) async {
    print("value:", i)
    // The delay makes the problem easier to reproduce

    try! await Task.sleep(nanoseconds: 2_000_000_000)
}

actor Counter {
    var count: Int = 0

    func increment() async -> Int {
        let oldValue = self.count
        //await log(oldValue) // uncomment this line to evidence the
problem
        let newValue = oldValue + 1
        self.count = newValue
        return newValue
    }
}

Task {
        let counter = Counter()
        async let c1 = counter.increment()
        async let c2 = counter.increment()
        await print("c1:", c1)
        await print("c2:", c2)
}
```

The result, if you keep the line containing `await log(oldValue)` commented, will normally be well behaved, meaning that you will get different values for `c1` and `c2`, namely 1 and 2, or 2 and 1, depending on the execution order.

If you delete the double slash at the beginning of that line, however, the `log` function, being asynchronous and long-lived, will cause `c1` and `c2` to be both logged before the increment, and both `c1` and `c2` to be printed with the same value of `1`. One of the two increments gets lost!

There are several techniques to circumvent this problem – for instance, you could complete the increment before the `async` call, or you could move the `await log(oldValue)` line just before the `return` statement of the `increment()` method. This would have the effect of separating the asynchronous code from the synchronous one and moving the data structure manipulation into synchronous code, where no asynchronous calls occur.

Another possible mechanism could be the rewrite of `increment()` with a `while` pattern that checks that `oldValue` is still unchanged, before incrementing it; otherwise, the improved `increment()` function "retries" the operation, keeping the value of `counter` in sync with the change introduced by the other competing task:

```
func increment() async -> Int {
    while true {
        let oldValue = self.count
        await log(oldValue)
        guard self.count == oldValue else { continue }
        let newValue = oldValue + 1
        self.count = newValue
        return newValue
    }
}
```

In general, the solution involves using the internal state of the actor to prevent reentrant code issues, and it might require some creativity.

A pattern that can also resolve the problem is using the actor as a state machine, with each state disallowing transitions that could be the result of concurrency problems arising from reentrancy.

Another notable difference between actors and classes is that actors do not support inheritance; the Swift language designers made this choice to simplify the implementation of actors, and to avoid the complications that would have arisen for developers had inheritance been implemented.

In the next section, we will examine a particular actor that is used at the system level to coordinate the behavior of the UI in SwiftUI and UIKit.

MainActor

`MainActor` is a special actor that is tied to the system level and is always present in a modern Apple app, that is based on a version of the operating system that is capable of supporting structured concurrency.

MainActor is tied to the main queue. Any update to the UI in Apple systems needs to be performed within the main queue.

Any code marked with @MainActor will execute on the MainActor, which is tied to the main queue, and this is particularly useful to ensure that UI update-related code is not executed on threads different from the main one.

For instance, the code shown in the following fragment would be executed in MainActor:

```
@MainActor
private func showAlert() {
        isAlertShown = true
}
```

And this would be needed if we wanted to be able to, for example, invoke the showAlert() function from a within background task, but with the need to affect the UI.

@MainActor can be used with closures, classes, structs, enums, functions, methods, and properties, besides ordinary actors.

Declaring a class with @MainActor ensures that all methods and computed properties belonging to that class will run on the main actor.

With structs and enums, you can't declare them wholly as @MainActor, but you can mark individual methods and properties (enums can only have computed properties).

By placing the @MainActor property wrapper before specific methods or functions, you can make sure that a method or function runs on the main actor without making the entire class run on it.

This also applies to other ordinary actors. However, be aware that declaring methods belonging to other actors as the @MainActor property wrapper can potentially lead to the creation of deadlocks and should be handled with care. This happens because actors are designed to be thread-safe, and switching between different actor contexts can be potentially risky.

SwiftUI explicitly requires UI operations to be run on the main queue. Therefore, when you modify @State, @Binding, or any other SwiftUI-specific property wrappers, they already automatically dispatch UI updates to the main queue. There is no need to explicitly mark that code as belonging to @MainActor.

Note that you can't "instantiate" the main actor. You can mark code to be run on the main actor, or you can execute methods belonging to MainActor, which is a singleton.

For instance, you can use its `run` method to execute a closure on the main actor. `MainActor.run` is declared as follows, meaning that it can allow for any closure, including those that return a result:

```
static    func   run<T>(resultType: T.Type, body: () throws -> T) async
rethrows -> T
```

So, if you want an arbitrary block of code to be run on the main actor, `Main.run{ }` is the simplest way to achieve that result, from anywhere in your code.

`MainActor` is a special case of a global actor, meaning that it can be accessed anywhere in your code, using its annotation.

Should you desire to have similar functionality to `MainActor`, with a global actor that you can access with an annotation of your choice, you only need to annotate a normal actor with `@globalActor`. This will be a normal actor that you can access anywhere.

In the following example, we will declare two custom global actors, `DatabaseActor` and `NetworkActor`:

```
@globalActor
struct DatabaseActor {
    static let shared = Actor()
}
@globalActor
struct NetworkActor {
    static let shared = Actor()
}
```

After this declaration, you will have annotations with the same name as the actors, `@DatabaseActor` and `@NetworkActor`.

The only thing you need to implement in your own actors to use them in this way is a static shared property.

To avoid concurrency problems due to the need to execute code (e.g., database code on a specific thread and network code on another specific one), you can declare two global actors, as we have just done, and use them to reference each of the two actors, easily, without the possibility of confusion.

You can also use this mechanism to easily group methods and entire types so that they share state in their own concurrency context.

Also, any code marked with your own custom global actor annotation or run with its `shared.run` method is guaranteed not to run on the main thread.

Bridging old GCD and structured concurrency

In general, if you can, you should avoid mixing concurrency paradigms. However, sometimes, you have old code that uses GCD and you want to use it, and maybe you can't or don't want to modify the old asynchronous code you need to invoke, adapting it to the more modern structured concurrency approach, because it may be part of a library, and you may not have access to the library source code.

`withCheckedThrowingContinuation` is a Swift function that bridges between asynchronous code and traditional completion handler-based code. It's particularly useful when you have an API that uses completion handlers and you want to use it within Swift's modern `async/await`-structured concurrency model.

The `withCheckedThrowingContinuation` function takes as an argument a closure that itself takes a single argument – a continuation. This continuation can be resumed exactly once, either by returning a value with `resume(returning:)` or by throwing an error with `resume(throwing:)`.

This function is useful when dealing with APIs that are callback-based (completion handlers) and you want to wrap them in a function that can be used with `async/await`.

For instance, let's wrap the following function example:

```
func fetchData(completion: @escaping (Result<String, Error>) -> Void)
{
    // Simulating a network request with a delay
    DispatchQueue.global().asyncAfter(deadline: .now() + 2) {
        let success = true // Change this to false to simulate an
error
        if success {
            completion(.success("Data fetched successfully"))
        } else {
            completion(.failure(NSError(domain: "", code: -1,
userInfo: [NSLocalizedDescriptionKey: "Failed to fetch data"])))
        }
    }
}
```

We can create a wrapper for the previous old-style `async` function using `withCheckedThrowingContinuation`, as shown in the following code snippet:

```
func fetchAsyncData() async throws -> String {
    try await withCheckedThrowingContinuation { continuation in
        fetchData { result in
            switch result {
            case .success(let data):
```

```
                    continuation.resume(returning: data)
            case .failure(let error):
                    continuation.resume(throwing: error)
            }
        }
    }
}
```

Finally, you can test the functionality of the fetchAsyncData wrapper function

by invoking it within a Swift Playground, where you will have copied both definitions of the fetchAsyncData and fetchData functions, as shown in the following code example:

```
import PlaygroundSupport
PlaygroundPage.current.needsIndefiniteExecution = true

Task {
    do {
        let data = try await fetchAsyncData()
        print(data)
    } catch {
        print("An error occurred: \(error)")
    }
}
```

Summary

In this chapter, we examined structured concurrency in Swift and explained why this new modern approach is preferable to the old ones. We examined the basic components of structured concurrency, including async/await, async let, tasks, task groups, and asynchronous sequences and streams. You were introduced to the preferred way to synchronize tasks, actors, including the MainActor and user-defined global actors. Finally, we learned how to use the new structured approach with old code that uses old concurrency models.

In the next chapter, we will introduce the SwiftData framework.

14

An Introduction to SwiftData

SwiftData is the new ORM framework introduced by Apple to replace **Core Data**. At the time of writing this book, you need to know both frameworks, with the view that in about two years, Core Data will only be used for legacy projects. New projects based on newer versions of the Apple operating system should preferably use SwiftData to implement persistency. SwiftData is less of a great choice if your existing users still use iOS 16 or previous versions of the operating system, or if you need features of Core Data that are yet to be introduced in this new framework. For more advanced uses, you may need to stick to Core Data right now.

This chapter will introduce this new persistence framework that is going to become increasingly important for SwiftUI-based development in the next few years.

SwiftData was announced at the **Worldwide Developers Conference** (**WWDC**) 2023. It solves the same problem as Core Data: it allows applications to persist data, that is, making sure that data is stored so that it is still accessible between two executions of an app.

SwiftData relies on modern structured concurrency and is Swift native, rather than being based on Objective-C. SwiftData aims not to have external dependencies and to have simpler code while being easier and more robust. It can coexist with Core Data in the same application project. This allows you to gradually replace Core Data, rather than forcing you to convert all your existing code at once.

SwiftData has been introduced in Xcode 15 and is currently supported on a range of Apple operating systems, including iOS 17, iPadOS 17, macOS 14, Mac Catalyst 17, tvOS 17, watchOS 10, and visionOS 1.0. visionOS 1.0 is in beta and at the time of writing this book requires Xcode 15.2.

In this chapter, we're going to cover the following main topics:

- SwiftData and Core Data
- The main features of SwiftData
- SwiftData and SwiftUI
- Binding changes
- Creating a data model

Technical requirements

You will require a recent Apple computer to run the examples and code in this book. In general, the more RAM and the more powerful your system, the better. The examples in this book have been tested on an M3 MacBook Pro running macOS 4.2 (Sonoma) with 48 GB of RAM. It will work just as well on an Intel machine.

Understanding the differences between SwiftData and Core Data

SwiftData has recently been introduced and has room to grow. It has some current limitations that Apple is likely to address in the near future.

Presently, SwiftData is missing some key features that are present in Core Data and allow some of the most advanced use cases:

- There is no equivalent of `NSCompoundPredicate`, so it is not possible to create complex predicates.

- There is no replacement for `NSFetchedResultController` for executing queries and reacting to changes.

- There is no support for derived attributes. **Derived attributes** can be defined and managed using the Core Data model editor in Xcode.

In Core Data, derived attributes can be based on the following:

- **Calculation**: Computed based on an expression that you specify. This expression can reference other attributes of the entity, as well as attributes of related entities.

- **Storage**: While derived attributes are computed, their values can be cached in the persistent store alongside other data, without needing to be recalculated, improving performance.

- **Updating**: Core Data updates the value of a derived attribute whenever any of the attributes it depends on change, for example, the `lastUpdated` property.

- **Expressions**: The expressions used to define derived attributes can use many operators and functions, allowing complex calculations to be performed.

In SwiftData, there are no sectioned *fetch requests*, which are useful when dealing with sectioned table views and collection views in UIKit.

SwiftData does not have the concept of child contexts, which can be handy for handling form input with validation before committing to the main context in Core Data.

Now, let's explore a comparison between SwiftData and Core Data in *Table 14.1*, which highlights the key features of SwiftData and their equivalents in Core Data:

SwiftData Feature	Corresponding Core Data Feature
`#Predicate`	`NSPredicate`
`FetchDescriptor`	`NSFetchDescriptor`
`FetchRequest`	`NSFetchRequest`
`MigrationStage`	`NSMigrationStage`
`ModelContainer`	`NSPersistentContainer`
`ModelContainer` supports iCloud if enabled	`NSPersistentCloudKitContainer`
`ModelContext`	`NSManagedObjectContext`
`PersistentModel` and `@Model` class	`NSManagedObject`
`SchemaMigrationPlan`	`NSEntityMigrationPolicy`
`SortDescriptor`	`NSSortDescriptor`

Table 14.1 – SwiftData and Core Data equivalents

Some of these and other features are going to be introduced in the future, as improvements of SwiftData. If any of these are fundamental for your specific use case, you should still be using Core Data.

> **Important note**
> Note that `#Predicate` and `@Model` are Swift macros that have been added with Swift 5.9. The hash symbol (#) marks free-standing macros that can produce code on their own, without being attached to a language entity, such as a class. The at symbol (@) in `@Model` instead marks a class macro, indicating that the class needs to be augmented and used as a data model.

In the next section, I will explain how SwiftData interacts with SwiftUI.

SwiftData and SwiftUI

SwiftData introduces a declarative Swift-native API. It allows developers to work with data persistence in iOS apps seamlessly, and like SwiftUI follows a purely declarative paradigm.

Let's take a look at the features of SwiftData:

- SwiftData can perform automatic migrations of the underlying model data, allowing you to maintain a consistent state for the data after application updates. It simplifies the boilerplate and error-prone code associated with data migrations.

- SwiftData has live updates. One of its main features is the live updates to SwiftUI views when the underlying data changes, without the need for manual refreshes. This is consistent with SwiftUI design and is facilitated through the `@Query` property wrapper, which we will cover later in this chapter in the *Fetching data* section.

- SwiftData requires minimal code and has a straightforward setup. It leverages Swift's modern structured concurrency features and does not require external dependencies; you don't need to link it as a framework.

- Like Core Data, it also integrates with CloudKit, allowing enhanced syncing on the cloud.

- Of course, being Swift native, and leveraging language features that are present only in Swift, there is no way SwiftData can be made compatible with Objective-C, unless you want to build that support from scratch yourself, which is probably unwise.

- SwiftData has richer, simpler-to-use features, compared to Core Data. With SwiftUI and SwiftData, developers can more easily configure their data store, enable or disable options, and enable undo and autosave functionalities. With Core Data, the developer would have needed to perform save activities manually, while SwiftData has an autosave functionality.

- Being Swift native, SwiftData has stricter data type checking. For instance, it ensures that data types used to filter data with predicates are correct at compile time.

In the next section, I will briefly mention the changes introduced in the binding mechanisms, as these affect the use of SwiftData and change a little from what we need to use in older versions of SwiftUI. In the meantime, be warned that there's also less documentation and experience available for SwiftData, but the situation is likely to improve rapidly.

Exploring changes in the binding mechanisms

1. With iOS 17, iPadOS 17, macOS 14, tvOS 17, watchOS 10, and visionOS 1.0, SwiftUI bindings have been simplified. To support these changes, you should perform the following tips on any existing code you want to modernize:

- Rather than using `ObservableObject` and `StateObject`, it is now possible to use the **Observation** pattern (`https://developer.apple.com/documentation/observation/`). If you already have code that was written for previous versions of the operating systems, you should replace classes inheriting from `ObservableObject` and `StateObject` with classes marked with the `@Observable` macro.

You should perform this change incrementally; it is not wise to change all your code base in one go. Notice that the @Observable macro can only be applied to classes, not value types such as enums and structs.

The properties of an @Observable class, if they are visible, are all observable. They don't need any more to be marked as @Published; the accessibility of the @Observable class will instead determine which of the properties are observable.

- If you don't want a specific property to be tracked, you can use the @ObservationIgnored macro to mark that property to be ignored.

- In SwiftUI, when a bound variable changes, the views that depend on that will get re-rendered on the screen. Due to performance improvements, now the view depending on that value will get re-evaluated only if the affected view actually needs to be redrawn and is affected by this change; if the bound variable change does not affect the view, the redraw of that view won't get triggered.

Thankfully, these changes in binding mechanisms lead to a reduction of complexity in programming. Now, rather than having to deal with six different choices, to be used in different situations, we have just three: @State, @Bindable, and @Environment.

Let's look at these in greater detail:

- @State is unchanged and is still used to bind a variable to the view that contains it. As a best practice, @State variables should be declared private, to make it apparent that they are used to bind the **private state**, that is, local, belonging to a view, and not exposed outside it.

> **Additional reading**
> @State is explained in full in the developer documentation: https://developer.apple.com/documentation/swiftui/state/.

- @Bindable is instead used to mark those properties of an @Observable class that you want to bind bi-directionally, that is, they are mutable. As before, you will need to mark each name of these properties with a dollar sign ($) prefix when you reference them. You can use @Bindable on the properties of an @Observable object.

- The main difference between @Bindable and the old @Binding is that while @Binding can only refer to an external variable to the view, @Bindable can reference any property in an @Observable, including any bindings to a SwiftData data model, global variables, properties that exist outside of SwiftUI types, or even local variables.

> **Additional reading**
> @Bindable is explained in full in the developer documentation: https://developer.apple.com/documentation/swiftui/bindable#.

- `@Environment` now works both for values that need to be bound globally, whether these are defined by the user, which previously required `EnvironmentObject`, and if they are provided by the system (the old `Environment`).

Additional reading

You will find a complete explanation of `@Environment` here: `https://developer.apple.com/documentation/swiftui/environment`.

`StateObject` was used before iOS 17 to preserve the state of an observable object when a view gets re-rendered. Achieving this with `@Observable` requires ensuring that the same instance of the `@Observable` class is used whenever the view is re-rendered.

The following code example shows the use of `@Bindable`:

```swift
import SwiftUI

@Observable
class Illumination {
    var isOn: Bool = false
}

struct MyView: View {
    @Bindable var lightBackground: Illumination
    var body: some View {
        VStack{
            Spacer()
            Toggle(isOn: $lightBackground.isOn) {
                Text("Lights")
            }.fixedSize()
        }
    }
}

struct ContentView: View {
    @State private var light = Illumination()

    var body: some View {
        VStack {
            MyView(lightBackground: light)
            if light.isOn {
                Text("On")
            }
        }
```

```
                    else {
                            Text("off")
                                    .colorInvert()
                    }
                    Divider()
                    Text("Example of a bindable var")
                            .foregroundStyle(light.isOn ? .primary :
Color.white)
                }
            .frame(maxWidth: .infinity, maxHeight: .infinity)
            .background(light.isOn ? Color.white : Color.blue)
        }
}

#Preview {
        ContentView()
}
```

You can declare a variable inside the view as @Bindable. A variable, to be @Bindable, needs to conform to Sendable and Identifiable. The result is shown in the following screenshot:

Figure 14.1 – An example of @Bindable

In the next section, I will explain how a data model is created in SwiftData.

Creating a data model

A data model is a class that represents the structure of data. SwiftData lets the developers design this using code, rather than with an editor inside Xcode.

Now, let's take a look at the components of a data model:

- **Model classes**: The core of the SwiftData data model is the model classes, which define the schema for a SwiftData application. This schema comprises entities (which map to database tables) with their attributes (which are equivalent to columns in a relational database model), together with relationships and constraints. This is conceptually no different from Core Data. However, now you do this with code, using Swift macro decorations.

  To create a data model with SwiftUI, after importing the SwiftData framework, you need to declare a Swift class, and adding in front of it the `@Model` macro, to convert it into a model managed by SwiftData. A class used for a model does not need to be declared final, but subclassing it would probably be unwise and create problems. We suggest, as a best practice, that you mark them with `final`.

  You can't use value types for this purpose; structs and enums can, however, be used as data within data models, together with every type that conforms to the `Codable` protocol.

- **Custom schema creation**: SwiftData constructs a custom schema using the models provided, mapping fields to the underlying storage. This mapping ensures that objects are fetched from the database when necessary and are automatically saved at appropriate times without additional developer intervention.

  This aspect of SwiftData also provides a mechanism, via the `ModelContext` API, allowing developers to have finer control over the process if so desired.

  You define models in Swift using the `@Model` macro, which automatically enables data persistence for the class it annotates. The `@Model` macro requires the type to be a class, not a struct, and it converts stored properties into getters and setters for interacting with SwiftData storage.

As an exercise, create a new app with Xcode 15, and select **Persistence**, indicating **SwiftData** as an option, as shown:

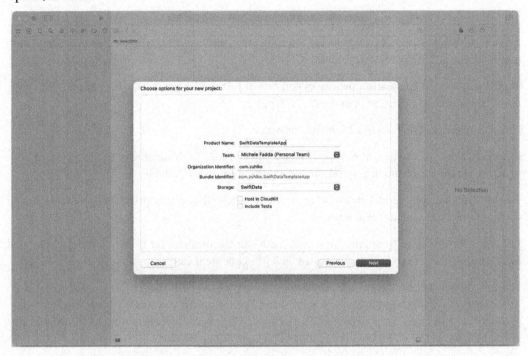

Figure 14.2 – Creating a SwiftData app using the template

Inspect the created code and run the app.

We will find that the Xcode template for SwiftData created an app containing three Swift source files: `Item.swift`, `ContentView.swift`, and a file containing the root composition, the `@main` struct. This last file and the struct inside it will have the name of the project, followed by `App.swift`.

In the `Item.swift` file, we will find our first data model.

Let's examine it:

```
import Foundation
import SwiftData


@Model
final class Item {
        var timestamp: Date

        init(timestamp: Date) {
```

```
                    self.timestamp = timestamp
        }
    }
```

A SwiftData model file needs two imports: `Foundation` and `SwiftData`. Despite SwiftData being useful for SwiftUI, it does not depend on it.

The data this small application processes consists of just the `Item` class, which contains a single property variable, `timestamp`, of the `Date` type.

The class needs an `Init` method, which is provided.

In a model class, you can have any property non-computed attribute belonging to `Int`, `Bool`, `String`, or any struct or enum, and in general, any type that conforms to Codable.

You can have as many model classes as are needed to describe your entities, one per "table" if you want to think in SQL-equivalent terms.

In the case of this simple app, the "source of truth" for the model layer is this class definition, and SwiftData will use this to keep the persisted data in a consistent state.

You can change the behavior of one property by using the `Attribute(_:originalName:hashModifier:)` macro and specify values for the options that drive the desired behavior. For instance, you can modify an attribute to be unique. This would be equivalent to adding a constraint to a table, in SQL parlance.

Let's do that. We'll modify the timestamp so that it becomes unique, this way:

```
    @Attribute(.unique)
    var timestamp: Date
```

The app will, of course, continue to work nicely after this simple change.

The root composition, the `<name-of-the-application>App.swift` file, will instantiate the `@main` struct of the app, with `sharedModelContainer` inside it.

The file created is the following:

```
import SwiftUI
import SwiftData

@main
struct SwiftDataTemplateAppApp: App {
    var sharedModelContainer: ModelContainer = {
        let schema = Schema([
```

```
                    Item.self
            ])
            let modelConfiguration = ModelConfiguration(schema:
schema, isStoredInMemoryOnly: false)

            do {
                return try ModelContainer(for: schema,
configurations: [modelConfiguration])
            } catch {
                fatalError("Could not create ModelContainer: \
(error)")
            }
        }()

    var body: some Scene {
        WindowGroup {
            ContentView()
        }
        .modelContainer(sharedModelContainer)
    }
}
```

This is similar to what the Core Data template does.

The model configuration contains the schema, that is, the set of model classes – in our case, just the Item class. That configuration is used to create a ModelConfiguration instance, which is in turn used to create a shared ModelContainer instance. Yes, this is an example of the **Singleton pattern**.

ModelContainer is then passed to WindowGroup using the .modelContainer modifier, which is the actual point of integration with the SwiftUI framework, where the model gets injected into the WindowGroup containing the ContentView view instantiated at app launch.

Note that, in Swift, .self is used to refer to the type itself, rather than an instance of the type. This can be used for various purposes, such as accessing static members or, as in this case, to pass the type as a parameter.

Finally, this is the ContentView file generated:

```
import SwiftUI
import SwiftData
struct ContentView: View {
    @Environment(\.modelContext) private var modelContext
    @Query private var items: [Item]

    var body: some View {
```

```
            NavigationSplitView {
                List {
                    ForEach(items) { item in
                        NavigationLink {
                            Text("Item at \(item.timestamp,
format: Date.FormatStyle(date: .numeric, time: .standard))")
                        } label: {
                            Text(item.timestamp, format: Date.
FormatStyle(date: .numeric, time: .standard))
                        }
                    }
                    .onDelete(perform: deleteItems)
                }
#if os(macOS)
                .navigationSplitViewColumnWidth(min: 180, ideal:
200)
#endif
                .toolbar {
#if os(iOS)
                    ToolbarItem(placement: .navigationBarTrailing)
{
                        EditButton()
                    }
#endif
                    ToolbarItem {
                        Button(action: addItem) {
                            Label("Add Item", systemImage:
"plus")
                        }
                    }
                }
            } detail: {
                Text("Select an item")
            }
        }

    private func addItem() {
        withAnimation {
            let newItem = Item(timestamp: Date())
            modelContext.insert(newItem)
        }
    }

    private func deleteItems(offsets: IndexSet) {
        withAnimation {
```

```
                for index in offsets {
                    modelContext.delete(items[index])
                }
            }
        }
    }

#Preview {
    ContentView()
        .modelContainer(for: Item.self, inMemory: true)
}
```

This is a `ContentView` view implementing a master-detail interface, using a `NavigationSplitView` to display a list of items and a detail view.

Conditional compilation is used to distinguish between the code supporting macOS and the code supporting iOS.

Within the `ContentView` struct, `@Environment(\.modelContext)` allows `ContentView` to access `modelContext` globally from the environment. `modelContext` is the SwiftData managed object context and is similar to Core Data's `NSManagedObjectContext`.

`@Query` is a property wrapper that automatically fetches data and provides it to the view. Here it fetches an array of type `Item`.

`NavigationView` contains `NavigationSplitView`. This view manages the display of two or more child views in a navigation interface.

`List` with `ForEach` creates a list of items, where each `Item` is displayed with a `NavigationLink`. This link shows more details about the item when tapped.

The `Text` view uses a `Date.FormatStyle` to format the `timestamp` property of each `Item`. This allows the date and time to be displayed in a user-friendly format.

`ToolbarItem` adds buttons to the toolbar. On iOS, and `EditButton` toggles the edit mode of the list, and on all platforms, the **Add Item** button creates new items.

The `private func addItem()` function creates a new `Item` with the current `Date` as a timestamp, inserting it inside `modelContext`.

The `private func deleteItems(offset:indexset)` function deletes items from the `modelContext` property, identifying them at the specified index set, and is called when the user deletes items from the UI.

The `withAnimation` block is used to perform the add and delete actions with animation.

Finally, the #Preview section configures the preview with a modelContainer property set up for Item objects and specifies that the storage should be in-memory, as you would expect for a preview.

The end result is shown in the following screenshot:

Figure 14.3 – The app created by the SwiftData template

In the next section, I will explain how to handle the different types of relationships among SwiftData objects.

Understanding relationships in SwiftData

Creating relationships between @Model classes in Swift, particularly when dealing with complex data models and SwiftUI, involves various techniques. These techniques mirror the types of relationships commonly found in databases and data modeling. Let's take a look at the different ways to create relationships in @Model classes.

One-to-one relationships

Use a property to store the related model's identifier or directly store an instance of the related model. A one-to-one relationship maps one object to a single instance of a related one, and you are not supposed to have multiple instances of the second object associated with the first one.

Let's look at an example of a one-to-one relationship:

```
class UserProfile: ObservableObject {
      @Published var userId: UUID
      // Other properties
}

class User: ObservableObject {
      @Published var id = UUID()
      @Published var profile: UserProfile
      // Other properties
}
```

The class User contains only one UserProfile instance: These two classes have a one-to-one relationship.

One-to-many relationships

A single instance of a model relates to multiple instances of another model. Use an array or a list to hold references to the many instances of the related model.

Let's look at an example of a one-to-many relationship:

```
class Post: ObservableObject {
      @Published var id = UUID()
      // Other properties
}

class User: ObservableObject {
      @Published var id = UUID()
      @Published var posts: [Post]
}
```

In the previous example, an array of Post is the many-to-one property associated with a User class (we can say that a User 'has-a' relationship with an array of Post.

Many-to-one relationships

Multiple instances of a model relate to a single instance of another model. It is similar to a one-to-many relationship, but the focus is on the reverse relationship. In a many-to-one relationship, multiple instances of one model (e.g., Child) are associated with a single instance of another model (e.g., Parent).

Implementation: Each Child instance holds a reference (like an ID) to its associated Parent. The Parent model doesn't necessarily hold a direct reference to its Child instances.

Let's look at an example of a many-to-one relationship:

```
class Parent: ObservableObject {
    @Published var id = UUID()
    // No direct reference to Child instances is needed here
}

class Child: ObservableObject {
    @Published var id = UUID()
    @Published var parentId: UUID   // Reference to a single Parent
}
```

In this example, multiple children have one parent. This is a many-to-one relationship.

Many-to-many relationships

Many-to-many relationships involve multiple instances of one model being associated with multiple instances of another model. This is typically implemented using a **join model** or an **intermediary structure** that holds references to both related models.

Let's look at an example of a many-to-many relationship:

```
class Student: ObservableObject {
    @Published var id = UUID()
    @Published var courses: [CourseEnrollment]
}

class Course: ObservableObject {
    @Published var id = UUID()
    @Published var enrolledStudents: [CourseEnrollment]
}

class CourseEnrollment: ObservableObject {
    @Published var studentId: UUID
    @Published var courseId: UUID
}
```

In this example, multiple students can be associated with multiple courses.

Each `Student` owns a list of `CourseEnrollment`, representing their enrollment in various courses.

Each `Course` tracks its enrolled students through `CourseEnrollment`.

`CourseEnrollment` is the join model, keeping references to both `Student` and `Course`.

Cascading deletion rules

Deletion rules specifically refer to the actions taken when a record is deleted.

They are created with the macro `@Relationship`.

For example, say we annotate the `var` posts within the declaration of `User` as follows:

```
@Relationship(deleteRule: .cascade) var posts = [Post]()
```

It means that whenever the SwiftData object containing the `posts` property is deleted, for example, a User, this will also delete all the posts related to the user.

Fetching data

To integrate with SwiftUI, we use the `@Query` annotation to fetch data and display it into SwiftUI views.

Here's an example:

```
@Query var posts: [Post]
var body: some View {
      List(posts) { recipe in
            NavigationLink(post.name, destination: PostView(post))
      }
}
```

The `@Query` annotation links the `posts` variable to the views so that SwiftData fetches them from the underlying database.

This has the effect of refreshing the views utilizing `posts` whenever the underlying data changes, without any action being necessary in the code.

Filtering data with predicates

To filter data in SwiftData, we use the `#Predicate` macro.

The same macro is used to filter data loaded with `@Query`, and also when selecting data to be deleted with `delete(model:)`.

For instance, if we had a database with albums of songs by bands, we could write a query such as this one to filter all the albums of the Beatles:

```
@Query(filter: #Predicate<Album> { album in
       album.band.name == "The Beatles"
}) var albums: [Album]
```

To allow the compiler to correctly handle the type information, with `#Predicate`, you need to identify the data type of the queried information, in our example, `Album`.

`#Predicate` is a macro that converts Swift code into a number of `PredicateExpression` objects. The predicate is checked at compile time for type safety, unlike `NSPredicate` from Core Data.

At the moment of writing, the process is not perfect, and `#Predicate` does not support all the features and operations on strings; sometimes, it even crashes due to bugs.

Let's look at an example. Predicates support the method `starts(with:`, and the following query is legal:

```
@Query(filter: #Predicate<Album> { movie in
       album.name.starts(with: "White Alb")
}) var albums: [Album]
```

But `hasPrefix()` and `hasSuffix()` are not supported. Similarly, `uppercased()` and `lowercased()` are not supported and may even crash.

If you want to perform a case-insensitive search, you can use the string modifier `.localisedStandardContains()`, instead.

So, SwiftData is an exciting new addition to the tools for handling data persistency in Apple systems and will eventually become the prevalent technology for this purpose in a few years. But it has some rough edges at the moment, so we would not suggest updating your existing projects using Core Data to SwiftData immediately.

Summary

In this chapter, I have given a brief introduction to SwiftData, a new persistency framework ORM that is designed to work with SwiftUI that will likely become increasingly more important, but at the time of writing this book is not completely mature yet. You have learned how to start a simple Xcode project that uses SwiftData and how different types of relationships can be specified in the data model. In the next chapter, we will talk about consuming data from REST services.

15
Consuming REST Services in SwiftUI

If you've been reading this book up to this point, you should be familiar with SwiftUI and its role in streamlining interface design. This chapter delves into utilizing REST services within a SwiftUI application. Considering the widespread need for iOS apps to communicate over the internet, network operations are routine. The aim here is to arm you with the skills required to incorporate the most prevalent method of network communication into your SwiftUI programming activities.

Understanding network data involves grasping HTTP requests, managing JSON data, and updating the UI in response to asynchronous events.

We'll begin by looking at how to use the `URLSession` class to execute HTTP requests. By using this adaptable API for network calls, you'll learn the ropes of retrieving data from RESTful endpoints.

JSON management plays a crucial role in interacting with REST services. We'll discuss how to employ Swift's Codable protocol to translate JSON into Swift formats and vice versa. This simplifies JSON handling, allowing you to concentrate on the core functionality of your app rather than the intricacies of JSON parsing.

Communication with the network layer typically happens through `ObservableObject` and the `@Published` properties, which change the UI when data changes. This ensures the UI shows the latest data. Another essential topic we will discuss is error handling. Various issues can cause network requests to fail. It is important to handle errors and offer feedback to the user when there is a failure. We will go over some tips for handling common errors in network requests and how to implement them in a SwiftUI context.

In this chapter, we're going to cover the following main topics:

- An overview of REST
- Implementing REST requests in Swift
- Codable, Encodable, and Decodable

- Using `URLSession`
- `URLProtocol`

Technical requirements

You require a recent Apple computer to run the examples and code in this chapter. In general, the more RAM and more powerful your system, the better. This chapter will work on an Intel MacBook Pro running macOS 13.1 (Ventura) with 16 GB of RAM. It will work just as fine on a more recent Apple Silicon machine.

For this chapter and the rest of the book, you need Xcode version 14.3 or later.

The examples in this chapter have also been tested on a MacBook Pro M3 with 48 GB of RAM, Xcode 15.2 running on macOS Sonoma 14.2.1.

You will find the code related to this chapter here: `https://github.com/PacktPublishing/An-iOS-Developer-s-Guide-to-SwiftUI`, under the `CH15` folder.

An overview of REST

REST is an acronym that stands for **Representational State Transfer**. REST is a set of principles for designing networked applications. It's used to build services that can be accessed over the web. When you hear about REST in the context of web and mobile development, it often relates to RESTful APIs or services, which allow different software systems to communicate with each other over the internet.

The phrase *Representational State Transfer* is used because, in REST, the state of a resource (such as an object, file, or service) is transferred through representations (typically JSON or XML data formats). When you interact with a web service using REST, you're essentially transferring a representation of the state of that resource between the client and the server. This allows a standardized way of interacting with web services, simplifying the creation and use of APIs.

To summarize, a RESTful service has the following properties:

- **Uses standard HTTP methods**: It uses HTTP methods, such as `GET` to retrieve data, `POST` to create new resources, `PUT` to update existing resources, and `DELETE` to remove resources.

- **Is stateless**: Each request from client to server must contain all the information the server needs to understand and complete the request. The server does not store the state of the client session.

- **Operates on resources**: Resources, such as user data or files, are exposed as URLs on the web. Each resource is identified by its **Uniform Resource Identifier** (**URI**).

- **Is client-server based**: The client, in our case, will be a Swift application, and the server (which hosts the RESTful service) will operate independently and communicate via requests (from client to server) and responses (from server to client).

- **Supports caching**: Responses must be defined as cacheable or non-cacheable, which helps in improving the application performance by reusing previously fetched resources.

For a Swift developer, interacting with RESTful APIs usually involves making network requests to specific URLs, handling the responses (often in JSON format), and integrating that data into your app. Swift's URLSession class is commonly used for this purpose, allowing you to create and manage HTTP networking requests.

The following picture illustrates the most used REST verbs (HTTP methods):

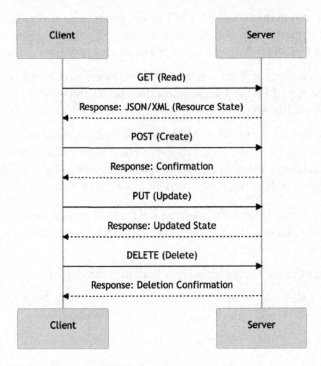

Figure 15.1 – Most commonly used REST verbs

Here is an explanation of the terms used with REST:

- **Request**: In the context of a RESTful API, a request is made by a client to a server. It is an action to be performed on a resource identified by a URI. A request is composed of several parts, including the HTTP method (verb), the headers, the URI, and optionally, the body.

- **Body**: The body of the request is the part of an HTTP message that contains the data being sent to the server. In RESTful APIs, the body typically contains data in formats such as JSON or XML when you need to send data to the server (e.g., with `POST` or `PUT` requests).

- **Response**: The response is what the server sends back to the client after receiving a request. It contains the status of the request (success or failure), an HTTP status code, headers, and sometimes a body with the requested information or details about any errors that occurred.

- **Status**: The status in the context of an HTTP response is a three-digit code that indicates the result of the request. It is part of the response and helps the client understand whether the request was successful if there was an error, and what type of error occurred.

- **URI**: A URI is a string of characters used to identify a resource over a network. In the case of RESTful APIs, the URI is the address where the resource can be accessed. It specifies the path to the resource on the server.

- **Headers**: Headers are part of the HTTP request and response message and provide metadata about the message. Headers can include a wide range of information, such as the content type of the message body, authentication tokens, and instructions on how to cache the data. Headers consist of key-value pairs and can be used for various purposes:

  - `Content-Type`: Specifies the media type of the resource or data in the body of the request/response. For example, `Content-Type: application/json` indicates that the body contains JSON data.

  - `Authorization`: Contains the credentials to authenticate a user agent with a server.

  - `Accept`: Specifies the media types that the client can understand, and the server can use this information to select an appropriate response content type.

  - `User-Agent`: Provides information about the client software that is making the request.

  - `Cache-Control`: Directives for caching mechanisms in both requests and responses.

The following table provides a summary of the main RESTful HTTP verbs (methods), their meanings, the request bodies they might include, and the typical response status codes for both successful and unsuccessful requests:

HTTP Verb	Meaning	Request Body	Successful Response	Failure Response
GET	Read	None	200 OK	404 Not Found
POST	Create	Resource representation	201 Created	400 Bad Request
PUT	Update/replace	Full resource state	200 OK	404 Not Found
PATCH	Update/modify	Partial resource state	200 OK	400 Bad Request
DELETE	Delete	None	200 OK	404 Not Found
HEAD	Read header	None	200 OK	404 Not Found
OPTIONS	Return HTTP verbs	None	200 OK	405 Method Not Allowed
CONNECT	Establish a tunnel	None	200 OK	405 Method Not Allowed
TRACE	Echo the request	None	200 OK	405 Method Not Allowed

Besides success and failure, the server can report other errors in response to client requests. The most important of these HTTP errors are as follows:

- **3xx Redirection**: These indicate that further action needs to be taken by the client to complete the request.

  - 301 Moved Permanently: The web resource has been moved to a new URI permanently
  - 302 Found: The web resource has been moved temporarily
  - 304 Not Modified: The web resource has not been modified and can be loaded from the client's cache

- **4xx Client Error**: These signify an error that the client is responsible for:

  - 401 Unauthorized: The client needs to authenticate itself to get the requested response
  - 403 Forbidden: The client does not have the right to access the content
  - 405 Method Not Allowed: The HTTP method is not supported for the request
  - 408 Request Timeout: The server timed out waiting for the request

- **5xx Server Error**: These codes indicate an error on the server side:

  - `500 Internal Server Error`: An unexpected error condition was encountered on the server

  - `501 Not Implemented`: The server either does not recognize the request method or is unable to fulfill the request

  - `503 Service Unavailable`: The server is not ready to handle the request, perhaps due to maintenance or overload

  - `504 Gateway Timeout`: The server, acting as a gateway, did not receive a timely response from an upstream server

The following are the verbs supported by HTTP, along with their syntax:

- `GET`: Used for retrieving data. A successful `GET` request normally returns a `200 OK` status code along with the data in the form of JSON or XML. A failure might result in a `404 Not Found` if the resource does not exist.

- `POST`: Used for the creation of a new resource. It often includes a request body that provides the data representing the new resource, commonly in JSON format. A successful POST request may return `201 Created` along with the location of the created resource. A failure could return `400 Bad Request` if the input data is invalid.

- `PUT`: Used for updating an existing resource or creating a new one at a specific URL. The request body contains the complete new state of the resource. A successful PUT request returns `200 OK`, while a failure returns `404 Not Found` if the resource to be updated doesn't exist.

- `PATCH`: Is like `PUT`, but it is used to partially update to a resource. The request body only needs to contain the changes, not the complete resource data. A successful `PATCH` request also returns `200 OK`, and a failure might result in `400 Bad Request` if the changes are not valid, for example, if the request parameters are not recognized.

- `DELETE`: Is used to delete a resource. It does not require a request body. A successful `DELETE` request usually returns `200 OK` with a response body that may or may not include a representation of the deleted resource. A failure might return `404 Not Found` if there's nothing to delete.

- `HEAD`: Identical to `GET` except that it does not return a message body in the response. It is used to obtain the metadata associated with the resource. Success and failure responses are the same as for a `GET` request.

- `OPTIONS`: Used to describe the communication options for the target resource. A successful `OPTIONS` request may return `200 OK` with the allowed HTTP methods in the headers. Failure might result in `405 Method Not Allowed` if the method is not available.

- CONNECT: Converts the request connection to a transparent TCP/IP tunnel, usually to facilitate SSL-encrypted communication (HTTPS) through an unencrypted HTTP proxy. Success and failure responses are similar to the other methods.

- TRACE: Echoes the received request, primarily for testing or diagnostic purposes. It returns 200 OK on success. TRACE is rarely used and is often disabled for security reasons.

These verbs are a part of the **HTTP/1.1 protocol**, and the status codes are standardized by the IETF in RFC 7231 (`https://datatracker.ietf.org/doc/html/rfc7231`).

Please note that the actual implementations you will meet as a developer will vary based on server configuration and specific APIs. It is the responsibility of the web service implementers to respect the standard and choose how to handle error responses, and the implementation may differ from the standard.

To pass parameters from the client to the server, different verbs use different mechanisms. Parameters can be passed from the client to the server using various methods, depending on the HTTP verb (REST verb) being used:

- GET: Parameters are passed in the URI query string. The query string is appended to the URI with a ? and then followed by key-value pairs separated by & for the first parameter and : for the successive parameters, for example, `/api/items?category=magazines&price=15`.

- POST, PUT, and PATCH: Parameters can be included in the request body. The body of the request is often formatted as JSON or XML. For example, a JSON body might look like this:

```
{
    "category": "magazines",
    "price": 15
}
```

These verbs can also pass parameters in the URI or the query string, but it's less common for the actual data to be passed this way.

- DELETE: Although it's less common to send a body with DELETE, it's possible to do so in the same way as POST, PUT, and PATCH. But more commonly, parameters are passed in the URI or query string to specify the resource to delete, for example, `/api/users/123`, where 123 is the ID of the user to be deleted.

- HEAD and OPTIONS: Parameters are typically passed in the URI query string, like with GET.

URL encoding

Parameters passed with HTTP requests are more often than not encoded using URL Encoding. **URL encoding**, or **percent encoding**, is a mechanism for encoding parameters in a URI. It replaces some characters with one or more character triplets that consist of the percent character, %, followed by two hexadecimal digits. The two hexadecimal digits represent the numeric value of the replaced character.

For example, the space character in a URL is replaced by %20 because the ASCII value for space is 32, which translates to 20 in hexadecimal. Similarly, an ampersand (&) becomes %26, as the ASCII value for & is 38, which translates to 26 in hexadecimal.

URL encoding is relevant to REST in the following:

- **Query strings**: When you pass parameters through the query string in a GET request, special characters must be URL encoded to ensure they are interpreted correctly by the server. For example, if a query parameter contains an ampersand or equals sign, which are characters with special meanings in URLs, they need to be encoded to avoid being misinterpreted as part of the URL structure itself.

- **Path**: If a resource identifier (part of the URL path, not the query string) includes characters that are not allowed in URLs, such as spaces or slashes, these must be URL encoded.

- **Form data**: When submitting data from a web form using the POST method, the content type is often application/x-www-form-urlencoded, and the body of the request is in the same format as a query string, with key-value pairs separated by ampersands and equal signs. Special characters in the keys or values are URL encoded.

- **Unicode characters**: URLs are limited to ASCII characters, so any Unicode characters must be represented using percent-encoded UTF-8 sequences.

- **Safety and idempotence**: In some cases, characters are encoded to prevent them from being misinterpreted as control characters by servers and intermediate devices, such as proxies and routers. This ensures that the HTTP methods such as GET, PUT, DELETE, PATCH, HEAD, and OPTIONS are safe (they should not alter server state) and idempotent, that is, the same request can be repeated multiple times without different outcomes. For example, if you delete a resource, it is gone, and deleting it again will not change the state beyond the first deletion.

It's important to handle URL encoding properly because handling it incorrectly can lead to security issues such as injection attacks, as well as functional errors where the server misinterprets the intended action of the client.

Hypertext Transfer Protocol (HTTP) and **Hypertext Transfer Protocol Secure (HTTPS)** are used for transmitting and receiving information across the internet. The primary difference between them is that HTTPS provides an additional layer of security and encrypts data.

HTTP is the standard protocol used in the transfer of hypertext documents through the World Wide Web. It operates at the application layer and loads web pages using hypertext links. However, the data transferred by HTTP is not encrypted; thus, the information can be easily intercepted.

HTTPS is essentially HTTP over a secure connection. It uses the SSL/TLS protocols for the encryption of communication and secure identification of a web server, ensuring that data transfer is secure. This is important for transactions that involve sensitive information, such as banking details or personal information, in order to prevent easy interception by hostile actors such as hackers.

Ports

Ports in internet protocols are so named as an analogy for doors in a building. Just as a building might have multiple doors for different purposes, such as entrance, exit, and deliveries, a computer uses ports to manage different types of internet traffic. Each port is given a number, called the **port number**, which identifies a specific service running on the computer.

When information is transmitted over the internet, the port number tells the receiving computer which program should handle the incoming data. For example, web browsers usually communicate through port 80 for HTTP or port 443 for HTTPS, while email services might use port 25 for **SIMPLE mail protocol** (**SMTP**, used for sending emails) or port 110 for **Post Office protocol** (**POP3**, used for receiving emails).

You could liken the computer's IP address to its street number, and the port number as a specific flat within that building. This system allows computers to run multiple services simultaneously without mixing up data, ensuring that emails are directed to the email service, web pages are delivered to the browser, and so on.

In the next section, we will explain how to implement these REST requests in Swift.

Understanding REST requests in Swift

We are now going to explain the process for handling HTTP or HTTPS requests.

Implementing RESTful services in Swift typically involves making HTTP requests to a server, handling the responses, and parsing the JSON data. The most common way to achieve this is by using the `URLSession` API, which provides the most common native framework for networking in Apple operating systems.

`URLSession`, which we will examine in full, is part of a larger system, the **URL Loading System**, provided by Apple's Foundation framework. The URL loading system is a set of classes designed to access content via URLs. It supports data retrieval, uploading, downloading, and some level of protocol-specific interactions.

The URL Loading System is built around the core concept of communicating with resources identified by URLs, making it suitable for a wide range of network operations, from simple fetch requests to complex network communications.

The URL Loading System consists mainly of the following key components:

- `NSURL`: Represents a URL that can be a file path or a web address.

- `URLRequest`: Encapsulates all the information about a request (such as the URL, HTTP method, headers, and body) that you want to load.

- `URLSession`: Coordinates network data transfer tasks. It's designed to handle a group of related network data transfer tasks. Sessions are configured using `URLSessionConfiguration`.

- `URLSessionTask`: The base class for tasks within a session. Tasks are divided into four main types:

  - `URLSessionDataTask`: This retrieves content from a server using HTTP GET or POST methods and returns data directly to the app in memory. Suitable for short, often interactive requests to a server.

  - `URLSessionUploadTask`: This is like `URLSessionDataTask` but optimized for uploading data. It can upload data from a file or memory.

  - `URLSessionDownloadTask`: This downloads files from a server directly to the local filesystem, making it ideal for large downloads that might need to continue in the background.

  - `URLSessionWebSocketTask`: This was introduced in iOS 13 and manages a WebSocket connection, sending and receiving messages.

- `URLSessionConfiguration`: Defines the behavior and policies to use when a session makes a network request. There are three types of configurations: **default**, **ephemeral**, and **background**.

- `URLSessionDelegate` and related protocols: Allows handling events for an entire session or individual tasks, such as authentication challenges, errors, or the need for more data.

The following are the types of connections supported by `URLSession`:

- **Default**: Default connections are the standard way to perform data tasks and upload tasks in iOS. These connections use a shared session configuration that leverages the default system settings for caching, cookie storage, and other network behaviors. When a `URLSession` is created with a default configuration, it uses global caching, cookie storage, and credential storage, making it suitable for most networking tasks that don't require any special configuration. Default connections are ideal for standard network requests where you want to take advantage of the efficiencies provided by system-wide configurations and caching.

- **Ephemeral**: Ephemeral connections are designed for situations where there should be no disk persistence of the data due to a network operation. When a session is created with an ephemeral session configuration, iOS sets up a session whose data is kept in memory and is not written to disk. This is especially useful for sensitive data that does not need to be stored or cached, therefore ensuring a higher level of privacy. Ephemeral sessions are used with private browsing modes in web browsers or for handling sensitive data that should never be cached or persisted.

- **Background**: Background connections enable performing network operations in the background even when the app is not visible. This is done through a background session configuration. A background session may be used for tasks such as downloading content, updating content in the background, and performing large uploads without needing the app to remain active. These tasks can continue in the background or even after the app has been suspended or terminated by the system. iOS manages these tasks and provides callbacks to your app to handle data, responses, and errors when the app is next active. Background connections are particularly useful for content apps that must preload content, apps that need to perform large uploads, and any other task that must continue without user interaction.

In the next section, we will examine the protocols used for encoding and decoding data in Swift, typically to and from JSON.

Codable, Encodable, and Decodable protocols

Let's now examine the protocols used in Swift for automatically encoding and decoding data, as these are fundamental in exchanging data over the Internet.

The **Codable** protocol in Swift is an alias that groups together both the **Encodable** and **Decodable** protocols. The Encodable protocol allows a Swift data type to be encoded, and Decodable allows it to be decoded.

If you specify Codable as a protocol conformance, the data type referred to will conform to both Encodable and Decodable. If you want to just use encoding, use Encodable; if you instead want to restrict the use to decoding, use Decodable.

Introduced in Swift 4, Codable makes it easy to encode and decode custom data types to and from JSON, XML, or even **property lists** (**plists**). This functionality becomes particularly valuable when working with networking code when you need to send and receive data to and from a server or when you are persisting data to the filesystem.

Swift can automatically generate the code needed to encode and decode the most common data types, provided that all their properties are themselves Codable. This significantly simplifies code.

The following data types are Codable:

- **Primitive types**: String, Int, Float, Double, Bool

- **Collections**: Arrays and dictionaries provided that both keys and values conform to Codable. Typically, the keys are String or Int. Sets are also Codable, provided that the element type conforms to Codable.

- **Complex types**: Structs, classes, and enums are Codable provided that all their properties are themselves Codable, including the associated values for enums. For a type to be Codable, all its properties must also be Codable. This recursive requirement means that you might sometimes need to provide a custom Codable conformance implementation for some of your types, especially if they contain properties that are not inherently Codable or if you need to transform data during encoding or decoding.

The following are special cases, requiring more attention from the developer:

- `Optional`: Optional types are Codable if the wrapped type conforms to Codable. This allows for encoding and decoding values that may be `nil`.

- `Date`: Represents specific points in time. `JSONEncoder` and `JSONDecoder` provide strategies (`dateEncodingStrategy` and `dateDecodingStrategy`) for encoding and decoding `Date` instances.

- `Data`: Represents binary data. Similar to `Date`, there are strategies (`dataEncodingStrategy` and `dataDecodingStrategy`) for handling the encoding and decoding of `Data` instances.

For custom types, conformance to Codable can be either synthesized by the compiler (if all properties are themselves Codable) or implemented manually by providing custom implementations of the relevant methods:

- **Customizable coding keys**: If your data type's property names don't match the keys in the encoded format, you can define a nested enumeration named `CodingKeys` that conforms to the `CodingKey` protocol. This enumeration specifies the mapping between your property names and the keys in the encoded data.

- **Custom encoding and decoding**: For more complex data structures or when you need more control over the encoding and decoding process, you can implement the `encode(to:)` and `init(from:)` methods manually.

- **Support for nested types and enumerations**: Codable supports complex data types, including structs with nested types and enums (with associated values, provided they are Codable as well).

- **Handling of missing and optional data**: When decoding, Codable can handle missing keys and values by marking properties as optional or providing default values.

- **Extensible to support custom formats**: While Swift provides `JSONEncoder` and `JSONDecoder` for working with JSON, you can extend the Codable functionality to support other formats by creating custom encoders and decoders.

In the following example, which can be run into a Swift Playground, we will decode JSON encoded data into a struct:

```
import Foundation

struct User: Codable {
      var id: Int
      var name: String
      var email: String

      // Use CodingKeys to map property names to keys in the JSON,
only the mapped keys will be converted.
      // user_id gets remapped to id and user_email to email
      // user_address to "
      enum CodingKeys: String, CodingKey {
            case id = "user_id"
            case name
            case email = "user_email"
      }
}


// Example User instance
let user = User(id: 1, name: "Ross Super", email: "ross@example.com")

// Create a JSONEncoder to encode the user
let encoder = JSONEncoder()
encoder.outputFormatting = .prettyPrinted // For readable JSON output

do {
      let jsonData = try encoder.encode(user)
      if let jsonString = String(data: jsonData, encoding: .utf8) {
            print("Encoded JSON: \n\(jsonString)")
      }
```

```
} catch {
    print("Encoding failed: \(error)")
}

// Simulate the reception of a JSON string from a server
let jsonString = """
{
    "user_id": 3,
    "name": "Ross Super",
    "user_email": "ross@example.com"
}
"""

// Create a JSONDecoder instance in order to decode the JSON string
back into a User struct
let decoder = JSONDecoder()

do {
    let jsonData = Data(jsonString.utf8)
    let decodedUser = try decoder.decode(User.self, from: jsonData)
    print("Decoded User: \(decodedUser)")
} catch {
    print("Decoding failed: \(error)")
}
```

The output on the console will be the following:

```
Encoded JSON:
{
    "email" : "ross@example.com",
    "id" : 1,
    "name" : "Ross Super"
}
Decoded User: User(id: 3, name: "Ross Super", email: Optional("ross@
example.com"))
```

The following are the advanced features of Codable:

- **Handling data at different hierarchies**: Sometimes, the data you need is nested within a hierarchy in the JSON structure. Besides converting the JSON keys to your preferred Swift property names, CodingKeys can be used to remap data that is contained within nested structures:

  ```
  struct Profile: Codable {
      var userName: String
      var emailAddress: String
  ```

```
        enum CodingKeys: String, CodingKey {
            case userName = "user/name"
            case emailAddress = "user/email"
        }
}
```

- **Conditional encoding and decoding**: You can conditionally omit certain properties from being encoded or decoded using the `encodeIfPresent` and `decodeIfPresent` methods.

The following example shows how `decodeIfPresent` is used:

```
struct Book: Codable {
    var title: String
    var author: String
    var publicationYear: Int
    var isbn: String?

    private enum CodingKeys: String, CodingKey {
        case title, author, publicationYear, isbn
    }

    init(from decoder: Decoder) throws {
        let container = try decoder.container(keyedBy:
CodingKeys.self)
        title = try container.decode(String.self, forKey:
.title)
        author = try container.decode(String.self, forKey:
.author)
        publicationYear = try container.decode(Int.self,
forKey: .publicationYear)
        isbn = try container.decodeIfPresent(String.self,
forKey: .isbn) // Handles `null` and missing values gracefully:
// The previous line attempts to decode the isbn value if it's
present in the JSON and not null; otherwise, it sets isbn to
nil.


    }
}
```

- **Customizing date and data encoding strategies**: JSONEncoder and JSONDecoder provide options to customize how dates and binary data are represented in JSON. For example, you can specify date formats using the .dateEncodingStrategy and .dateDecodingStrategy properties. For example, the following will specify the date encoding strategy for a JSONDecoder and JSONEncoder to be in iso8601 format (an example data in ISO8601 could be 2024-02-18T12:45:00Z, where the date-time corresponds to 18 February 2024 at 12:45:

```
let encoder = JSONEncoder()
encoder.dateEncodingStrategy = .iso8601

let decoder = JSONDecoder()
decoder.dateDecodingStrategy = .iso8601
```

In the next section, we will examine how to use URLSession in detail.

Using URLSession

URLSession is the class that provides an API for performing HTTP requests and managing network data transfer tasks in iOS and macOS.

In order to get data from a URL with URLSession, you need to perform the steps illustrated in the following sequence diagram:

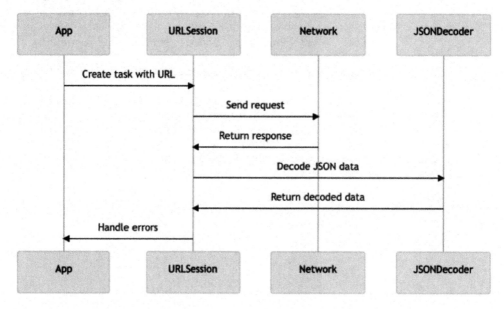

Figure 15.2 – Conceptual flow for performing a GET with URLSession

Implementing HTTP methods

HTTP methods (GET, POST, PUT, DELETE, etc.) are specified by setting the HTTP method of a URLRequest.

As an example, let's create a POST request.

A POST request submits data to a specified resource (it creates the resource on the server, e.g., a new user):

```
let url = URL(string: "https://example.com/post")!
var request = URLRequest(url: url)
request.httpMethod = "POST"
request.setValue("application/json", forHTTPHeaderField: "Content-
Type")
let postData = ["key": "value"]
let jsonData = try! JSONSerialization.data(withJSONObject: postData,
options: [])
request.httpBody = jsonData

let task = URLSession.shared.dataTask(with: request) { data, response,
error in
     // Handle response here
}
task.resume()
```

The previous code fragment creates and sends a POST request to https://example.com/post with a JSON body with the data {"key": "value"}. It sets the request's content type to application/json, serializes the postData dictionary into JSON format for the request body, and starts the network task with the shared URLSession. When the task is completed, the closure { data, response, error in ... } will be executed, handling the response, the data received, or any errors that occurred. The task.resume() call is in this case required to start the network task since tasks are initialized in a suspended state.

Setting headers

Headers are set on the URLRequest object using the setValue(_:forHTTPHeaderField:) method, as shown in the following code fragment:

```
var request = URLRequest(url: URL(string: "https://example.com")!)
request.setValue("application/json", forHTTPHeaderField: "Accept")
request.setValue("Bearer secureToken", forHTTPHeaderField:
"Authorization")
```

Handling errors

Errors are handled in the completion handler of the `dataTask`. The `error` parameter provides information about task-level errors, such as network connectivity issues. HTTP errors, such as `404` or `500`, can be detected by inspecting the `HTTPURLResponse` object, as in the following example:

```
let task = URLSession.shared.dataTask(with: request) { data, response,
error in
    if let error = error {
        print("Task error: \(error.localizedDescription)")
        return
    }

    guard let httpResponse = response as? HTTPURLResponse,
(200...299).contains(httpResponse.statusCode) else {
        print("Server error")
        return
    }

    // Process successful response here
}
task.resume()
```

Let's use a Swift Playground as a demonstration of a simple fetch of data using `async/await`:

```
// Make an indefinite execution to allow asynchronous tasks to
complete
import PlaygroundSupport
PlaygroundPage.current.needsIndefiniteExecution = true

import Foundation

// Define a struct that conforms to Codable for the JSON Post
struct Post: Codable {
    let userId: Int
    let id: Int
    let title: String
    let body: String
}
// Define an async function to perform the fetch
func fetchPost() async throws -> Post {
    guard let url = URL(string: "https://jsonplaceholder.typicode.
com/posts/1") else {
        throw URLError(.badURL)
    }
```

```
        let (data, response) = try await URLSession.shared.data(from:
url)

        guard let httpResponse = response as? HTTPURLResponse,
httpResponse.statusCode == 200 else {
            throw URLError(.badServerResponse)
        }

        let post = try JSONDecoder().decode(Post.self, from: data)
        return post
}

// Use a Task to call the async function and handle the result or any
errors
Task {
        do {
            let post = try await fetchPost()
            // Use the data (for example, print it to the console)
            print("Post Title: \(post.title)")
        } catch {
            print("Error: \(error.localizedDescription)")
        }
}
```

The preceding code fragment defines an asynchronous function, `fetchPost`, that fetches data from a URL and returns an instance of `Post`. Firstly, it attempts to create a URL object. If the URL is invalid, it throws a `URLError`. Then, using `URLSession`, it asynchronously fetches data from the URL. In this example, we are using the more modern version, `let (data, response) = try await URLSession.shared.data(from: url)`, so there's no need to resume a `dataTask`.

If the HTTP response status code is not `200`, that is, it's been successful, it throws a `URLError`. Then, this code fragment decodes the fetched data using a `JSONDecoder` into an instance of `Post` and returns it.

Finally, the code fragment includes a `Task` block that calls the `async` function, `fetchPost()`, handling the result by printing the post's title to the console or catching and printing any errors that could occur.

I will now give a complete example of accessing a REST service and displaying the fetched data with SwiftUI. For demonstration purposes, I will use a mock API available at `https://jsonplaceholder.typicode.com/users` that provides a list of fake user data.

To practically perform a GET request in a simple example app, follow these steps:

1. We will begin by setting the App struct:

```
import SwiftUI

@main
struct UrlSessionExampleApp: App {
    var body: some Scene {
        WindowGroup {
            UserListView()
        }
    }
}
```

2. Then, let's create a data structure for User:

```
import Foundation
// Define a struct that conforms to Codable to decode the data
struct User: Codable, Identifiable {
    let id: Int
    let name: String
    let username: String
    let email: String
}
```

3. Next, let's create a UserService class that performs the data fetch:

```
import Foundation

// Define a service to fetch and decode the user data
class UserService {
    func fetchUsers() async throws -> [User] {
        guard let url = URL(string: "https://
jsonplaceholder.typicode.com/users") else {
            throw URLError(.badURL)
        }

        let (data, _) = try await URLSession.shared.
data(from: url)

        let decoder = JSONDecoder()
        let users = try decoder.decode([User].self, from:
data)
```

```
                        return users
        }
}
```

4. Create an `ObservableObject` model to link to the `View` as follows:

```
import SwiftUI

// Define the Model
@MainActor
class UserListModel: ObservableObject {
        @Published var users: [User] = []
        @Published var errorMessage: String? = nil

        let service = UserService()

        func loadUsers() async {
                do {
                        let users = try await service.fetchUsers()
                        self.users = users
                } catch {
                        self.errorMessage = error.localizedDescription
                }
        }
}
```

5. We then need a list to display the loaded data:

```
import SwiftUI

// Define the list view
struct UserListView: View {
        @StateObject var viewModel = UserListModel()

        var body: some View {
                NavigationView {
                        List(viewModel.users) { user in
                                NavigationLink(destination:
UserDetailsView(user: user)) {
                                        HStack {
                                                VStack(alignment: .leading)
{
                                                        Text(user.name)
                                                                .font(.headline)
                                                        Text(user.email)
```

```
                                                          .font(.
subheadline)
                                          }
                                  }
                          }
                  }
                  .navigationTitle("Users")
                  .onAppear {
                      Task {
                              await viewModel.loadUsers()
                      }
                  }
                  .alert("Error", isPresented: Binding<Bool>.
constant($viewModel.errorMessage.wrappedValue != nil), actions:
{}, message: { Text($viewModel.errorMessage.wrappedValue ?? "")
})
                  }
          }
}
#Preview {
      UserListView()
}
```

6. And finally, create a details view to display the details when the user taps on a list's cell:

```
import SwiftUI

struct UserDetailsView: View {
      let user: User

      var body: some View {
              VStack {

                      Text(user.name)
                              .font(.title)
                      Text(user.username)
                              .font(.headline)
                      Text(user.email)
                              .font(.subheadline)
              }
              .navigationTitle(user.name)
              .navigationBarTitleDisplayMode(.inline)

      }
}
```

```
#Preview {
      UserDetailsView(user: User( id: 2,
            name: "Jerome",
            username: "Jerry",
            email: "jerry@example.com"))
}
```

This was a simple example that showed how to use URLSession and doesn't include all the necessary error handling or the full UI you might want for a production app. Publishing a full example of a production-quality network library would be beyond the scope of this book. However, you can build on these examples to add complete error handling and support for all HTTP verbs, and so on.

Certificate Pinning

Certificate pinning is a method of securing mobile and web application communication involving the SSL/TLS protocol (used to implement HTTPS) between client and server. This is done by "pinning" a server's certificate or public key directly within the application.

When the application issues network requests to the server, it checks that the certificate or public key of the server against the one that has been pinned (stored within the mobile application). If the server certificate does not match the pinned version, it issues an error as someone else is impersonating the server.

In the context of the development of Swift for iOS applications, certificate pinning helps protect network communications from man-in-the-middle attacks. Here is a high-level explanation of how you might go about implementing certificate pinning in Swift:

1. **Get the server's certificate or public key**: First, you must get the certificate or public key of the server you want to pin to. You can either export the certificate from the server or use a network tool to capture it at the time a secure connection is established.

2. **Add the certificate or public key to the app**: With the server's certificate or public key in place, you need to add it to your app's bundle, so that the app can access it at runtime for comparison against the server's certificate during the TLS handshake.

3. **Certifying and checking certificates or public keys**: After your app makes a network connection, you will capture the server's certificate from the TLS handshake. You can either use the URLSession delegate methods or use a networking library such as Alamofire that supports certificate pinning.

4. **Comparing the public key**: Get the public key from the certificate that the server presented during the handshake. Compare the extracted public key with the one you've pinned within your app. If they match, then the connection is secure, and the connection should continue with the requests. If the certificate does not match, we need to end the connection to prevent potential man-in-the-middle attacks as the connection is not secure.

URLProtocol

URLProtocol is a part of the URL Loading System in the Foundation framework. It provides a powerful mechanism for intercepting, inspecting, modifying, and even mocking HTTP requests and responses in your iOS, macOS, watchOS, and tvOS applications. It serves as the backbone for customizing the behavior of URLSession tasks and allows developers to implement custom network protocols, perform custom actions on network requests, and handle custom networking scenarios.

These are the key features and uses of URLProtocol:

- **Custom protocol handling**: URLProtocol allows you to implement support for custom URL schemes beyond the standard http, https, file, and so on. This can be useful for handling specific use cases within your app, such as routing internal app requests through a custom scheme.

- **Request and response interception**: URLProtocol provides a way to intercept all network requests and responses made by URLSession. This is particularly useful for debugging, logging network traffic, or implementing custom caching strategies.

- **Mocking network responses**: In testing environments, URLProtocol can be used to mock network responses. This is invaluable for unit testing and UI testing, where you want to test the app's behavior under controlled network conditions without making actual network requests.

- **Modifying requests and responses**: URLProtocol allows the modification of requests before they are sent to the server and responses before they are returned to the caller. This includes altering HTTP headers, changing request methods, and modifying the body of requests and responses.

URLProtocol is an abstract class, and its functionality is defined by subclassing it and implementing its core methods. The steps involved in using URLProtocol are as follows:

- **Subclassing URLProtocol**: Create a subclass of URLProtocol and implement the required methods, such as canInit(with:) to determine if this protocol can handle a given request, canonicalRequest(for:) to return a standardized version of a request, startLoading() to start loading the request, and stopLoading() to stop loading the request.

- **Registering the custom protocol**: Before your custom protocol can intercept requests, register it using URLSessionConfiguration. You can achieve this by adding your URLProtocol subclass to the protocolClasses property of a URLSessionConfiguration instance.

- **Handling requests**: In a URLProtocol subclass, the startLoading() method is where you handle incoming requests. Within this method, you can modify the request, serve a response from the cache, load a response from a local file, or generate a response programmatically.

- **Sending responses**: Use the `client` property, which receives an object conforming to the `URLProtocolClient` protocol, to send responses back to the URL Loading System. This includes sending response data, response headers, loading errors, and indicating that loading has finished.

As an example of using `URLProtocol`, let's examine the problem of the **Thundering Herd** in network communication. Suppose you have an app, and you program it to try to fetch data every hour. What would happen? Why isn't this a good choice? Even worse, if there is an error, what is likely to happen?

If our app is very popular and has many users, it will behave as its own denial of service attack due to the thundering herd problem.

The **Thundering Herd** problem is one of the performance issues that arise in computer systems, especially in web servers and databases and for other multi-threaded or multi-processed systems. Basically, this happens when a significant number of threads or processes wake up together to respond to the same event and create a tremendous demand on system resources due to contention. This issue is illustrated by the analogy of a herd of animals that suddenly start running in the same direction when a stimulus occurs. In computer systems, consider several processes or threads that were "sleeping" and were waiting for a certain condition to be met, such as data becoming available, a lock getting released, and so forth. When this condition is met, all waiting processes are awakened simultaneously to check if they can proceed. However, usually only one or a few of them can make progress (for example, acquire the lock or process the available data), while the rest would either go back to sleep or wait again.

In our case, all clients will request data from the server, at the same time, and some of them will likely fail due to the server being overwhelmed. If we retry after a non-randomized time, many clients will retry at the same precise intervals in a synchronized way. If the clients instead retry at a randomized interval, this won't happen as the requests will be spread more evenly in time, preventing the server from becoming overloaded.

Let's give an example of implementing an exponential backoff with randomization.

The retry time will increase exponentially but with a random element so that different client requests will be spread over time and will not happen at the same intervals:

```
import Foundation

import PlaygroundSupport
PlaygroundPage.current.needsIndefiniteExecution = true

// Exponential Backoff Class inheriting from URLProtocol
class ExponentialBackoffURLProtocol: URLProtocol {
    static var requestCount = 0

    override class func canInit(with request: URLRequest) -> Bool {
```

```swift
                return true
        }

        override class func canonicalRequest(for request: URLRequest) ->
URLRequest {
                return request
        }

        override func startLoading() {
                Self.requestCount += 1

                // Calculate the backoff delay
                let backoffTime = pow(2.0, Double(Self.requestCount)) +
Double.random(in: 0...1)

                // Start timing the request
                let startTime = Date()

                DispatchQueue.global().asyncAfter(deadline: .now() +
backoffTime) {
                        // Randomly decide whether to simulate an error
                        let simulateError = Bool.random()

                        if simulateError {
                                let error = NSError(domain:
"ExponentialBackoff", code: 1, userInfo: [NSLocalizedDescriptionKey:
"Simulated error"])
                                self.client?.urlProtocol(self,
didFailWithError: error)
                        } else {
                                // Normally, here you would load actual data,
for demonstration we're just finishing successfully
                                let fakeResponse = HTTPURLResponse(url: self.
request.url!, statusCode: 200, httpVersion: nil, headerFields: nil)!
                                self.client?.urlProtocol(self, didReceive:
fakeResponse, cacheStoragePolicy: .notAllowed)
                                self.client?.urlProtocolDidFinishLoading(self)
                        }

                        // End timing and print the duration
                        let endTime = Date()
                        let duration = endTime.timeIntervalSince(startTime)
                        print("Request \(Self.requestCount) finished in \
(duration) seconds with \(simulateError ? "an error" : "success")")
                }
        }
```

```swift
        override func stopLoading() {
                // Implement to support cancellation, if needed
        }
}




struct Post: Codable {
      let userId: Int
      let id: Int
      let title: String
      let body: String
}

func fetchPost() async {
      do {
              let url = URL(string: "https://jsonplaceholder.typicode.
com/posts/1")!
              let (data, response) = try await URLSession.shared.
data(from: url)

              guard let httpResponse = response as? HTTPURLResponse,
httpResponse.statusCode == 200 else {
                      throw URLError(.badServerResponse)
              }

              let post = try JSONDecoder().decode(Post.self, from: data)
              print("Post Title: \(post.title)")
      } catch {
              print("Error: \(error.localizedDescription)")
      }
}

// Inject the custom URLProtocol for exponential backoff
let config = URLSessionConfiguration.default
config.protocolClasses = [ExponentialBackoffURLProtocol.self]
let session = URLSession(configuration: config)

// Run the async function
Task {
      await fetchPost()
}
```

This code fragment shows how to implement an exponential backoff mechanism in Swift by subclassing URLProtocol with a custom class named ExponentialBackoffURLProtocol.

The exponential backoff approach is designed to progressively increase the delay between retry attempts following a failure in network requests. This mechanism helps reduce server load and enhances the reliability of network communication overall.

The ExponentialBackoffURLProtocol class overrides methods from URLProtocol to implement the logic for the exponential backoff.

The core of this logic is implemented within the startLoading method, where the backoff time is calculated based on the number of requests made.

The method then simulates a network request and randomly simulates errors. If an error is simulated, the method notifies the client of the failure; otherwise, it simulates a successful response.

The fetchPost() function is an async function that fetches a post from a specified URL using URLSession. It utilizes a URLSession configured with a custom URLSessionConfiguration that includes the ExponentialBackoffURLProtocol class. This allows the exponential backoff mechanism to be triggered for requests made within this session.

Summary

In this chapter, we have given an overview of REST HTTP services and examined the URL Loading System in Swift. We have examined how to handle REST requests and how to integrate them into SwiftUI. Finally, we have shown how it is possible to redefine URLProtocol in order to implement features not normally implemented by URLSession. In the next chapter, we will have a look at Vision Pro, the innovative spatial computing system just introduced by Apple.

16

Exploring the Apple Vision Pro

The Apple Vision Pro is an advanced mixed-reality headset introduced by Apple, marking the company's entry into the spatial computing domain. It offers a fully immersive three-dimensional user interface, controlled intuitively through eyes, hands, and voice inputs. The device's design features a curved glass display with an aluminum alloy frame. Apple Vision Pro supports applications written using Metal, ARKit, and SwiftUI.

Its display system is based on two separate micro-OLED screens, providing more than 4K resolution per eye. The Vision Pro is driven by an M2 chip for the operating system and graphics, and a new R1 chip that processes the inputs from twelve cameras, sensors, and microphones. The Vision Pro has a Spatial Audio system that creates an immersive sound experience, making it feel like audio is emanating from the surrounding environment.

Security is achieved using Optic ID for secure authentication through iris scanning, similar to Apple's Face ID and Touch ID technologies. Designed for both plugged-in and portable use, the headset provides up to two hours of usage with an external battery. Additionally, it supports custom optical inserts for users needing prescription lenses designed by Carl Zeiss AG. The operating system of this new device is called **visionOS**, and it is capable of connecting to a Mac as a display and supports Bluetooth accessories for text input.

In this chapter, we're going to cover the following main topics:

- Tools for visionOS development
- An overview of Unity and RealityKit
- Beginning development with visionOS
- First steps with visionOS development

Technical requirements

This chapter requires a recent Apple Silicon Mac with Xcode 15.2 running on macOS 14.2 (Sonoma).

Developing for visionOS requires an Apple Silicon Mac and development can't be done on an Intel Mac; you are practically expected to use an Apple Silicon Mac to develop for visionOS. Given the requirements of visionOS, the higher the amount of RAM available, the better. The examples shown in this chapter have been verified on an M3 MacBook Pro with 48 GB of RAM.

Tools for visionOS development

To install the visionOS development system, you only need to download the optional visionOS simulator when installing Xcode. Otherwise, you can go to **Xcode | Settings** and select the **Platforms** tab. The following screenshot shows the **Platforms** tab in the Xcode preferences:

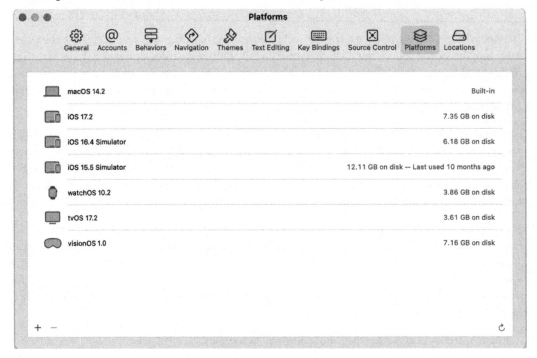

Figure 16.1 – Verifying that the visionOS platform is installed

If visionOS has not been downloaded already, it will show a **GET** button next to its size. The visionOS simulator download is around 7 GB in size, in addition to Xcode itself. A visionOS application can contain one or more **windows**, **spaces**, and **volumes**. Let's understand these further:

- **visionOS windows** are SwiftUI scenes that can contain traditional 2D views and controls. They appear as floating 2D windows.

- **visionOS volumes** can add 3D depth and are SwiftUI scenes that include 3D content made with **RealityKit** or **Unity**, creating user experiences that can be viewed from any angle in the shared space or in an application full space.

- **visionOS spaces** represent a new way of interacting with apps and content in "spatial computing." There are different types of spaces for apps:

  - **Shared Space**: This is the default mode where visionOS apps launch. In Shared Space, multiple apps can run side by side, like how multiple applications can be open at the same time on a desktop. Here, users can open, close, and rearrange windows and volumes that show content.

  - **Full Space**: For a more immersive experience, a visionOS application can open a dedicated Full Space. In this mode, only the content of that specific app appears, providing an environment where the app can fully immerse people in its experience. In Full Space, apps can use windows and volumes or create unbounded 3D content, fully immersing the user in an environment.

To design 3D content for visionOS, you can use RealityKit and Unity, which we will examine in the next section.

An overview of Unity and RealityKit

Unity is a third-party 3D game engine and can be downloaded from `https://unity.com`. Unity is normally used to produce high-end 3D games. It is quite expensive if used professionally within a corporation, but there is a free tier license available for students and small businesses or individual developers. Unity is programmed in C#, not Swift, and it includes its own development environment.

Unity 3D is a powerful and widely used 3D engine and development platform that enables developers to build immersive real-time 3D applications, games, and simulations. It's well known for its versatility across various platforms, including consoles, mobile devices, desktops, and the web. Unity has introduced what they call "PolySpatial technology," which is designed to power Unity content within the shared space on Apple Vision Pro. This includes support for immersive applications that can run side by side and windowed applications, which are the simplest way to bring existing mobile and desktop applications to visionOS.

You can find more information about the support of Unity for visionOS here: `https://create.unity.com/spatial`

While not as powerful as Unity, **RealityKit** is better integrated within the Swift programming environment. RealityKit is a framework developed by Apple to simplify the creation and rendering of **augmented reality** (**AR**) experiences. Now, Apple prefers to describe this as "spatial computing" rather than augmented reality, and according to the the visionOS specific app submission guide (`https://developer.apple.com/visionos/submit/`), you should avoid calling your visionOS apps "AR" or "augmented reality" in the description or within their name.

RealityKit offers a set of tools and APIs that enable developers to produce realistic 3D and augmented reality content. Augmented reality refers to the capability to superimpose computer-generated graphical objects to the scene observed in real time. At the moment, this is achieved using cameras to capture a video stream that is superimposed digitally with content before showing it to the user, as no transparent screen capable of displaying information to the user is currently technically viable.

The features of RealityKit are as follows:

- **Photorealistic rendering**: RealityKit renders 3D scenes with realistic lighting and shadows.

- **3D object anchoring**: This allows precise placement and tracking of 3D objects in the real world using ARKit's tracking capabilities. This includes support for anchoring objects to specific points or surfaces in the user's environment.

- **Animation and audio support**: RealityKit supports animations and spatial audio, which can be used to create engaging and interactive AR experiences.

- **Multiuser AR experience**: ARKit potentially enables the creation of shared AR scenes, where multiple users can interact with the same virtual environment at the same time.

- **Swift support**: RealityKit works seamlessly with Swift, allowing iOS and visionOS developers to integrate AR into their applications.

- **Live video feed**: RealityKit merges the live video feed from the device's camera with the 3D content generated by the device, creating a blend of the real and virtual scenes.

- **Collision detection and physics**: RealityKit, like a 3D game engine, includes a physics simulation engine, as well as collision detection to prevent 3D objects from unrealistically intersecting.

SwiftUI can be used to program new visionOS apps, while visionOS is also able to display existing iOS and iPadOS apps. RealityKit is integrated with SwiftUI and can be used to build applications having 3D content, effects, and visual effects.

RealityKit uses MaterialX, an industry standard adopted by visual effects and movie companies to specify shaders. The specifications of the MaterialX standard are available at `https://materialx.org`.

ARKit is a framework that can show 3D content on surfaces belonging to the surroundings of the user, for example, placing a superimposed 3D model of a train on the top of a table that is physically present in the user's room.

To create scenes containing 3D content, Apple has designed an application called **Reality Composer Pro**, which is included with versions of Xcode starting from 15.1 onward.

Reality Composer Pro

Although developers can load USDZ files and other assets directly in visionOS, RealityKit compiles assets within Reality Composer Pro projects in binary files, which load more efficiently than loading from individual files.

You can also, to some extent, produce 3D content using the more limited version of **Reality Composer** for iPad, which is available on the App Store. To access the Reality Composer Pro tool from Xcode, you will need to open the **Xcode | Open Developer Tools** menu and select **Reality Composer Pro**.

RealityKit supports multiple lighting modes, allowing you to see 3D models in different lighting scenarios and you can use Reality Composer Pro to preview and test these modes.

Reality Converter, available as a separate download from the Apple developer website, `https://developer.apple.com`, is an application that allows you to view and convert 3D content on a Mac to the USDZ format required by RealityKit. It supports many different traditional 3D formats, including `.obj`, `.gltx`, and `.fbx`, and converts them to Pixar's `.usdz` file format, which supports 3D objects, material properties, and textures together with their metadata. Interestingly, Apple does not directly support the `.dae` Collada file format within RealityKit and ARKit, but developers can use multiple ways to convert from `.dae` to `.usdz`, and most 3D editors and animation packages, including Blender and Maya, have support for that conversion with plugins.

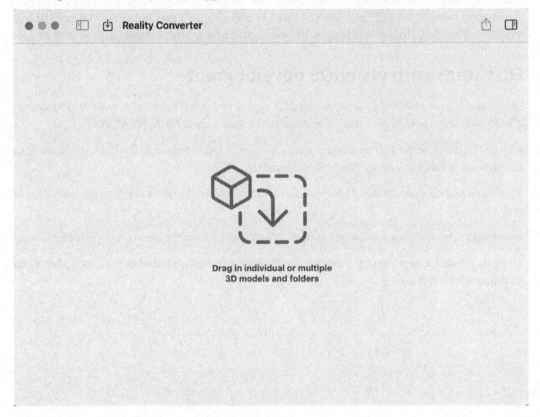

Figure 16.2 – Reality Converter

As every file format supports different features, and sometimes each file format represents the same data in fundamentally different ways, the resulting USDZ converted models may differ from the source models. Apple also supplies several Python programming language scripts designed to help developers work with USDZ files, also available as a separate download from the Apple Developer website: `https://developer.apple.com/augmented-reality/tools/`.

It is worth noticing that for obvious performance optimization reasons, Reality Converter only supports single-sided geometry, that is, a 3D model will appear completely transparent if observed from its inside, while it will be visible if observed from the space outside the model. Reality Converter also removes double-sided geometry attributes during data import.

The entire UV preview surface specification detailing the full capabilities of the USDZ format is available from Pixar at the following URL: `https://graphics.pixar.com/usd/docs/UsdPreviewSurface-Proposal.html`

Additional information on the USDZ and MaterialX support in Apple visionOS is available in the presentation videos of WWDC2023 here: `https://developer.apple.com/videos/play/wwdc2023/10086`. In the next section, we will explain how to start a visionOS project in Xcode.

First steps with visionOS development

Everything you have learned so far about SwiftUI applies to visionOS and is the same if you are using Windows-based visionOS apps. Let's create our first Xcode project for Apple Vision Pro.

A SwiftUI application for visionOS comprising a window is rather similar to the applications you have already seen in this book for mobile and desktop devices.

Your views will conform to the `View` protocol and are built in the same way you are familiar with right now.

In this section, we will examine how this process differs, slightly, from the development for other devices.

To create a SwiftUI app, start by selecting the Xcode template for **visionOS** apps, as shown in the following screen capture:

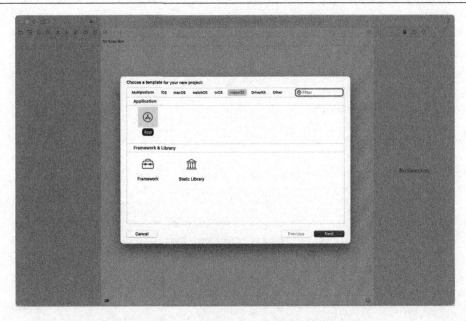

Figure 16.3 – The Xcode template for visionOS apps

Let's start with the simplest configuration you can use, as shown in the following screen capture. Please set it with exactly the options shown:

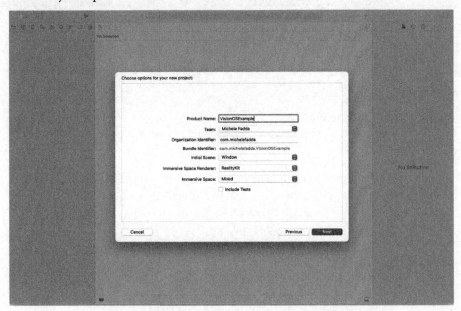

Figure 16.4 – Configuring your first visionOS app template

The code created by the template for the `ContentView.swift` file is the following:

```swift
import SwiftUI
import RealityKit
import RealityKitContent

struct ContentView: View {

    @State private var showImmersiveSpace = false
    @State private var immersiveSpaceIsShown = false

    @Environment(\.openImmersiveSpace) var openImmersiveSpace
    @Environment(\.dismissImmersiveSpace) var dismissImmersiveSpace

    var body: some View {
        VStack {
            Model3D(named: "Scene", bundle: realityKitContentBundle)
                .padding(.bottom, 50)

            Text("Hello, world!")

            Toggle("Show Immersive Space", isOn: $showImmersiveSpace)
                .toggleStyle(.button)
                .padding(.top, 50)
        }
        .padding()
        .onChange(of: showImmersiveSpace) { _, newValue in
            Task {
                if newValue {
                    switch await openImmersiveSpace(id:
"ImmersiveSpace") {
                    case .opened:
                        immersiveSpaceIsShown = true
                    case .error, .userCancelled:
                        fallthrough
                    @unknown default:
                        immersiveSpaceIsShown = false
                        showImmersiveSpace = false
                    }
                } else if immersiveSpaceIsShown {
                    await dismissImmersiveSpace()
                    immersiveSpaceIsShown = false
                }
```

```
                }
            }
        }
    }
}

#Preview(windowStyle: .automatic) {
    ContentView()
}
```

This `ContentView` SwiftUI code creates an interface for an application on visionOS using RealityKit. It includes a 3D model display, a toggle button to control the display of the immersive augmented reality space, and logic to handle the opening and closing of this space based on user interaction.

The RealityKit framework is used here to integrate 3D objects into an AR environment, leveraging ARKit for environmental tracking and sensing.

The following is an explanation of the previous code:

- `ContentView`: This uses `@State` properties to manage the view's state and `@Environment` properties to interact with environmental data.

  - State variables:

    - `showImmersiveSpace`: This controls whether the immersive AR space is displayed or not.

    - `immersiveSpaceIsShown`: This is another boolean `@State` variable that equals true if the immersive space is currently shown.

  - Environment: `openImmersiveSpace()` and `dismissImmersiveSpace()`: These functions are provided by the environment and handle the display and dismissal of the immersive space.

- body: The `body` property defines the view's layout. It contains a vertical stack (`VStack`) with a 3D model (`Model3D`), a text component, and a toggle button.

  This is the screen that will be displayed as a floating window within the 3D space.

  - `Model3D`: This displays a 3D model named `Scene` from `realityKitContentBundle`. This is a part of RealityKit's functionality to render 3D objects.

  - `Text("Hello, world!")`: This is a simple text label.

  - `Toggle`: This is a toggle switch that binds to the `showImmersiveSpace()` state variable. When toggled, it should trigger the display or dismissal of the immersive AR space.

    - `.onChange`: The modifier observes changes in the `showImmersiveSpace` variable. When the state changes, `.onChange` either opens or dismisses the immersive space.

- `openImmersiveSpace()`: The function called to open the immersive space, with different outcomes (`opened`, `error`, `userCancelled`) handled through a `switch` statement.
- `dismissImmersiveSpace()`: The function called to dismiss the immersive space.

The `ImmersiveView.swift` file controls the display of the immersive space, which on a visionOS device is the space surrounding the user and is shown here:

```
import SwiftUI
import RealityKit
import RealityKitContent

struct ImmersiveView: View {
    var body: some View {
        RealityView { content in
            // Add the initial RealityKit content
            if let scene = try? await Entity(named: "Immersive", in:
realityKitContentBundle) {
                content.add(scene)
            }
        }
    }
}


#Preview {
    ImmersiveView()
        .previewLayout(.sizeThatFits)
}
```

The App file is the following. The only difference between a visionOS application and a normal SwiftUI application is that a visionOS application, besides the window group containing `ContentView`, also declares `ImmersiveSpace`, the 3D content of the app:

```
import SwiftUI

@main
struct VisionOSExampleApp: App {
    var body: some Scene {
        WindowGroup {
            ContentView()
        }

        ImmersiveSpace(id: "ImmersiveSpace") {
```

```
                ImmersiveView()
            }
        }
    }
```

As a result, the preview shows the window of our visionOS app floating in a simulated environment of a fictional living room, as shown in the following screen capture:

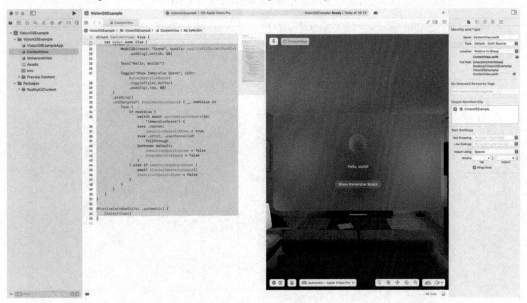

Figure 16.5 – The preview of a visionOS app window in Xcode

The icons shown at the bottom of the preview allow you to control the position and orientation of the viewer inside the simulated space and choose other visualization modes.

On a real physical device, the Vision Pro would capture the visual environment using its 12 cameras and would track the eyes of the user to display a scene that superimposes rendered graphical objects onto the existing external user environment in a way similar to ARKit on iPad but completely immersive, tridimensional, and stereoscopic, by showing an appropriate image to each eye of the user.

At the bottom of the preview canvas, you will find a number of control icons, grouped in five main bars, as shown in the following screenshot:

Figure 16.6 – visionOS preview controls

These controls, from left to right, are as follows:

- The two buttons in the first pane on the left allow you to alternate between displaying rendered simulated space rather than a wireframe model of the shared space.

- A 3D wireframe will be rendered in shades of gray, without textures, and showing the boundaries of the simulated space in yellow, together with the measures in centimeters, as shown here:

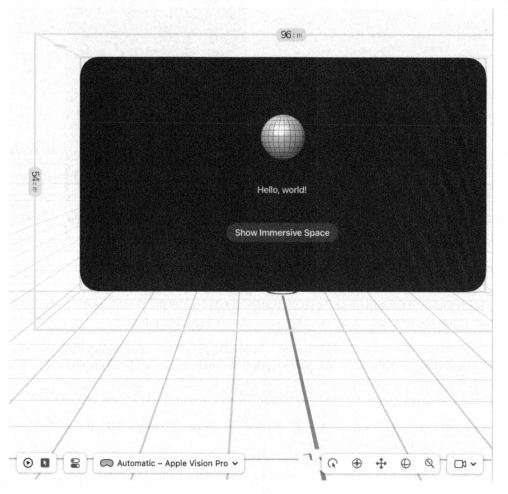

Figure 16.7 – The wireframe view

The window size is shown as 54 cm by 96 cm, inside a 40 cm deep box.

- The second pane contains the canvas device settings. Currently, this control allows you to customize the dynamic font size.

- The third pane allows you to choose different devices. At the moment, only Vision Pro supports this mode, but other devices will be introduced at a later time.

- If you are familiar with 3D video games, you can also use the keyboard to navigate the 3D scene using the WASD keys:

  - *W*: Moves the camera viewpoint forward.

  - *A*: Moves the camera viewpoint left.

  - *S*: Moves the camera viewpoint backward.

  - *D*: Moves the camera viewpoint right.

- The fourth pane contains keys allowing you to control the navigation within the 3D scene. From left to right, these buttons are as follows:

  - **Select**: This changes the pointer to select mode.
  - **Rotate Camera**: This switches to a mode that allows the mouse or the trackpad to rotate the camera on its vertical or horizontal axes.
  - **Strafe**: This switches to a mode that allows the camera to be moved left or right with the mouse without changing the camera angle.
  - **Rotate View**: This switches to a mode that allows the mouse or trackpad to rotate the view vertically or horizontally without changing the position of the camera.
  - **Zoom**: This switches to a mode in which the mouse or trackpad allows zooming in or out of the scene (up and right zoom in, left and down zoom out).

- The fifth pane in *Figure 16.6* contains two buttons: the first selects the simulated user scene used within the simulator and preview, and the second selects predefined viewpoints such as top, front, back, left, right, leading, and trailing. You will have encountered similar predefined views allowing you to observe a 3D scene from multiple predefined points of view if you have used 3D graphical editors before.

- Some of these allow observing the scene from above, from the left, from the right, and so on.

The visionOS simulator only displays the simulated user environment and uses the same controls as the preview for the navigation, as shown in the following screen capture:

Figure 16.8 – Showing the user space, a simulated one within the simulator

When the **Show immersive space** button on the floating app window displayed in the virtual space is pushed, the immersive environment gets displayed. In the visionOS Xcode default template, this immersive environment comprises two 10 cm radius spheres that are displayed superimposed on the user environment:

Figure 16.9 – The visionOS simulator – user immersive space shown

The default material is **grid material**, which is shown as a uniform gray with a square grid net.

This 3D immersive content can be edited within Reality Composer Pro directly from Xcode, by selecting the immersive content. In our case, it's two spheres – one to the left and one to the right, as shown in the following screen capture:

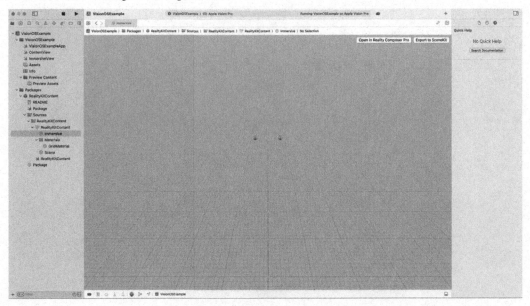

Figure 16.10 – Previewing RealityKit content within Xcode

By tapping the **Open** button in Reality Composer Pro on the top of the Xcode canvas, you can edit this 3D content within Reality Composer Pro.

Here, we can import other 3D models, and associate them with materials, which we can also edit, to change the color and light reflection properties. As in a video game, you can import textures as bitmap images, or edit uniform colors directly.

You can't directly change the color of the spheres. To change them, you need to create materials with the surface colors you want to apply to them first.

Let's create **Purple** and **Green** materials by selecting **Create Material**, and then changing the diffuse colors as shown here:

Figure 16.11 – Editing materials with Reality Composer Pro

In our example, we can set the diffuse color of the sphere on the left to purple by clicking on the **Diffuse Color** button and selecting the color corresponding to hexadecimal #762348 in the system color picker within Xcode, as shown here:

Figure 16.12 – You can edit colors using the color picker view of Xcode

We produce a green color in the same way, setting the diffuse color to hexadecimal #007617 and setting the **Metallic** property to 0.8.

Feel free to experiment with material creation. If you have used 3D editing software before, this will be rather familiar.

By selecting each sphere, we then change the radius from 10 to 30. Then we save all files from within Reality Composer.

If we run the project again from Xcode, the changes to the 3D content we have just made, that is, changing the colors and sizes of the spheres are shown in the visionOS simulator as shown here:

Figure 16.13 – The modified 3D content displayed within the simulator

RealityKit allows much more. For example, it allows animating 3D objects, and more complex interactions.

Please consult the Apple Developer website for more information: https://developer.apple.com/augmented-reality/realitykit/

In this section, I have shown how to interact with a simple visionOS project and how it is possible to edit the materials inside 3D models used in RealityKit directly within Xcode.

Summary

In this chapter, you have learned how to create a basic project for visionOS in Xcode, how to use the simulator and previews, how to navigate in 3D space, and how to edit the 3D content associated with it with Reality Kit Composer Pro.

This concludes the book. I hope it has equipped you with a good understanding of SwiftUI, covering its core components, layout system, and data management. Through examples, you've learned how to build user interfaces and handle user interactions. As SwiftUI develops, remember to revisit the fundamentals discussed here and explore new features and developments. Keep experimenting to refine your skills and adapt to the progress of app development. I hope to have given you inspiration for your continued growth.

Index

X

Z

packtpub.com

Subscribe to our online digital library for full access to over 7,000 books and videos, as well as industry leading tools to help you plan your personal development and advance your career. For more information, please visit our website.

Why subscribe?

- Spend less time learning and more time coding with practical eBooks and Videos from over 4,000 industry professionals

- Improve your learning with Skill Plans built especially for you

- Get a free eBook or video every month

- Fully searchable for easy access to vital information

- Copy and paste, print, and bookmark content

Did you know that Packt offers eBook versions of every book published, with PDF and ePub files available? You can upgrade to the eBook version at packtpub.com and as a print book customer, you are entitled to a discount on the eBook copy. Get in touch with us at customercare@packtpub.com for more details.

At www.packtpub.com, you can also read a collection of free technical articles, sign up for a range of free newsletters, and receive exclusive discounts and offers on Packt books and eBooks.

Other Books You May Enjoy

If you enjoyed this book, you may be interested in these other books by Packt:

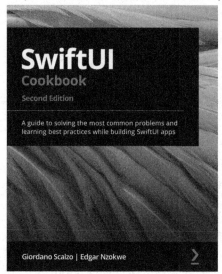

SwiftUI Cookbook

Giordano Scalzo | Edgar Nzokwe

ISBN: 978-1-80323-445-8

- Explore various layout presentations in SwiftUI such as HStack, VStack, LazyHStack, and LazyVGrid
- Create widgets to quickly display relevant content at glance
- Get up to speed with drawings in SwiftUI using built-in shapes, custom paths, and polygons
- Discover modern animation and transition techniques in SwiftUI
- Add user authentication using Firebase and Sign in with Apple
- Manage concurrency with Combine and async/await in SwiftUI
- Solve the most common SwiftUI problems, such as integrating a MapKit map, unit testing, snapshot testing, and previewing layouts

iOS 15 Programming for Beginners

Ahmad Sahar | Craig Clayton

ISBN: 978-1-80181-124-8

- Get to grips with the fundamentals of Xcode 13 and Swift 5.5, the building blocks of iOS development
- Understand how to prototype an app using storyboards
- Discover the Model-View-Controller design pattern and how to implement the desired functionality within an app
- Implement the latest iOS features such as Swift Concurrency and SharePlay.
- Convert an existing iPad app into a Mac app with Mac Catalyst.
- Design, deploy, and test your iOS applications with design patterns and best practices.

Packt is searching for authors like you

If you're interested in becoming an author for Packt, please visit authors.packtpub.com and apply today. We have worked with thousands of developers and tech professionals, just like you, to help them share their insight with the global tech community. You can make a general application, apply for a specific hot topic that we are recruiting an author for, or submit your own idea.

Share Your Thoughts

Hi,

I am Michele Fadda author of *An iOS Developer's Guide to SwiftUI*. I really hope you enjoyed reading this book and found it useful for increasing your productivity and efficiency using SwiftUI.

It would really help me (and other potential readers!) if you could leave a review on Amazon sharing your thoughts on this book.

Go to the link below to leave your review:

`https://packt.link/r/1801813620`

Your review will help me to understand what's worked well in this book, and what could be improved upon for future editions, so it really is appreciated.

Best Wishes,

Michele Fadda

Download a free PDF copy of this book

Thanks for purchasing this book!

Do you like to read on the go but are unable to carry your print books everywhere?

Is your e-book purchase not compatible with the device of your choice?

Don't worry!, Now with every Packt book, you get a DRM-free PDF version of that book at no cost.

Read anywhere, any place, on any device. Search, copy, and paste code from your favorite technical books directly into your application.

The perks don't stop there, you can get exclusive access to discounts, newsletters, and great free content in your inbox daily

Follow these simple steps to get the benefits:

1. Scan the QR code or visit the following link:

https://packt.link/free-ebook/9781801813624

2. Submit your proof of purchase.
3. That's it! We'll send your free PDF and other benefits to your email directly.

Printed in Great Britain
by Amazon

60477867R00252